SEXUALITY IN CHINA

SEXUALITY IN CHINA

HISTORIES OF POWER & PLEASURE

EDITED BY

HOWARD CHIANG

UNIVERSITY OF WASHINGTON PRESS

Seattle

Sexuality in China was made possible in part by a grant from the Chiang Ching-kuo Foundation for International Scholarly Exchange.

UNIVERSITY OF WASHINGTON PRESS
www.washington.edu/uwpress

LIBRARY OF CONGRESS CATALOGING-IN-PUBLICATION DATA
Names: Chiang, Howard, 1983– editor.
Title: Sexuality in China : histories of power and pleasure / edited by
    Howard Chiang.
Description: Seattle : University of Washington Press, [2018] | Includes
    bibliographical references and index. |
Identifiers: LCCN 2017049032 (print) | LCCN 2017053700 (ebook) |
    ISBN 9780295743486 (ebook) | ISBN 9780295743462 (hardcover : alk. paper) |
    ISBN 9780295743479 (pbk. : alk. paper)
Subjects: LCSH: Sex—China—History. | Sex customs—China—History.
Classification: LCC HQ18.C6 (ebook) | LCC HQ18.C6 S44 2018 (print) |
    DDC 306.70951—dc23
LC record available at https://lccn.loc.gov/2017049032

To Lois

CONTENTS

ACKNOWLEDGMENTS

My passion for the study of history began when I took an undergraduate course on the history of gender and sexuality with Lois Banner at the University of Southern California. I was then a premed student working on a dual-degree track in the sciences (biochemistry and psychology). Lois completely changed my view of history and eliminated the anxiety I felt entering the world of humanities as a science major. What began as a general education class that I intended to take only for a pass-or-fail grade evolved into a life-changing experience that motivated me to pursue a career as a historian. Lois became an informal mentor throughout my undergraduate education, and under her tutelage, I completed several projects in the history of sexuality that won distinctions. By offering me guidance and support in this intellectual journey, she eased my "coming out" transition as I learned to take pride in the history and heritage of people like me. Today I constantly look for ways to improve my teaching, hoping to cultivate among students the same excitement and achievement that I felt fifteen years ago as a nonspecialist learning about history. For these reasons, it is to Lois that I dedicate this book.

The editorial support, encouragement, and expertise of Lorri Hagman at the University of Washington Press played an instrumental role in bringing this volume to fruition. Two anonymous readers offered thoughtful comments that helped to improve the individual chapters and the book as a whole. The contributors have worked hard with me in completing this collection. I thank each of the individuals mentioned above and hope that they are as pleased about the final product as I am.

CHINESE DYNASTIES AND HISTORICAL PERIODS

Xia	ca. 2100–ca. 1600 BCE
Shang (Yin)	ca. 1600–ca. 1028 BCE
Zhou	ca. 1027–ca. 256 BCE
Qin	221–207 BCE
Han	206 BCE–220 CE
Three Kingdoms period	220–280
"Six Dynasties" period	222–589
Sui	581–618
Tang	618–907
Five Dynasties and Ten Kingdoms period	907–979
Song	960–1279
Yuan (Mongol)	1260–1368
Ming	1368–1644
Qing (Manchu)	1644–1911
Republican period	1911–1949
Maoist period	1949–1978
Reform period	1978–

SEXUALITY IN CHINA

INTRODUCTION

Writing the History of Sexuality in China

HOWARD CHIANG

BORN IN THE 1970S, THE HISTORY OF SEXUALITY HAS BECOME AN established area of critical inquiry,[1] yet the most vibrant body of secondary literature in this field remains primarily concerned with Western Europe and North America. Over time, the field has moved decidedly toward a social constructionist paradigm that distinguishes erotic orientation from reproduction, views categories of sexuality as cultural constructs, and challenges essentialist understandings of sexual desire and practice as universal across time and place.[2] Although studies in the history of sexuality in other regions have begun to mature in the new millennium, historians of Asia, the Middle East, Africa, and South America have engaged in serious conversations with historians of Western sexuality rather late. These dialogues tend to emanate from a more explicit interest in transnational, imperial, postcolonial, or global history.[3] Consequently, the historiography of non-Western sexuality is often broached under the lingering shadow of the theories, categories, themes, and debates derived from European and American historical analyses.

The concept of sexuality poses a pressing problem for scholars of China, not the least because the word itself has no precise literal translation in Chinese. Nonetheless, for a long time, historians of China (and East Asia more generally) have produced in-depth studies on topics that are typically associated with the idea of sexuality in the English-speaking world.[4] In this regard, the landmark contribution of Robert Hans van Gulik, *Sexual Life in Ancient China* (1961), has been heralded as a groundbreaking work, but it is also often challenged and revised for its Orientalist burdens.[5] Feminist historians of China, such as Charlotte Furth, Gail Hershatter, and Emily

Honig, began to pay more explicit attention to sexuality in the late 1980s and 1990s, primarily in response to the growing influence of cultural theory on the study of women's history.[6] This arose from the earlier turn to social history, whereby the history of the oppressed subjects (usually absent in grand historical narratives) pushed historians to think deeper about the issues of power, representation, and language.

The focus on discourse, interpretation, and meanings, therefore, has defined an important agenda among historians of sexuality. French philosopher Michel Foucault's *History of Sexuality, Vol. 1* has influenced many of the subsequent explorations of these themes in the history of Western sexuality.[7] This has led some scholars to argue that sexuality itself is a rather recent phenomenon—a decisively *modern* product of history.[8] Although the Orientalist overtone of Foucault's work is no less problematic than that of van Gulik's, the concept of sexuality as a Western invention continues to haunt the investigative thinking of Chinese historians on matters related to erotic pleasure, sexual practices, and the body. Even so, the social constructionist paradigm descending from Foucault's work offers a useful template for the denaturalization of sexual binary categories that appear as ostensibly immutable and fixed, in the Chinese context or otherwise.[9]

This volume brings together for the first time the perspectives of scholars who have helped shape the field of the history of Chinese sexuality in distinct ways, but who have not previously had the chance to come together and synthesize their varying expertise across different periods of Chinese history. While it does not claim exhaustive coverage, *Sexuality in China* aims to provide a useful tool for teaching, presenting a wide range of perspectives that feature the different temporal, regional, methodological, and theoretical strengths of the contributors. Presented in a loose chronological thread, the following chapters introduce students to some of the major debates, sources, theories, and empirical contours of current historical work on Chinese sexuality, from the ancient times to the present. Centering on the theme of power (an important analytic since Foucault's impact on the field), the volume argues that despite the difficulty of translating the idea of "sexuality" into Chinese—or precisely because of it—the history of sexuality in China provides a promising platform for stimulating, robust dialogues with a broad interdisciplinary reach. The diverse and contested nature of this field encourages innovative methodologies, critical approaches, and the creative use of different sources in historical research on human sexual experience. As both Chinese history and the history of sexuality are growing fields, this book is the first of its kind to bring the two

    HOWARD CHIANG

fields together with an emphasis on methods and historiography, providing rich directions for future research and debates.

POWER AND PLEASURE

In the preface to *Gender and Sexuality in Modern Chinese History*, Susan Mann underscores the repressive strictures of the heteronormative state as a central theme in her compelling survey of Chinese people's modern intimate experience: "The prominent role of the government in defining gender relations and sexuality is a unique, enduring feature of Chinese history that sets the Chinese experience apart from other modern industrial nations."[10] Through their relation to marriage (or nonmarriage), for instance, men and women earned morally charged social recognitions. Although men and women bore an uneven relationship to the institution of marriage, the state still imposed an entrenched set of regulations on "acceptable" gender conventions.[11] A famous example of changing state regulations occurred in 1950, when the New Marriage Law of the People's Republic of China catalyzed an unprecedented divorce tide in China, with an estimate of over one million divorce cases in 1953.[12] Although this may suggest a pivotal turning point in the undermining of Chinese patriarchy, many scholars have documented the uneven implementation of the New Marriage Law on the local level, as well as the enduring obstacles and predicaments that thwarted its full realization.[13] Without exceptionalizing the Chinese state, this volume similarly maintains the family as a site intensely regulated by the state, where men's control over women's bodies contributed to the social differentiation of female agency and identities.

Chapter 1, by Debby Chih-yen Huang and Paul R. Goldin, treats marriage as a useful lens for viewing the socially imbued hierarchies of men and women. Through the prism of the state-sanctioned practice of polygyny, Huang and Goldin examine the enduring pronouncement of patriarchy and how it shaped Chinese women's self-understanding and social positioning in subtle ways. Frequently justified as a means to increase fertility, polygyny, as it was practiced in China since the Bronze Age, sometimes indexed the symbolic value of a man's wealth and status, which the elaborateness of a wedding ceremony would only capture in part. Ultimately, polygyny assured the social mechanisms by which women understood their status in society based on their role in the family. The difference between being a principal wife and a concubine, for example, had direct bearing on a woman's inheritance rights and her maternal experience with the descendants of the family's patriline. Social motherhood notwithstanding, a wife could secure her status in a polygynous household through a mother-son bond (which in turn shows that a son's self-perception crucially relied on his unique identification with his biological mother). Yet, as Huang and Goldin also point out, the distinction between a wife and a concubine became increasingly fluid over the course of the Song and Yuan dynasties. As a social unit and organization of power relations, the family defined a realm in which the Chinese state thus exercised a flexible degree of governance. Even though the focus of their analysis is on early to middle-period China, Huang and Goldin remind us of the immense challenges presented by the sex ratio imbalance today despite the fact that polygyny has been banned by the Chinese government since the 1950s.

It is not surprising that surviving documentation of human sexual experience from the past is scattered and incomplete. When people disclose information about their sexual lives in a factual manner or metaphorically, public record—usually censored in one way or another—rarely captures the true extent of what happened in the bedroom (or elsewhere). This poses a significant degree of methodological difficulty for studying the history of sexuality. Furthermore, different social groups leave behind disproportional measures of historical voice, making it a challenge to deduce broader generalizations about erotic desire and sexual practice in a particular region or a given time period. These observations have long been acknowledged by historians of sexuality in the West, but they are equally germane to the field of Chinese history. Meanwhile, scholars of China often carry a double burden. While resisting the temptation to narrate the history of sexuality in China as a variant of Western modernity, they must also avoid romanticizing the cultural difference between China and the rest of the world as the basis for a more "tolerant" Chinese past.[14] Bringing to the fore questions concerning historical evidence and practice, this volume complicates the form of attachments scholars develop to the sources available for their scrutiny and the kind of histories they write.

In chapter 2, Ping Yao provides an authoritative overview of the historiography of sexuality in imperial China, showing that the historian's pleasure in history writing derives from the power of source discovery and a passion for hermeneutics. Yao surveys scholarship on sexuality in Chinese history through a close examination of how scholars utilize sources in their research, exploring ways that the availability and genre of sources shape key themes and trends in the evolving historiography. Scholarship on sexuality in early medieval China has focused overwhelmingly on Daoist conceptions of sexuality—a result, Yao explains, of the accessibility of a

   HOWARD CHIANG

considerable quantity of Daoist texts, such as *The Classic of the Plain Girl* (Sunüjing), *Secret Instructions of the Jade Bedchamber* (Yufang mijue), and *Liturgy of Passage of the Yellow Writ of Highest Clarity* (Shangqing huang-shu guodu yi). In the Tang dynasty, as the literati came to dominate the definitions of sexuality and the Buddhist discourse on sexuality staked its influence, an enormous amount of erotic literature developed; as a result, Tang sexuality scholars can cover a much broader scope and draw on a more diverse body of source materials. Research on the Song period, mean-while, relies on more limited extant textual sources, and historians of the period frequently examine Confucian ideals of gender and sexual relations. Scholarship on sexuality during late imperial China has proven to be most vibrant due to two important factors: the maturation of the field of late imperial Chinese studies, and the period's rich and engrossing source materials, ranging from didactic texts and religious scripts to novels, plays, woodblock prints, court cases, and sex manuals.

In contrast to Yao's historiographical survey, chapter 3, by Keith McMa-hon, employs the fine-grained approach of cultural history. It focuses on a single eighteenth-century novel, *Preposterous Words* (Guwangyan), to illus-trate a common theme in pornographic fiction linking social decline and sexual disorder. The novel embodies this theme in the form of the impotent man and the sexually voracious woman, whom it portrays in grotesque and titillating detail. Only a man—ideally a monk—with a herculean penis can outdo her. What is this organ like? It appears in many works, and in *Prepos-terous Words* most explicitly: it moves and sucks and bites on its own, and no woman can withstand it. The literal form that *Preposterous Words* gives this phallus stands for the ideal male self-image couched within the porno-graphic imagination of the late imperial novel. But it is only the supreme monk who need have such an organ; the model man is more refined, never so crude. He is both a literary and sexual talent.

In theoretical terms, the distinction between the monk and the scholar is one between the ideal the man imagines he needs to be (the sexually skilled monk); and the ideal the man envisions in the social context (one who does his best given the pressures of existing in a society of other men and women). The monk never marries; he skips from one woman to the next, conquering them all, never tying himself down. But the man of nor-mative society must marry. In the Ming and Qing novel, he marries the talented woman, but in *Preposterous Words* the blind prostitute is his sym-bolically sightless but sublime female counterpart. Their coupling repre-sents the defeat of the evil and corrupt society. The story of their romantic and sexual superiority provides the formula for the redemption of the social order, a formula that lasts in literature until at least the end of the Qing dynasty. In a word, *Preposterous Words* interweaves ethics and aesthetics, using pornography—itself a powerful medium for exploiting but also arousing pleasure—as a critique of the sexually decadent world of the late Ming dynasty and a method for conceptualizing an alternative world of social and sexual harmony.

SEXUAL MODERNISM

When the Xinhai Revolution established the Republic of China in 1911, its social and cultural impact was immediately reflected in the changing identity of ordinary people. Men's cutting of the queue and women's unbinding of their feet paralleled the new fashions, etiquettes, rituals, and customs adopted in schools, homes, wedding ceremonies, and other public and private venues.[15] Concurrent with the sweeping intellectual transformations of the 1920s and 1930s, natural science began to reauthorize the boundaries of gender, and sexuality emerged as an epistemic mainstay in political and cultural debates.[16] "What emerged was a type of 'lattice knowledge,'" to quote one of the earliest studies of sexual modernism in Republican China, "a body of knowledge in flux, characterized by interactions, overlaps and echoes, by constant change and endless combinations."[17] In the last decade or so, an outpouring of scholarship has illuminated the bold and colorful sexual culture of the Republican period.[18] This volume includes three chapters that deepen our understanding of Republican-era sexuality by showing how the modernizing rhetoric of the May Fourth period revolutionized the structures of sexual desire and thereby lent historical weight to such new sexual categories as "heterosexuality," "homosexuality," and "transsexuality."

Informed by the social constructionist paradigm, historians of Western sexuality have foregrounded the historicity of heterosexuality and eschewed an understanding of opposite-sex desire as a naturalizing force or an immutable construct.[19] In dialogue with this approach, chapter 4, by Mirela David, analyzes the philosophical debates on free love, eugenics, and individualism in 1920s urban China. These debates liberated heterosexual pleasure from the burdens and constraints of traditional (often dubbed Confucian) Chinese culture. In assessing the fascinating hold that British philosopher Bertrand Russell and Swedish feminist author Ellen Key had on the editors and writers of the *Ladies' Journal* (Funü zazhi), David argues that the reception of Russell and Key in May Fourth China deserves careful scrutiny: it helps outline a historical backdrop against which Chinese public intellectuals promoted a liberal vision with notable eugenic confines, even as they proclaimed an individual's right to love free of social bondage. Key's articulation of a new morality—in terms of evolutionary humanism and as encapsulated in the unity of body and soul—was the guiding principle for Zhang Xichen's editorial politics in the *Ladies' Journal*. Zhang and fellow editor Zhou Jianren's theorizations of a new sexual morality incorporated Key and Havelock Ellis's belief in the compatibility of humanistic individualism with the social outlook of eugenics. Following Russell, Key, and Ellis, these seminal Chinese male feminists envisaged the imperative of the robust individual as the harbinger of this new modern sexual ethics. In line with ongoing scholarship on the political pluralism of early Republican China, David's chapter depicts the cultural authority of Western science and eugenic ideas as coconstitutive of May Fourth–era enlightenment, reshaping common attitudes toward proper gender expressions and the fulfillment of heterosexual desire.[20]

Whereas David historicizes heterosexual romance, chapter 5, by Peter J. Carroll, traces a lateral genealogy of female homosexuality. During the Republican period, cities constituted both the site and substance of gender transformation; urban space both accommodated and contributed to the refashioning of modes of maleness and femaleness, including same-sex sexuality. Carroll's chapter examines a key event in the distillation of Republican ideas regarding female same-sex relations: the murder of Liu Mengying by Tao Sijin and subsequent scandal in Hangzhou. The basic story is rather simple and, although lurid and fatal, not that unusual in terms of police blotter stories. On February 11, 1932, twenty-two-year-old Tao Sijin, a student at the National Hangzhou Art Academy, fatally stabbed her lover, Liu Mingying, twenty years old, also a student at the academy. Liu was left dead on the ground with several dozen wounds, and Tao, covered in a mixture of Liu's blood and her own, lay in a semiconscious state near her lover.

The ferocity of the attack was documented in police photos of Liu's nude corpse, published in the media. The subsequent investigation, trial, and unsuccessful appeal by Tao were prominent news items throughout Jiangnan and beyond for over a year. Drawing on foreign social scientists such as Cesare Lombroso and Edward Carpenter, Chinese researchers such as Pan Guangdan, and a range of received opinion, commentators parsed the Tao-Liu case in a diverse set of popular and academic publications, including educational journals, newspapers, women's magazines, and fiction. The media coverage captured the growing anxiety about the Xinhai Revolution's dark side, construing the epidemic of same-sex love among students as a dire consequence of the expansion of women's public presence. Carroll's chapter extends the existing historiography of Republican-era homosexuality, spotlighting the cultural absorption and dissemination of sexological ideas in urban media and revealing the limitations of conceptualizing queerness through the legal framework of sodomy (*jijian*) alone.[21] The Tao-Liu case, meanwhile, imparts greater global historical texture to well-known lesbian love-murder stories in the twentieth century, such as the Alice Mitchell–Freda Ward case in the United States and the Mahin Padidarnazar–Zahra Amin case in Iran.[22]

Historians, especially after Foucault's seminal work, have tended to privilege science and medicine as the epistemic leverage for the formation of modern gender and sexual identities.[23] Whereas Carroll's chapter rethinks this relationship for lesbianism in the context of early-twentieth-century urban China, chapter 6 joins the work of historian Joanne Meyerowitz and traces the historical shaping of transsexual subjectivity in Nationalist mainland China and Taiwan.[24] My analysis focuses on two widely publicized episodes of human sex change: the case of female-to-male Yao Jinping in mid-1930s Shanghai and the story of male-to-female Xie Jianshun in early 1950s Taiwan. Originating from different historical contexts, the two examples illuminate the significance of the urban press in influencing popular categorizations of gender and sexuality through its interaction with medical and scientific knowledge. Major urban newspapers and tabloid print media enabled writers with sufficient cultural capital to comment on these rare and fascinating stories of bodily transformation. Meanwhile, these published writings and their circulations provided other intrigued readers with an unusually wide range of perspectives on the topic. The press also became a central vehicle for the agents of elite medico-scientific discourse to engage with the wider public, filtering novel and complicated ideas about sex plasticity for lay readers. This social milieu unveils the underappreciated process whereby common understandings of sexuality were shaped not only by dominant secular discourses of medical science, but also by the participants in the media—a quotidian venue for voicing competing visions for themselves and the nation. In sum, sexual modernism in Republican China coalesced around coeval developments of heteroerotic, homosexual, and transgender identities, reflecting a restructuring of the relationship between scientific knowledge, mass culture, and sexual politics.

MASCULINE ANXIETIES

If the sexual revolution of the May Fourth period gave birth to such fictional but powerful characters as Ding Ling's Sophia, a woman who freely expressed her erotic feelings through newfangled vocabularies, the image of

HOWARD CHIANG

a modern sexualized person was virtually demolished in the Maoist period.[25] Between the 1950s and 1970s, men and women were encouraged to subsume their erotic subjectivity under the interest of the Chinese Communist Party state, leading many critics to characterize this period in terms of a pervasive "erasure" of gender and sexuality that contrasted sharply with the political heterogeneities of the 1920s and 1930s.[26] The gender-neutered Red Guard figure epitomizes the ways in which the alleged Communist Party vision of gender equality was performatively embodied in the self-presentation of Maoist revolutionaries.

More recently, drawing on memoirs, fictions, plays, and scientific publications, scholars such as Harriet Evans, Wendy Larson, Emily Honig, and Rosemary Roberts have tried to "sexualize" the Maoist era.[27] As feminist historians continue to debate on the recodifications of gender and sexuality and their implications for the feminist cause in early PRC history, recent path-breaking studies have begun evaluating the effects of state transformation on men and their identities in the reform and postsocialist periods.[28] The last part of this volume features the work of some of these scholars. In contrast to chapter 1, which examines the subjugation of women under patriarchy's shadow, these final chapters put the spotlight on the evolving configurations of masculinity in the age of China's rising status as an economic powerhouse and as HIV/AIDS becomes a pressing global health problem.

Chapter 7, by Shana Ye, challenges the dichotomy of socialist state oppression and postsocialist desire that pervades existing historical scholarship on gender and sexuality in the People's Republic of China.[29] Calling for a reparative return to what she calls "queer socialism," Ye theorizes an alternative genealogy that equips the queer socialist closet with the hefty weight of history. Legal cases of sodomy have attracted a significant measure of critical attention, given sodomy's centrality in historicizing male homosexuality; Ye instead proposes an approach that highlights the kind of historical injury embedded within these cases, exploring the ethical and affective investments scholars put into constructing historical narratives about Chinese queerness from the perspective of the global neoliberal present.[30] By drawing attention to an important source type—the *tanbai jiaodai* (honest confessions) narrated by men who engaged in same-sex behavior during the Cultural Revolution—Ye delineates these narrative spaces as a queer counterpublic, in which subjects are coerced to speak about the most intimate spheres of their personal lives. Such "evidence" of queerness serves a function beyond the additive nature of representation. While it presents historians a supplementary understanding of queer existence in the Maoist period, it also underscores the value of privileging disruption in the search for surprises and otherness, giving credence to reparative—rather than recuperative—imaginations of queerer and more diverse pasts.

Based on long-term anthropological fieldwork in Beijing and Chengdu in the 1990s and 2000s, chapter 8, by Everett Yuehong Zhang, explores the complaint of many Chinese men—both in the clinics of men's medicine and in the general population—about the inadequacy of their sexual organs. Worry about male genital size dates back to ancient times, but China's modern encounters with Western industrial countries, and the ensuing comparison with white Westerners, ushered in a collective sense of Chinese male sexual inferiority. Men's exposure to pornography and public showers fostered a sense of penis envy in settings with other men; men's fragility and anxiety were further elevated by their sense of being unable to fulfill women's desires.

Instead of attributing this complex sentiment in post-Mao China to China's semicolonial history, Zhang suggests that the Maoist socialist state, despite its fierce attack on Western imperialism, may be partly to blame, having created a false image of Maoist socialist utopic superiority that—contrary to its intention of strengthening China's pride—exacerbated Chinese men's self-doubt. Moreover, the widespread teleological logic of modernity contributed to men's collective sense of inferiority, despite China's rapid economic development and rise. Concluding with a proposal encouraging "enlightened confidence," Zhang's chapter reveals the ways in which men attributed their masculinity being under siege to China's global self-repositioning and translated this general social uncertainty into a personal anxiety fixated on a physical organ.

China has a long-celebrated history of courtesanship that eventually led to a demand for prostitution among the merchant class that grew toward the end of the Qing dynasty.[31] Courtesans and prostitutes were a sign of male nobility and an entitlement for men of the noble and merchant classes of imperial China. A change in attitude came with the rise of the Communist Party. Mao outlawed prostitution as a social evil and worked to oppress sexuality in China in general. Prostitution has once again emerged in post-Mao China—but under the global term "sex work," translated as *xing gongzuo*. The approach to sex work in China has, likewise, adopted the global paradigms applied to sex work, which are largely framed by the HIV/AIDS movement. Mention of the term "sex work," globally, automatically invokes images of marginalized women at risk for HIV infection.

Probing the often-overlooked detrimental effects of prostitution on heterosexual male clients, chapter 9, by Elanah Uretsky, contends that such a perspective is counterproductive to sex workers and the aims of the sex

    HOWARD CHIANG

work movement globally. The term "sex work" was developed to legitimize prostitutes as social contributors through their occupational role. Association with the stigma of AIDS, however, has once again resurrected the image of sex workers as carriers of dirt and disease, thwarting the goal of the sex work movement. In China, women from all classes—and not just the ones typically associated with poverty and marginalization—engage in the transactional exchange of sex often referred to as "sex work." As Uretsky demonstrates, sex is often an equally relevant part of work for elite Chinese men living in postsocialist China. These men utilize sex to demonstrate the loyalty necessary to access state-owned and controlled resources in a market economy governed under a Leninist system. For many, it is an unofficial part of their work. The exchange of sex in such contexts typically cements social relations, rather than occurring as individual behavior. Uretsky argues for an approach to sex work in China that applies the term to all people who include sex in the duties they perform as part of their work. This revisionist approach transforms what is normally considered a consumerist act of pleasure into something that ultimately serves an occupational role for men seeking economic and political success in China.

PERVERSE POSSIBILITIES

Covering a wide range of topics—polygamy, pornography, free love, eugenics, sexology, crime of passion, homosexuality, intersexuality, transsexuality, masculine anxiety, sex work, and HIV/AIDS—this book samples a variety of sources and approaches in order to consider sexuality as a useful category of analysis in the study of Chinese history. Presented here is a snapshot of the state of the field, as well as suggestive points of departure for viewing Chinese history in a sexy, powerful, and pleasurable light. While the following chapters mark the rise of a new era in both Chinese studies and sexuality studies, they present only fragments of the larger history yet to be written. This volume does not claim comprehensive coverage. Rather, it tries to capture a new phase in the way scholars from different disciplines think about the past, showcase new directions in Chinese history and the history of sexuality, and provoke new historical interpretations of a complicated phenomenon. If Foucault was correct in claiming that "the nineteenth-century transformations made sexuality the truth of our identification and the basis of our becoming subjects," what these chapters accomplish collectively is less turning sexuality into the truth of Chinese historiography than transforming the category of sexuality into an unpredictable, exciting referent for future inquiries into the past.[32]

1   For an early set of exemplary anthologies that helped to shape the field, see Snitow et al., *Powers of Desire*; Vance, *Pleasure and Danger*; and Duberman et al., *Hidden from History*. See also D'Emilio, *The World Turned*.

2   See Stein, *Forms of Desire*.

3   See, for example, Bleys, *The Geography of Perversion*; McClintock, *Imperial Leather*; Murray, *Homosexualities*; Stoler, *Carnal Knowledge and Imperial Power*; Aldrich, *Colonialism and Homosexuality*; Crompton, *Homosexuality and Civilization*; Aldrich, *Gay Life and Culture*; Canaday, "Thinking Sex in the Transnational Turn"; and Buffington et al., eds., *A Global History of Sexuality*.

4   See, for example, Hinsch, *Passions of the Cut Sleeve*; McMahon, *Misers, Shrews, and Polygamists*; Pflugfelder, *Cartographies of Desire*; Volpp, "Classifying Lust"; Frühstück, *Colonizing Sex*; Theiss, *Disgraceful Matters*; McMahon, *Polygamy and Sublime Passion*; and Vitiello, *The Libertine's Friend*.

5   Van Gulik, *Sexual Life in Ancient China*; Furth, "Rethinking van Gulik Again."

6   See, for example, Furth, "Androgynous Males and Deficient Females"; Honig and Hershatter, *Personal Voices*; Zeitlin, *Historian of the Strange*; and Furth, *A Flourishing Yin*.

7   Foucault, *The History of Sexuality, Vol. 1*.

8   See Halperin, *One Hundred Years of Homosexuality*; Halperin et al., *Before Sexuality*; Sedgwick, *Epistemology of the Closet*; Davidson, *The Emergence of Sexuality*; and Traub, *Thinking Sex with the Early Moderns*.

9   See Murphy and Spear, eds., *Historicising Gender and Sexuality*; Rupp, *Sapphistries*; Doan, *Disturbing Practices*; Lanser, *The Sexuality of History*; and Chiang, "Revisiting Foucault."

10 Mann, *Gender and Sexuality in Modern Chinese History*, xvii.

11 See Sommer, *Sex, Law, and Society in Late Imperial China*; and Sommer, "The Gendered Body in the Qing Courtroom."

12 See Diamant, *Revolutionizing the Family*.

13 See Hershatter, *The Gender of Memory*; and Santos and Harrell, eds., *Transforming Patriarchy*.

14 Mann, *Gender and Sexuality in Modern Chinese History*, xvi.

15 See Harrison, *The Making of the Republican Citizen*; Glosser, *Chinese Visions of Family and State, 1915–1953*; and Ko, *Cinderella's Sisters*.

16 See Wang, *Women in the Chinese Enlightenment*; Barlow, *The Question of Women in Chinese Feminism*; Chiang, "Epistemic Modernity and the Emergence of Homosexuality in China"; and Chiang, *After Eunuchs*.

17 Dikötter, *Sex, Culture and Modernity in China*, 12.

18 See Hershatter, *Dangerous Pleasures*; Sang, *The Emerging Lesbian*; Tsu, *Failure, Nationalism, and Literature*; Lee, *Revolution of the Heart*; Kang, *Obsession*; and Chiang, *After Eunuchs*.

19 See Katz, *The Invention of Heterosexuality*.

HOWARD CHIANG

20   See Schwarcz, *The Chinese Enlightenment*; Mitter, *A Bitter Revolution*; and Leary, "Intellectual Orthodoxy, the Economy of Knowledge, and the Debate over Zhang Jingsheng's Sex Histories."

21   See, for example, Wang, "Shame, Survival, Satisfaction."

22   Duggan, *Sapphic Slashers*; Najmabadi, *Professing Selves*, 75–119.

23   See, for example, Terry, *An American Obsession*; Oosterhuis, *Stepchildren of Nature*; and Minton, *Departing from Deviance*.

24   Meyerowitz, *How Sex Changed*.

25   Barlow and Bjorge, *I Myself Am a Woman*, 49–81.

26   See Meng, "Female Images and National Myth"; and Yang, "From Gender Erasure to Gender Difference."

27   Evans, *Women and Sexuality in China*; Larson, "Never This Wild"; Honig, "Socialist Sex"; and Roberts, *Maoist Model Theatre*.

28   On rethinking socialist feminism, see Wang, *Finding Women in the State*. On the impact of state transformation on men and masculinity in the People's Republic of China, see Kleinman et al., *Deep China*, 106–51; Zhang, *The Impotence Epidemic*; and Uretsky, *Occupational Hazards*.

29   See, for example, Rofel, *Desiring China*.

30   On historical approaches to Chinese male homosexuality based on the legal relevance of sodomy, see Sommer, *Sex, Law, and Society in Late Imperial China*; Kang, "The Decriminalization and Depathologization of Homosexuality in China"; and Wang, "Shame, Survival, Satisfaction."

31   See Henriot, *Prostitution and Sexuality in Shanghai*.

32   Najmabadi, "Beyond the Americas," 17.

CHAPTER 1

POLYGYNY AND ITS DISCONTENTS

A Key to Understanding Traditional Chinese Society

DEBBY CHIH-YEN HUANG AND PAUL R. GOLDIN

AS EARLY AS THE BRONZE AGE, A PATTERN THAT WOULD GO ON TO characterize Chinese society for millennia had already taken hold: polygyny at the top of the social pyramid; and competition for women, frequently leading to violence, at the bottom.[1] Many aspects of traditional Chinese society become comprehensible if one bears this fact in mind. Pure arithmetic makes it impossible for *all* men in a society to engage in polygyny, so one can use the number of women sexually available to a man as a rough but telling index of his social standing. For the overwhelming majority of males, this number would have been zero or one, but even those with one wife might have considered themselves fortunate. One of the most important milestones in a man's life would have been attaining the requisite wealth and stability to support a wife; the thousands, if not millions, of men who could never afford a family became a permanent source of social unrest. It stands to reason that almost all healthy females were partnered at least once during their lifetimes, typically at an early age—either as wives (*qi*), if their families were relatively prosperous, or as concubines (*qie*), if their families needed the cash that would be offered for them.

With few exceptions (to be discussed below), men were permitted to marry just one wife at a time—polygamy in this sense was normally forbidden—but they could acquire any number of concubines.[2] In the family hierarchy, the principal wife (*diqi*) ranked second only to her husband, whereas a concubine was always inferior to the wife, even if her relations with the husband were more intimate. This inferiority was reinforced in part by the wife's particular privileges, and in part by the divergent manner in which wives and concubines entered the household.

One reason why polygyny was accepted throughout premodern Chinese history is that marriage was not construed according to the Judeo-Christian understanding of a union of two souls before God. But that can be only part of the explanation, because the same reasoning would permit polyandry as well, yet polyandry was never institutionalized.[3] Even Chinese literati who were attracted to Christian teachings were reluctant to give up their concubines. Because it contravened Christian doctrine, polygyny was regarded by missionaries as a prime impediment to Christianizing the Chinese people.[4] Michele Ruggieri (known also as Luo Mingjian), a Jesuit priest who traveled to China in 1583, wrote: "If one woman cannot have two men, how can one man own two women?"[5] In his reckoning, polygyny was at odds with the Sixth Commandment (or Seventh, according to the Septuagint and the Talmud): "Thou shalt not commit adultery." Xu Guangqi (1562–1633), a famous literatus, claimed: "Nothing about observing the Ten Commandments is difficult—except for not taking concubines."[6] Polygyny was an elemental component of traditional Chinese culture, and it was enshrined in Chinese myth as well: the sage king Yao, we are told, gave not one, but *both* of his daughters to his fellow sage king Shun in marriage.[7]

Chinese Catholic converts such as Xu Guangqi restated a position with ancient roots: Polygyny was justified as a means of increasing fertility. By taking concubines, a male of sufficient means could ensure the continuity of his patriline—a demonstration of his filial piety (*xiao*). At the same time, however, these men risked discord at home, because resentment could grow between wives and concubines in the domestic realm. For the sake of maintaining family harmony, many Chinese wives accepted it as their duty to manage the household and bear many descendants. However, not every woman shared these ideals or realized them in the same fashion. Some resorted to outbursts of jealousy in order to defend their marriage, status, and legacy.

Conflicts between a son of the principal wife (*dizi*) and a son of a concubine (*shuzi*) show that, in polygynous households, descendants identified themselves with both their fathers and their birth mothers. Most fathers seem to have regarded their sons equally, whether their mothers were wives or concubines, because they were all his descendants by blood. (This accounts for the traditional Chinese practice of equally distributing a father's property among his sons.) But the same did not necessarily hold for mothers, who were not always related to their husband's children. There could be considerable strife within a polygynous household.

A man might take concubines for yet another reason: they could serve as tokens of his wealth and status. This tendency exacerbated the complementary predicaments of lower-class men and women. The commodification of the female body drove many women into polygynous households, and also made it harder for poor men to establish monogamous households of their own. Men who had no opportunities for marriage were called "rootless rascals"[8] (*guanggun*) in the Qing dynasty (1644–1911). They were excluded from the regular family order because of the skewed sex ratio in the general population and the disproportionate number of women claimed by rich households. The skewed sex ratio was an enduring problem in China caused by a combination of factors: female infanticide,[9] to be sure, but also shorter female lifespans attributable to unequal access to resources and, above all, the considerable dangers of childbirth.[10] Polygyny in elite households further reduced the supply of marriageable women—a process already recognized in antiquity[11]—resulting in a socially destabilizing surplus of males. Since the family structure formed the basis of traditional Chinese society, men without such ties were viewed as sexual predators and threats to the social order. Polygyny is thus not only a tale of patriarchy, but also a key to understanding profound social tensions in traditional China.

THE PRIVILEGED STATUS OF THE WIFE

In traditional China, a woman's social status was defined by the role that she played in her family.[12] A wife was her husband's mate and the hostess in the household.[13] She shared her husband's class, whether he was a peasant, merchant, or official; accordingly, the clothes she could wear and the etiquette she was expected to display depended on her husband's background and achievements. The primary wife's stature was cemented by the wedding ceremony and the funeral rites that would be held for her, as well as her legal rights. Only a bride formally taken as a wife could address the patriline's ancestors as her husband's partner. Not only was the bride herself accepted into the patriline, but her relatives were also integrated into her husband's network as affines. A wife who ritually mourned her husband's parents could never be divorced.[14] When a wife died, all of her husband's recognized children, whether borne by her or not, assumed full mourning obligations for her, but her dowry was distributed only to her own sons and daughters.[15] Despite the vicissitudes of rituals and laws over the centuries, the superiority of the wife over any concubine was ensured by such institutions.

The wedding ceremony consisted of six basic procedures: making a proposal of marriage (*nacai*), requesting the bride's name and date of birth

    DEBBY CHIH-YEN HUANG AND PAUL R. GOLDIN

(*wenming*), sending news of divination results and betrothal gifts (*naji*), sending wedding presents to the bride's house (*nazheng*), requesting the date of the wedding (*qingqi*), and fetching in the bride in person (*qinying*). The details of each ritual could vary.[16] A woman was recognized as a man's wife only after the completion of all these procedures. Their importance is illustrated in the preface to a memorial poem about a faithful maiden, composed by Mao Qiling (1623–1713). Wang Ziyao, the eighteen-year-old heroine, was betrothed to a man from the Su family who died while still her fiancé. After observing the mourning period, she insisted on being married to her dead spouse in order to serve his parents. The Su family accordingly held a wedding ceremony for her. Maiden Wang was ritually ushered into her new home by her sister-in-law; she bowed with her fiancé's portrait in the Su lineage hall, and was formally introduced to her parents-in-law.[17] The rituals on her wedding day served to confirm her status as Mr. Su's wife.[18]

Some scholars have observed that a wife's identity was constructed when she offered sacrifices in her husband's ancestral shrine (*miaojian*).[19] The couple thereby embodied the idea that "the husband and wife are one body" (*fuqi tongti* or *fuqi yiti*)—which is to say that a husband and wife shared social status and family responsibilities.[20] For example, during the Eastern Han dynasty (25–220 CE), when an official's wife was granted an audience with the empress on the occasion of the New Year, her dress, adornments, and carriage all had to conform to her husband's official rank.[21]

In the same vein, joint burial of a husband and wife was customary. The grave was regarded as a re-creation of the house that the couple had dominated when they were alive.[22] This aspect of the practice was particularly prominent in Han tombs, where the rear room was furnished with a portrait of the deceased couple as a representation of the ideal afterlife—an extension of life in which concubines were absent.[23] Joint burial also conveyed the intimacy and complementarity of a married couple by juxtaposing their physical remains, expressing the idea that each spouse was not only half of a larger body (*banti*), but also an equivalent counterpart (*qiti*).[24]

Once a wife's legitimacy was established, her unique position was protected by law. According to the legal code of the Tang dynasty (618–907), a bigamist husband would be punished by at least a year of penal servitude, and the second marriage would be annulled.[25] Yet although marrying more than one wife at a time was generally illegal, it was occasionally allowed as a wartime exception or through the intervention of imperial power. For example, in 257 CE, Wu Gang, a married senior secretary of the Wei kingdom (220–265), was sent to the Wu kingdom (229–280) as a wartime hostage. There, he remarried, then returned to the north with his second family after the fall of Wu in 280. Instead of criticizing him, the government endorsed both marriages on account of the physical separation caused by the wars, though only the eldest son of the first principal wife was recognized as the heir to his lineage.[26]

The principal wife also enjoyed certain special rights of inheritance. During the Western Han dynasty (202 BCE–8 CE), both widows and daughters were eligible to inherit a man's noble rank and property, as well as to become the head of the household that he left behind.[27] Although widows were later denied the right to inherit their husbands' rank, from the Han dynasty (206 BCE–220 CE) to the Song dynasty (960–1279), they still could inherit their husbands' property.[28] However, from the Ming dynasty (1368–1644) onward, a widow acted solely as the custodian of her husband's property because she was no longer eligible to inherit it herself. This denial of widows' inheritance emerged from the increasing urge to keep property within the patriline. As compensation for lost rights of inheritance, more and more officials supported a widow's right to choose an heir instead of simply naming the closest relative of the dead husband. Allowing the widow to select her husband's heir reflected an effort to protect her from being completely dispossessed.[29]

The most reliable way for a bride's natal family to secure her status and well-being was to provide her with a dowry. According to Song dynasty sources, the list of dowry items would be specified before the wedding day. When the bride's parents prepared a dowry for their daughter, they would let her bring betrothal gifts back from her new family. The value of the betrothal gifts was usually smaller than that of the dowry. From the Song dynasty onward, the dowry would consist of landed and movable property, and its size depended on the wealth of the bride's family and the importance that they attached to the marriage.[30] However, before the Song, dowries containing land were rare; a bride's trousseau would have consisted mainly of chattel, such as jewelry, movables, and even bondservants. The conventional term for this trousseau, "cosmetics case" (*zhuanglian*), bespoke the personal nature of the assets.[31]

A proper dowry dignified a bride when she entered a new family. Her possessions were enumerated in detailed lists and were distinguished from the patrimony of her husband's family.[32] Her ownership of the dowry was protected by law; even the patriarch of her husband's family could not expropriate it,[33] and only her own children could inherit it after her death.[34] Her quasi-autonomous control of her own property buttressed her status within her husband's household. The dowry would contribute to the new couple's economic base, which they could manage without intervention

   DEBBY CHIH-YEN HUANG AND PAUL R. GOLDIN

from either family. In addition, the dowry sustained affinal connections. A husband could look forward to worldly favors, such as opportunities for advanced education and official posts, from his affines.[35] In return, the wife's natal family would expect financial support for the wife's parents, care for widowed and orphaned affinal kin, assistance with funeral arrangements, and so on.[36]

Wives' autonomy declined dramatically during the Yuan dynasty (1260–1368). Yuan lawmakers prohibited a widow from taking her dowry if she planned to leave her late husband's family. Consequently, unless she remained with her in-laws, she could hardly sustain herself without some kind of financial support from either her natal family or a new husband. This weakened economic condition forced the wife to submit further to patriarchal authority, as her obligations to her husband's patriline now persisted even after his death.[37]

THE FLUID STATUS OF THE CONCUBINE

The concubine's inferiority was fixed by the manner in which she joined the household: She was not married to a husband but was "collected" or purchased by a master (*naqie*). In other words, although she would enter into a legal relationship with a husband, she was not regarded as his spouse.[38] This accounts for her lack of inheritance and custodianship rights. Masters who permitted their concubines to manage domestic affairs were criticized because taking a concubine as one's wife was socially unacceptable and indeed legally prohibited.[39]

A concubine's position within a household was further defined by the services that she performed, such as bearing children, serving as a sexual outlet, or helping to establish sociopolitical networks. With such diverse functions, concubines could fall into different categories: high-ranking concubines (*yingqie*), "minor wives" (*xiaoqi*), "attendant-concubines" (*shiqie*), "courtesan-concubines" (*jiqie*), and so on.[40] However, a concubine's position was not fixed; it could change over time, at the whim of the master or with the help of her children. Thus some concubines could, over time, earn more dignity within their households. A concubine's position also depended on her relations with the rest of the household; some concubines navigated these hazards more skillfully than others.

In Zhou times (ca. 1027–ca. 256 BCE), *yingqie* were high-status concubines who were brought into an aristocratic family by the bride herself. The bride's relatives, usually her parents, would send bronze vessels, concubines, and servants on the occasion of the marriage. This ceremonial gift was called *ying*.[41] In practice, *ying* constituted a type of sororal polygyny, because the two *yingqie* would be a niece (*zhi*) and a younger sister of the bride (*di*). The blood relationship between the bride and the sororal concubines ensured the latter's high status vis-à-vis other concubines who might be added in the future, and also reassured the bride's natal family that the sororal concubines would support her in her new home. They would assist her in childbearing or childrearing, and in maintaining relations between the two lineages even if the bride was eventually divorced from the master.[42]

Sororal polygyny served both to produce offspring and to further diplomatic ends. A bride who came with sororal concubines was usually a daughter of a ruling house who was betrothed to the sovereign of another state. In an age of multistate politics, her marriage was not a personal affair only, but part of her natal kingdom's geopolitical strategy.[43] If the bride or one of the sororal concubines gave birth to an heir, the relationship between the two states would grow even closer. In order to strengthen such alliances, states whose ruling families had the same surname as the bride's family would also send concubines on the occasion of the marriage, since states with rulers of the same surname were regarded as natural allies.[44]

In contrast to sprawling aristocratic families, peasant households, at least in the Han period, were usually nuclear families comprising a couple and their children, as we know from both textual and archaeological evidence.[45] But this does not mean that peasants never took concubines: Other evidence suggests that even commoners could engage in polygynous marriage. The Western Han government categorized women as "wives" (*qi*), "side-wives" (*pianqi*), "lower wives" (*xiaqi*), or mere "cohabiting bondservants" (*yubi*).[46]

A side-wife was a freewoman who was not enumerated together with her husband or children on a population register; she might have lived outside the husband's household, in her own residence or that of her natal family. A side-wife probably did not rely totally on her husband to support her, unlike a wife, lesser wife, or cohabiting bondservant.[47] A lower wife, like a side-wife, was a freewoman;[48] she cohabited with the husband, but was inferior to the wife. Children of side-wives and lower wives were eligible to inherit any noble rank possessed by the father if there was no principal son to serve as the main heir.[49] A cohabiting bondservant, in contrast to side-wives and lower wives, was unfree, though she would be liberated after her master's death if she had given birth to a child.[50] (Otherwise, she would probably be sold.) It is uncertain whether a free side-wife or lower wife had inheritance rights like those of the principal wife.[51]

     DEBBY CHIH-YEN HUANG AND PAUL R. GOLDIN

The term "minor wife" (*xiaoqi*) also appears frequently in the textual tradition, as a respectful term of address. A minor wife would be listed alongside the "major wife" (*daqi*), or principal wife, in the population register of Changsha in the kingdom of Wu. (The prefixes "major" and "minor" indicate that the minor wife was inferior.[52]) Though it is still hard to gauge the extent of this inferiority, the fact that the minor wives of the politically indicted Chunyu Zhang (d. 8 BCE) were able to avoid being impounded as government slaves upon his conviction (on the grounds that they had left him before his arrest) suggests that a minor wife was not permanently bound to her husband.[53]

A concubine's identity was fluid because she was not necessarily a permanent member of the household. A concubine of low status, such as an attendant-concubine or a courtesan-concubine, could be bought and sold with impunity or exchanged between friends,[54] transferred from one household to another. Moreover, a concubine would probably be expelled from the household when her master was ready to marry a principal wife, even if she had borne him a child. She would typically go back to her natal family or enter another household as a wife and concubine.[55] However, bearing a child could have positive consequences. A bondservant could be reregistered as a concubine on account of her child;[56] similarly, a concubine could resist being cast out after her master-husband's death by claiming that she needed to take care of her children.[57]

A concubine could earn more respect at home if she had a son who passed the civil service examinations and became an official. In order to deepen the candidate pool, sons of concubines from elite families were allowed to take the examinations. Candidates were expected to exhibit their knowledge of the classics and present it in a satisfactory literary style.[58] If they were lucky, they would be appointed to official posts shortly after passing the civil service examinations, commencing careers involving travel from their residences to their assigned offices (and occasionally to the imperial capital).[59]

Concubines could benefit from the necessary domestic adjustments. Because a Tang gentleman would usually delay marriage until he passed the examinations, his household would probably be managed by a concubine. When a married official was assigned to a post far away from home, he might ask his wife to stay with his parents, and bring a concubine with him instead. Thus, a concubine who managed domestic affairs for a gentleman would become an indispensable member of his household, securing her own position as well as that of her children. Or if her son passed the civil service examinations, she could leave the household for the sake of attending her son on official business. Her inferior legal status could even be overturned if her son, now powerful and respected, petitioned authorities to confer on her a title commensurate with his own official rank. Even the son's father could not request this.[60]

The status of a concubine underwent two major transformations over the course of the Song and Yuan dynasties. First, in the Song dynasty, a concubine who was leased to a private individual (*dianqie*) probably no longer remained attached to his household when her contract expired.[61] Second, concubines could be accepted as fuller family members if they bore children; motherhood even became a stereotypical role in Yuan funerary texts for concubines.[62] These transformations could elevate a concubine above chattel status, and some elite men of the period may have gradually elided the distinction between wife and concubine.

The blurry line between a wife's and concubine's status can be seen in the figure of the "equal-status wife" (*liangtou da*, perhaps a southeastern regionalism) in late imperial China. An equal-status wife was acquired by a married man who spent considerable time without his wife's company while on business in other provinces. She was usually a woman of good family and was married, with due rituals, because the man was separated from his sexual partners or wished to forge new sociopolitical networks. The man usually granted the equal-status wife principal status in the new household, and treated any children borne by her as principal sons. However, even though "equal-status wives" were socially acceptable, bigamy was unquestionably illegal. Therefore, even though an "equal-status wife" may have acted like a wife, she was still considered a type of concubine.[63]

Similar ambiguity between marriage and concubinage arose through "combined succession" (*jiantiao*), which permitted an only son to serve as heir to both his father and his father's brother(s) if there was no other suitable candidate in his family. The single heir would be allowed to have two wives; the principal wife produced offspring for the main branch, and the secondary wife produced offspring for the secondary branch. In this manner, the property from each branch would be inherited by different descendants, ensuring the continuity of the respective patrilines.[64] Although combined succession was widely practiced, it was not legalized until 1775.[65] Moreover, Qing lawmakers still endeavored to protect the principal wife's unique position by considering the secondary wife as a concubine or regarding the second marriage as bigamous. This attitude toward the secondary wife was later confirmed by the Daliyuan, the highest court of appeals in Republican China.[66] However, the Nanjing government observed that, in the countryside, the secondary wife was always considered the principal wife of

     DEBBY CHIH-YEN HUANG AND PAUL R. GOLDIN

the second branch, and her equal standing was ensured by both verbal and written agreements.[67] Combined succession highlighted conflicts between legal ideology and social reality.

ANTAGONISM IN THE HOME

A woman's maternal experience in a polygynous household was determined by the circumstances of childbirth and by the woman's status in the family.[68] Giving birth differentiated a birth mother (*shengmu*) from a "foster mother" (*houmu* or *yangmu*) or "loving mother" (*cimu*). The term "foster mother" denoted a principal wife who adopted a son from her husband's paternal relatives with the approval of the patriarch or a matriarch. A "loving mother" was a concubine appointed by her master to take care of another concubine's child. In both sets of cases, maternity was established by discharging the dictates of the master; the woman had no biological bond with the child. Both "foster motherhood" and "loving motherhood" can be regarded as forms of social, rather than biological, motherhood.

Social motherhood denotes maternity as defined by a woman's relationship with the head of a household,[69] and the terminology denoting varieties of motherhood in traditional China could be highly ramified. In a polygynous household, the principal wife was the legal mother (*dimu*) of all children recognized by her husband. A concubine could be regarded as a "concubine-mother" (*shumu*) to all the master's children, but she did not hold maternal authority at home because she was ranked below the wife. If a man married more than once, the children of his new wife would recognize the former wife as "former mother" (*qianmu*), and the children of his former wife would recognize the new wife as "stepmother" (*jimu*). If the former wife or a concubine-mother left the household in divorce, she would be called the "divorced mother" (*chumu*) of her children. If the former wife or an expelled concubine later remarried, she would be called "remarried mother" (*jiamu*) by her birth children, who would remain in the father's household. Within the fierce crucible of a polygynous household, social motherhood was a childless woman's guarantee of security, allowing her to sustain her position in the family by acquiring factitious offspring. Because the institution of polygyny established roles for women too, some of which could be powerful, wives did not always oppose it; indeed, many worked to advance it.[70]

However, not every woman felt that she had found the right niche. For example, Lady Liu, the primary wife of the Jin dynasty statesman Xie An (320–385), is said to have rejected her husband's request for female entertainers and concubines. Later, Xie's nephews on both sides of the family discussed the canonical *Book of Odes* with her, implying that she should learn the virtue of suppressing jealousy from such poems as "Guanju" ("The chanting ospreys") and "Zhong si" ("The locusts"). Detecting sarcasm in their voice, she asked, "And who wrote those songs?" They replied, without hesitation, "The Duke of Zhou." Lady Liu then made a witty retort: "The Duke of Zhou was a man and wrote them for himself, that's all. Now if it had been the Duchess of Zhou, the tradition wouldn't have contained these words!"[71]

Occasionally, men objected to polygyny as well. Writing sometime around the year 300, the philosopher Bao Jingyan criticized it as a harmful byproduct of the political system: while the elite accumulated women in their harems, many ordinary men remained unmarried. After reporting this opinion, the author Ge Hong (283–343) defended the tradition by declaring that the appropriate number of concubines for the king was set by the sages in accordance with Heaven's wishes. The purpose of royal concubines, he said, was to foster the sovereign's erotic love, help the queen manage the palace, and assist at ancestral sacrifices. He went on to add that, according to the ancient ritual text *Zhouli* (Rites of Zhou) and the geographical treatise of the *History of the Han*, there are more women than men in the world anyway.[72] (We now know that, for most periods of Chinese history, this latter statement was simply untrue.)

A principal wife might also have regarded concubines and maids as an existential threat; they might usurp her husband's favors, her wifely authority, and her son's share of the patrimony.[73] During the Six Dynasties period (222–589), elite wives were sometimes taught to deploy exhibitions of jealousy in order to secure their positions and prevent their husbands from taking concubines. Calculated jealousy of this type was usually directed at concubines and maids, rather than the husband.[74] Because concubines and maids lived with the wife in the inner chambers, where the husband could not intrude at will, he could not always protect them from his wife's verbal and physical abuse.[75]

Conflict between a wife and concubines undermined the patriline, and was also considered a sign of a husband's inability to handle affairs. In order to maintain familial harmony, men of the Six Dynasties period urged their wives to comply with the ethics of female submission through reprimands and various threats and punishments, such as divorce, flogging, and even the death penalty. Outbursts of jealousy were regarded as vicious conduct on the part of women, to be corrected through discipline at the hands of men.

By the seventh century (at the latest), jealousy was taken as an inherent and innate disposition of women, thought to cause female illnesses that

    DEBBY CHIH-YEN HUANG AND PAUL R. GOLDIN

were curable through therapeutic rituals or prescriptions.[76] In late imperial China, therapy for women's jealousy was incorporated into complex medical theories: "Congested anger" (*yunu*), a gendered symptom present only in women, resulted from hatred of polygynous marriage, and would make a woman suffer from "liver fire" (*ganhuo*). *Yunu* was remediable by formulas designed to clear *ganhuo*.[77] A jealous woman was construed as disruptive to familial order, and treatments for jealousy were efforts to return the family to normalcy—that is, harmonious polygyny.

Childbirth was not the only task that a primary wife was expected to assume, especially in well-to-do families.[78] As a partner of the head of the household, she took responsibility for household management, productivity, and networking. In comparison to the aforementioned tasks, which required education and ingenuity, it was easy to find a surrogate for childbirth—a concubine or a maid, for whom fertility was the only requirement.[79] Thus, maternal identity encompassed more than just biological motherhood; it also reflected the wife's upbringing and character.[80] Both childbirth and childrearing forged emotional ties with the children in the family, and need not have been undertaken by the same mother.

The mother-son bond could produce several layers of emotional commitment. First, it was manifested financially in the distribution of the mother's dowry, as only her natural children could inherit such property. Second, it was manifested sociopolitically in the status and prestige of the mother and her descendants. A son's status was usually contingent on whether his mother was a wife, a concubine, or simply a maid;[81] but a concubine-mother's status could be elevated at her filial son's request.[82] Third, the emotional bond between a mother and her natural son would often be enhanced because they faced the same rivalries and crises.[83]

For an extreme case, consider Yan Tingzhi (d. 748), a Tang-era official who behaved indecorously toward his wife, Lady Pei; he preferred his concubine, Xuanying. Yan Tingzhi's eight-year-old principal son, Yan Wu (726–765), asked his mother, Lady Pei, about his father's patent antagonism. Lady Pei wept and said that Yan Tingzhi was cold to her because she was ugly. Yan Wu flew into a rage and vented his fury upon the concubine, smashing her head to pieces. The facts were concealed by attendants, who reported the death to Yan Tingzhi as an accident. However, Yan Wu admitted that he intentionally killed Xuanying because of his father's discrimination against his mother, asking, "How is it possible for a man of ministerial rank to favor his concubine but treat his legal wife frigidly?"[84]

Unlike his mother, Yan Wu was loved and respected by his father. Yan Wu hated the concubine not because *he* was mistreated by Yan Tingzhi, but because *his mother* felt mistreated by him. Lady Pei's emotional connection with her son led Yan Wu to transform his father's coldness toward his mother into an intolerable offense.

WOMEN'S BODIES IN PERIL

The vulnerability of the concubine's body was a consequence of a stratified society. Yan Wu was punished neither by his father nor by any judge for murdering Xuanying because she was regarded as a mere possession, not a free human being with commensurate legal protections. The practice of *zheng* in early China also reveals the tenuousness of a concubine's position. *Zheng* referred to the act of copulating with a deceased father's concubine—a predictable byproduct of polygyny. The very existence of this term suggests that the behavior was not exceptional, but a well-developed social practice during the Spring and Autumn period (771–476 BCE), and possibly a general Eurasian cultural feature.[85] In that era, a concubine's body was understood as a heritable possession; even a noblewoman or princess might be unable to stop a young heir intent on enjoying his new property. For example, the concubine Jiang of Yi was silent when her master's son, Lord Xuan of Wei (r. 718–700 BCE), committed *zheng* with her. Her antipathy could be inferred only after she committed suicide.[86]

The female body was also regarded as a limited resource that could not be allowed to go to waste. Empress Guo of Wei (184–235), for example, prohibited her relatives from collecting concubines because she wanted to ensure that soldiers could find wives during a national shortage of women.[87] Centuries later, the Mongol invasion introduced practices resembling the levirate; in most such cases, men would inherit their older brothers' widows, but sometimes a son would inherit his father's wives (other than his birth mother), or a nephew his uncle's widow, and so on. By this mechanism, a household could forgo the costs of betrothal gifts for younger brothers, maximally exploit the widow's productive and reproductive capacity, and retain the late husband's assets in the same patriline.[88] (Many of the complexities of Chinese polygyny derived from the need to clarify and protect rights of inheritance.) In pursuit of such efficiencies, more and more households, particularly poorer ones, proposed levirate marriages for their younger sons.[89] Widows could not easily reject levirate marriages because, as we have seen, they could scarcely survive on their own. Among their few other options were to rely on their natal families' wealth or to resort to the chastity cult—that is, forcing their in-laws to support them as "chaste widows" (*zhenfu*) by renouncing any future husband.

     DEBBY CHIH-YEN HUANG AND PAUL R. GOLDIN

Naturally, polygyny also reduced lower-status men's chances of entering into wedlock. The profusion of poor males with scant hope of marriage came to be regarded as a serious social issue in the Qing dynasty. In Qing legal documents, such men were conceived as vagrants disposed to seducing, raping, or abducting chaste women. In addition, they posed an existential threat to the dynasty, because their very existence, divorced from traditional family bonds, contravened the conscious efforts of the Qing government to organize society household by household.[90] Some Qing women responded to sexual molestation by committing suicide in order to force abusers to pay for their transgressions; judges were not pleased when women of good character killed themselves under such circumstances, and usually found responsible parties to punish. The female body could be converted into a ferocious incarnate denouncement, but only at the ultimate cost.[91]

THE OUTLOOK TODAY

Polygyny was abolished in China by the New Marriage Law of 1950, at a time when the Communist Party was eager to eradicate concubinage and other forms of sexual servitude.[92] Sociologists have begun to report, however, what any astute visitor to China has surely already observed: informal concubinage has rapidly reemerged among the wealthy.[93] In the absence of sanctioned institutions and precedents, the judicial system is struggling to decide how "second wives" (*ernai*) should be treated.[94] China is repeating the pattern of the past in other respects too: according to the 2015 census, males now outnumber females by some thirty-three million, and the sex ratio is one of the worst in the world.[95] If history is any guide, there will be discontent.

NOTES

1   Polygyny can frequently be inferred from the practice (called *xunzang*) of interring a deceased lord's concubines and servitors with him. See, generally, Ebner von Eschenbach, "In den Tod mitgehen." Gideon Shelach-Lavi (private communication) observes that polygyny is scarcely attested in Neolithic contexts, and therefore seems to be associated with the rise of Bronze Age states. Yu et al., "Shifting Diets and the Rise of Male-Biased Inequality on the Central Plains of China during Eastern Zhou," confirms that males and females appear to have had equal status in Neolithic farming communities.

2   See, for example, Liu, *Zhongguo gudai xing wenhua*, 143–50; and more generally, Zhang, *Duoqi zhidu*. (Note that, strictly speaking, the commonplace

Chinese term *duoqi zhidu*—literally, "system of multiple wives"—is inaccurate, because in a normal household there could be just one principal wife.)

3   For a recent study of informal polyandry, especially among the poor, see Sommer, *Polyandry and Wife-Selling in Qing Dynasty China*. Polyandrous domestic arrangements were never legal, and those who entered into them were always in danger of punishment, which could be severe. More generally, see Chen, *Zhongguo hunyin shi*, 44–46.

4   Brockey, *Journey to the East*, 300–301.

5   Luo, *Tianzhu shengjiao shilu*, 833–34.

6   Li, *Lixiu yijian*, 465–66.

7   See, for example, Birrell, *Chinese Mythology*, 74–76.

8   This translation comes from Sommer (*Sex, Law, and Society in Late Imperial China*, 14), who describes *guanggun* as "the superfluous rogue male who threatens the household order from outside." For another recent treatment, see Jiang and Sánchez-Barricarte, "Bare Branches and Social Stability."

9   For an early, casual reference to female infanticide, see Chen, *Han Feizi xin jiaozhu*, 1,006.

10   See Waltner, "Infanticide and Dowry in Ming and Early Qing China," 196–204.

11   See Chin, *Savage Exchange*, 200f.

12   Ebrey, *The Inner Quarters*, 44ff.

13   Bray, *Technology and Gender*, 5, 55; and Liu, "Zheng wei yu nei?" 58–59.

14   See Tai, "Divorce in Traditional Chinese Law," 90.

15   Bray, *Technology and Gender*, 351.

16   See Chen, *Zhongguo hunyin shi*, 99–102; and Dull, "Marriage and Divorce in Han China," 42ff. For practices in the Song dynasty, see Ebrey, *The Inner Quarters*, 82–98; for the late imperial period, see Bray, *Technology and Gender*, 339.

17   Mao, *Xihe ji*, 186.2a–186.4b.

18   See Lu, *True to Her Word*, 168–72.

19   Ch'ü, *Law and Society in Traditional China*, 102.

20   Taniguchi, "Kandai no kōgō ken," 1,588–89.

21   Hoshina, "Kandai no josei chitsujo"; and Ch'ü, *Law and Society in Traditional China*, 140–41.

22   Lewis, *The Construction of Space in Early China*, 8, 57–59.

23   Barnhart et al., *Three Thousand Years of Chinese Painting*, 34.

24   Chen, *Zhongguo hunyin shi*, 286–88.

25   Ch'ü, *Law and Society in Traditional China*, 123–24.

26   Chen, *Sanguo zhi*, 770, 1,154; and Du, *Tongdian*, 1,894–95.

27   Liu, *You Zhangjiashan Hanjian* Ernian lüling *lun Hanchu de jicheng zhidu*, 120–21, 149–162. The primary wife's unique rights of inheritance are ignored by Vankeerberghen ("A Sexual Order in the Making," 127), who argues for "the lack of sharp lines of division between the various women in a [Han dynasty] household."

28 Li, "Han Tang zhi jian nüxing caichanquan shitan"; and Bernhardt, *Women and Property in China*, 53–59.

29 Bernhardt, *Women and Property in China*, 47–72.

30 Ebrey, *Women and the Family in Chinese History*, 68–87; and Birge, *Women, Property, and Confucian Reaction in Sung and Yüan China*, 31.

31 Birge, *Women, Property, and Confucian Reaction in Sung and Yüan China*, 61; and Li, "Han Tang zhi jian nüxing caichanquan shitan."

32 Birge, *Women, Property, and Confucian Reaction in Sung and Yüan China*, 37, 140.

33 Ebrey, *Women and the Family in Chinese History*, 83; Birge, *Women, Property, and Confucian Reaction in Sung and Yüan China*, 61, 140; and Bray, *Technology and Gender*, 265.

34 Birge, *Women, Property, and Confucian Reaction in Sung and Yüan China*, 63. Bray (*Technology and Gender*, 139, 171) stresses that a woman of late imperial China would be willing to contribute economically to her nuclear family—i.e., her husband and children—rather than her husband's patriline.

35 Bossler, *Powerful Relations*, 137–42; Birge, *Women, Property, and Confucian Reaction in Sung and Yüan China*, 65.

36 Ebrey, *Women and the Family in Chinese History*, 84ff. For the Tang dynasty, see Chen, *Tangdai de funü wenhua yu jiating shenghuo*, 23–196.

37 Birge, *Women, Property, and Confucian Reaction in Sung and Yüan China*, 198, 279–80.

38 Ebrey, *Women and the Family in Chinese History*, 42.

39 Chen, *Tangdai de funü wenhua yu jiating shenghuo*, 305–18; MacCormack, "A Reassessment of the 'Confucianization of the Law' from the Han to the Tang"; and Liao Yifang, *Tangdai de muzi guanxi*, 165–66.

40 Bossler, *Courtesans, Concubines, and the Cult of Female Fidelity*, 65.

41 Chen, "Liang-Zhou hunyin guanxi zhong de 'ying' yu 'yingqi,'" 197.

42 Thatcher ("Marriages of the Ruling Elite in the Spring and Autumn Period," 31, 44) regards *yingqie* as secondary wives instead of high-status concubines.

43 Thatcher, "Marriages of the Ruling Elite in the Spring and Autumn Period," 46–48.

44 Chen, "Liang-Zhou hunyin guanxi zhong de 'ying' yu 'yingqi,'" 213–22.

45 Lewis, *The Construction of Space in Early China*, 7, 79, 87. The register of soldiers guarding the frontier town Juyan also indicates that frontier households mainly consisted of the husband, the wife, and their descendants; sometimes, but not always, they lived with their parents and siblings. See also Du, *Gudai shehui yu guojia*, 790–92.

46 Sasaki, "Handai hunyin xingtai xiaokao"; also Wang, *Gushi xingbie yanjiu conggao*, 219–31.

47 See Sasaki, "Handai hunyin xingtai xiaokao"; and Barbieri-Low and Yates, *Law, State, and Society in Early Imperial China*, 448, 601. Another indication that side-wives enjoyed relatively high rank within the family is that the law

explicitly forbade beating the parents of one's father's side-wives (Barbieri-Low and Yates, 405).

48 Despite Barbieri-Low and Yates, *Law, State, and Society in Early Imperial China*, which states that "[*xiaqi*] were unofficial wives, basically sex slaves who were bought from human traffickers and resided with the other wives and concubines" (865).

49 See Liu, *You Zhangjiashan Hanjian* Ernian lüling *lun Hanchu de jicheng zhidu*, 30, 42, 71, 95; and Vankeerberghen, "A Sexual Order in the Making," 125.

50 Zhang, "Shi Zhangjiashan Hanjian zhong de 'yubi'"; Barbieri-Low and Yates, *Law, State, and Society in Early Imperial China*, 861.

51 Liu, *You Zhangjiashan Hanjian* Ernian lüling *lun Hanchu de jicheng zhidu*, 120–21, 149–62.

52 See Hinsch, *Women in Early Imperial China*, 41.

53 Wang, *Gushi xingbie yanjiu conggao*, 254–65.

54 Bossler, *Courtesans, Concubines, and the Cult of Female Fidelity*, 79–84, 227–28.

55 In this respect, the concubine's natal family served as her shelter (Liao Yifang, 161–64).

56 Liu, "Wei Jin Nanbeichao shidai de qie," 9, 16–17; and Bossler, *Courtesans, Concubines, and the Cult of Female Fidelity*, 57.

57 Liao, *Tangdai de muzi guanxi*, 173.

58 See, for example, De Weerdt, *Competition over Content*, 2ff.

59 Hu, "Qianli huanyou cheng dishi, meinian fengjing shi taxiang."

60 Liao, *Tangdai de muzi guanxi*, 167–77.

61 Ebrey, *Women and the Family in Chinese History*, 46–52.

62 Bossler, *Courtesans, Concubines, and the Cult of Female Fidelity*, 334–35, 345–57.

63 Hsieh, *Concubinage and Servitude in Late Imperial China*, 44.

64 Ibid.; Ch'ü, *Law and Society in Traditional China*, 124; and Lu, *Qingmo Minchu jiachan zhidu de yanbian*, 145.

65 Bernhardt, *Women and Property in China*, 44–45.

66 Ibid., 76.

67 Wang, "Lishishang de 'pingqi' xianxiang jiqi falü wenti chutan," 48–50.

68 For discussion of the varieties of motherhood in the early imperial China, see Zheng, *Qinggan yu zhidu*, 21–59, 140–48.

69 See Bray, *Technology and Gender*, 103, 281, 351.

70 Ibid., 281, 351, 356, 364.

71 Liu, *Shih-shuo hsin-yü*, tr. Mather, 378.

72 Yang, *Baopuzi waipian jiaojian*, 560. Balazs did not discuss this aspect of Bao's critique in his famous study *Chinese Civilization and Bureaucracy* (242–46).

73 Bray, *Technology and Gender*, 355.

     DEBBY CHIH-YEN HUANG AND PAUL R. GOLDIN

74 Lee, "Querelle des femmes?" 68–97.

75 Ebrey, *The Inner Quarters*, 167, 230; and Bray, *Technology and Gender*, 147, 355.

76 Lee, "Querelle des femmes?" 77–85.

77 Kuriyama, "Angry Women and the Evolution of Chinese Medicine," 184–85.

78 Bray, *Technology and Gender*, 281.

79 Bray (*Technology and Gender*, 350, 365) argues that class distinctions were also incorporated into medical theories of reproduction.

80 Ibid., 281, 348, 364.

81 Zheng, *Qinggan yu zhidu*, 115–50. During the Western Han period, a son's inheritance was determined by his mother's status. However, from the Southern Song dynasty (1127–1279) onward, the mother's status was irrelevant; only paternal recognition mattered. See Liu, *You Zhangjiashan Hanjian* Ernian lüling *lun Hanchu de jicheng zhidu*, 95, 162; and Bossler, *Courtesans, Concubines, and the Cult of Female Fidelity*, 246–48.

82 Zheng, *Qinggan yu zhidu*, 61–114.

83 Liao, *Tangdai de muzi guanxi*, 161–66.

84 Wang, *Tang yulin jiaozheng*, 329; Ouyang Xiu et al., *Xin Tangshu*, 129.4484.

85 See Goldin, "Copulating with One's Stepmother—Or Birth Mother?"; and Dong, *Zhongguo gudai hunyin shi yanjiu*, 22–28.

86 Yang, *Chunqiu Zuozhuan zhu*, 146.

87 Chen, *Sanguo zhi*, 165. In times of war, the sex ratio is usually skewed in the opposite direction (because so many able-bodied men have been killed); Empress Guo's concern may indicate that the overall ratio was already seriously imbalanced.

88 See Birge, *Women, Property, and Confucian Reaction in Sung and Yüan China*, 204–206; and Dong, *Zhongguo gudai hunyin shi yanjiu*, 73ff.

89 Ch'ü, *Law and Society in Traditional China*, 96–99.

90 Sommer, *Sex, Law, and Society in Late Imperial China*, 96–101.

91 Theiss, *Disgraceful Matters*, 192–209.

92 See, for example, Tran, *Concubines in Court*, 175–97; and Huang, "Divorce Law Practices and the Origins, Myths, and Realities of Judicial 'Mediation' in China," 177.

93 See, for example, Yuen et al., *Marriage, Gender, and Sex in a Contemporary Chinese Village*.

94 Pan, "Transformations in the Primary Life Cycle," 32.

95 Yuen Yeuk-laam, "China Census Shows Continuing Gender Imbalance, Aging Population."

CHAPTER 2

BETWEEN TOPICS AND SOURCES

Researching the History of Sexuality in Imperial China

PING YAO

THE HISTORY OF CHINESE SEXUALITY HAS GROWN TO BECOME A vibrant field of research in recent decades, largely thanks to considerable advances in gender studies and to China scholars' keen awareness of the diverse sources they can tap for their research.[1] Not surprisingly, the availability and the types/genres of the sources have defined scholars' research directions and the ways they approach their topics. Scholarship on sexuality in early China through the third century, for example, focuses largely on the medical texts discovered in the Mawangdui tombs in Hunan Province in the 1970s, which date to the second century BCE, and to a lesser degree, on early Daoist texts. The result has been a bulk of publications exploring how Daoism and medical knowledge shaped the perception and practices of sexuality in early China.

With a large number of extant Daoist texts readily available, scholarship on sexuality in early medieval China (220–589) has been devoted overwhelmingly to perception of sexuality as seen in Daoist rituals and practices. During the Tang dynasty (618–907), the literati elite became a dominant force in defining sexuality, and perception of sexuality as well as writing about sexuality changed considerably; scholarship on Tang sexuality is more extensive in its topics and source materials. In contrast, with much more limited breadth in terms of extant texts, studies on the Song period (960–1279) tend to look into Confucian ideals of sexual relations or cautionary tales of sexual misconduct. Scholarship on sexuality in late imperial China (from 1368 through 1911) is abundant and continues to grow; the enormously rich sources available—ranging from didactic texts, family precepts, and religious scripts to novels, plays, woodblock prints, sex manuals, and legal cases—have made the field an exciting one to watch.

As the number of publications on the history of Chinese sexuality has increased drastically,[2] this chapter looks into how scholars utilize sources in their research in a selective fashion, exploring the ways that the availability, types, and genres of sources influence the written history of sexuality in imperial China. It focuses on the topics of perception of sexuality and sexual practice; regulation of sexual conduct; and femininity, masculinity, and eroticism.

PERCEPTION OF SEXUALITY AND SEXUAL PRACTICES IN DAOIST TEXTS

The earliest extant texts specifically addressing Chinese sexuality are Han Daoist medical texts unearthed from the Mawangdui archaeological site in Changsha between 1972 and 1974. The so-called Mawangdui medical manuscripts (Mawangdui *yishu*) include fourteen medical texts; among them are *Ten Interviews* (Shiwen), *Discourse on the Culminant Way in Under-Heaven* (Tianxia zhidao tan), and *Conjoining Yin and Yang* (He yinyang). These texts have provided scholars with rich sources on sexuality in the Han and the earliest known sexual culture in Chinese history.

Study of the Mawangdui medical manuscripts was pioneered by Donald Harper. In 1987, Harper published the first English-language philological study of a Chinese sexology text, "The Sexual Arts of Ancient China as Described in a Manuscript of the Second Century BC"; the article proposed that the Mawangdui manuscripts reflected the sexual culture of the Warring States and Qin-Han periods (221–207 BCE and 206 BCE–220 CE, respectively). In addition to overviewing the manuscripts, Harper examined *Conjoining Yin and Yang*, providing a translation and an extensive analysis of the first section of the text.[3] Later, Harper published a more comprehensive study on the Mawangdui medical manuscripts, as well as full translations of all fourteen medical texts, expanding his interpretation of Daoist influence on early understanding of sexuality and sexual practice.[4]

Overall scholarly consensus is that the Mawangdui medical manuscripts bear the distinctive tendency of combining Daoist beliefs with medical knowledge. Some texts stress sexual intercourse as resembling the union of *yin* and *yang*; others discuss sex's benefits for physical well-being.[5] Perceptions of gender and sexuality as seen in the texts are twofold. On one hand, the manuscripts emphasize the importance of women's pleasure during intercourse, and state that all human beings need a healthy balance of *yin-qi* and *yang-qi*, which can be achieved through intercourse. On the other hand, as Paul Goldin has pointed out, the texts were clearly "written exclusively for men": "For the sex act to have any medical value," he writes, "the male had to make sure that the female reached orgasm and emitted her *yin-qi*." (This probably is the main reason why ancient Chinese literature offers so few instances of homoeroticism.)[6]

In his pioneering 1961 study on sexuality in Chinese history, *Sexual Life in Ancient China*, Robert Hans van Gulik writes, "During the Han period there existed a number of handbooks of sexual relations, written in the form of dialogues between the Yellow Emperor and one of his teachers, or one of the Instructresses on Sex." Van Gulik explains, "The underlying thought of the handbooks was [mainly] Taoist," adding that "the Confucians approved of the principles set forth therein—with the understanding of course that these principles were applied only and exclusively inside the bedchamber." In van Gulik's analysis, "The differences between the two schools in their attitude to this subject was only a matter of emphasis," with "the Confucianists stressing eugenics and the obtaining of offspring," and "the Taoists stressing the sexual disciplines for prolonging life and for obtaining the Elixir of Immortality."[7]

Scholars have generally argued that post-Han discourse on sexuality, in the period from 220 to the Tang, presented a more pronouncedly Daoist concept of uniting *yin* and *yang* through intercourse.[8] Such understanding is, again, largely based on the available sources on sexuality, which are dominantly Daoist texts: the third- or fourth-century *Secret Instructions of the Jade Bedchamber* (Yufang mijue)[9] and the third- or fourth-century *Scripture of the Yellow Court* (Huangting jing),[10] for instance, alongside the fourth- or fifth-century *Liturgy of Passage of the Yellow Writ of Highest Clarity* (Shangqing huangshu guodu yi).[11] These texts show that post-Han Daoist thought considered attaining *yin-qi* crucial for reaching this-worldly immortality; since sexual intercourse constitutes a prominent technique to reach this goal, early literature on the art of the bedchamber appears to promote, to use van Gulik's phrase, "sexual vampirism."[12] *Liturgy of Passage of the Yellow Writ of Highest Clarity* stipulates that sexual intercourse formed part of the liturgy in the Daoist initiation ritual; called "the harmonization of *qi*" (*heqi*), the process involved combining male sexual energy ("yellow *qi*") and female sexual energy ("red *qi*") to realize the harmony of the universe.[13] Such perception of sexual practice was clearly influenced by the Taoist principle of *yin-yang*.[14]

                    PING YAO

While acknowledging Daoist influence on the perception of sexuality and gender during this period, scholars also find that such perception was far from uniform. In his recent essay "Birthing the Self," Gil Raz analyzes discussions of embryology in two post-Han texts—the *Shangqing Scripture of Nine-Fold Cinnabar for Transformation of Fetal Essence* (Shangqing jiudan shanghua taijing zhongji jing) and the *Central Scripture of Laozi* (Laozi zhongjing). Raz finds that these texts were aimed at male practitioners, who were urged to meditate on the process of gestation and return to an embryonic stage—and then give birth to a perfect self or a perfect embryo, which would ascend to the heavens upon the death of the gross physical body. The positive attitude toward *yin* in Daoist texts does not seem to carry over to actual women; in fact, Daoist embryology links mundane gestation and birth from female wombs to the inevitable cause of death.[15]

Douglas Wile is another scholar whose research relies on acute analysis and translations of Daoist texts; his 1992 book *Art of the Bedchamber* is probably the first comprehensive anthology of the Chinese sexological classics. Wile's book translates Mawangdui medical texts, such as the aforementioned *He yinyang*, and *Discourse on the Highest Tao under Heaven* (Tianxia zhidao tan); post-Han Daoist classics on sexuality, such as *The Classic of the Plain Girl* (Sunüjing),[16] *Prescriptions of Su Nü* (Sunüfang), *Essentials of the Jade Chamber* (Yufang zhiyao), *Secrets of the Jade Chamber* (Yufang mijue), and *Master Dongxuan* (Dongxuanzi); Tang and post-Tang medical manuals and household handbooks, such as *Health Benefits of the Bedchamber* (Fanghong buyi), *The Dangers and Benefits of Intercourse with Women* (Yunü sunyyi), *The Wondrous Discourse of Su Nü* (Sunü miaolun), *True Classic of Perfect Union* (Chunyang yanzheng Fuyou Dijun jiji zhenjing), and *Exposition of Cultivating the True Essence* (Zijin Guangyao Daxian xiuzhen yanyi); elixir literature such as *Seeking Instructions on the Golden Elixir* (Jindan jiuzheng pian), *True Transmission of the Golden Elixir* (Jindan zhenchuan), *Summary of the Golden Elixir* (Jindan jieyao), *Secret Principles of Gathering the True Essence* (Caizhen jiyao), and *The Rootless Tree* (Wugenshu); and Daoist texts on women's practice, such as *Queen Mother of the West's Ten Precepts* (Xiwangmu nüxiu zhengtu shize), *Essentials of the Golden Elixir Method for Women* (Nüjindan yaofang), *Master Li Ni-wan's Precious Raft of Women's Dual Practice* (Niwan Li zushi nüzong shuangxiu baofa), and *Correct Methods for Women's Practice* (Nügong zhengfa).[17]

In discussing historical perceptions of sexuality and sexual practice, Wile relies almost exclusively on these Daoist texts. He concludes that ten "formative [premises] of experience" are reflected in these classics: (1) "energy is lost through ejaculation"; (2) "the activation of sexual energy (*ching*) floods the entire system with positive vital energy (*chi*)"; (3) "sexual potency declines with age"; (4) "ejaculation, although depleting physical reserves, has the opposite effect on sexual desire"; (5) "sexual energy is capable of transfer from one organism to another"; (6) "the period from infancy to puberty is characterized by abundant *yang* energy (*ching-ch'i*) and an absence of seminal (or menstrual) leakage and sexual desire," and this period represents "a time of wholeness" and "physiological integrity"; (7) "abstinence from intercourse, whether voluntary or enforced, was observed to produce both psychological and physiological aberrations"; (8) men and women differ in arousal rate (men being faster than women); (9) "the mingling of sexual essences has the power to create new life"; and (10) "sexual compatibility is the foundation of conjugal harmony," while "harmony requires a detailed understanding of the partner's emotional state and arousal rate."[18]

Kristofer Schipper, a pioneer of scholarly writing about sexuality in Daoist texts, concluded in the late 1960s that sexual practices in Chinese history could be divided into three types: "science" (art of the bedchamber), "magic" (sexual alchemy and orgiastic ritual), and "mystique" (spiritualized sexual fantasy and mystical marriage meditation).[19] Many scholars have since followed in his footsteps, and the dominance of Daoist texts as primary sources for understanding early Chinese sexuality and sexual practices has rarely been challenged.

SEXUAL REGULATION IN DIDACTIC SOURCES, LEGAL DOCUMENTS, AND MISCELLANEOUS NOTES

Didactic sources, ritual codes, legal codes, legal cases, and miscellaneous notes are rich documents for scholars who wish to fathom various historical attempts to regulate sexuality in China. (Here, didactic sources used by scholars include clan regulations, family precepts, Confucian literary essays, and local gazettes.) The most discussed topic in such research is probably female chastity. As Weijing Lu outlines in her book *True to Her Word: The Faithful Maiden Cult in Late Imperial China*, late imperial China witnessed tremendous attempts by the state and the Confucian elite to mold people's behavior along moral lines; concurrent to this was an increasingly large number of chaste widows, relative to earlier dynasties.[20] Scholars such as T'ien Ju-K'ang, Katherine Carlitz, Charlotte Furth, Susan Mann, and Janet Theiss have examined how orthodox gender values were propagated in state laws, household instructions, lineage rules, and didactic and vernacular literature.[21] Other scholars have found that while neo-Confucianism laid the foundation for such moralism of female virtues, the Mongol empire's unique culture and ethnic agendas made the practice of widow chastity a much broader practice, economically and legally.[22]

More recently, Weijing Lu has expanded such inquiry to include Confucian discourse on both sexes during the late imperial period. Discussing essays written by Confucian moralists at the time, and records of their life stories, Lu notes that while Confucian social norms traditionally privileged males in sexual conduct and attributed sexual purity as a mainly female virtue, Confucian moralists' writing about sexual abstinence during the mourning period offers us evidences that this was one of the few instances in which male sexuality was regulated, disciplined, and morally judged. Lu argues that the rule of sexual abstinence was created "in the context of Confucian discourse on ritual and filial piety"; abstinence was part of an extensive mourning regimen that demanded self-restraint in order to fulfill spiritual devotion. Over the course of imperial history, while the rule was codified and applied to commoners, it grew to become a focal point of moral performance for the Confucian elite, representing the most daunting—and most prized—of all mourning rituals guiding the personal conduct of Confucian men.[23] Elsewhere, Lu notes that the promotion of the so-called faithful maiden—a young woman who chose to stay chaste when her fiancé died—was also linked to the moral performance and expression of the Confucian elite.[24]

Naturally, legal codes and records of legal cases provide excellent resources in understanding how sexuality was regulated as well as the historical and social contexts behind it. One of the most influential studies in this topic is Bettine Birge's 1995 article on levirate marriage and widow chastity. In the piece, Birge articulates how levirate marriage—a common practice among the Mongols, wherein a deceased man's brother was obligated to marry his widow—was legalized for all people in the Yuan empire. As such, a widow's rights to return home or remarry were drastically reduced, as her husband's family would control her fate and her property, including her dowry. The enforcement of the law also caused serious confusion and conflict, as it was incompatible with traditional Chinese notions of incest. To ease the contradictions, the Yuan court promulgated a new provision to allow widows to evade levirate marriage by staying chaste. Birge suggests that this break from traditional Chinese practice led to the full-fledged widow chastity cult during the Ming and Qing period. Birge's study is largely based on *The Collection of Laws of the Yuan Dynasty* (Yuan dianzhang), a collection of imperial edicts, provisions, and legal documents dating from 1234 to 1322, compiled by regional officials who handled day-to-day legal cases. The Mongol rulers encouraged the use of precedents as a source of law, and the legal collection above has helped scholars discern how sexuality was perceived and sanctioned during the Yuan dynasty.[25]

Matthew Sommer is another scholar who has utilized legislative initiatives and legal case records as the main source of his studies on late imperial sexuality. His monograph *Sex, Law, and Society in Late Imperial China* examines the regulation of sexuality in Qing dynasty legislation and central court practice. The book also delineates broader historical changes, social context, and to some extent, perceptions and practices of sexuality among the general populace.

Sommer finds that the guiding principle for regulating sexuality from the medieval period through the early Qing dynasty may be termed "status performance"—meaning that men and women had to perform the roles conferred upon them by their particular legal status (such as, for example, the principle of female chastity, which applied mainly to elite women). But he adds that the Qing dynasty, especially the Yongzheng reign (1678–1735), also "marks a watershed in the regulation of sexuality, when the age-old paradigm of status performance yielded to a new one, gender performance." In particular, Sommer notes changes in the following areas: the prohibition of prostitution; the curtailing of sexual use of servile women; harsher penalties for both rape and consensual-but-illicit sexual intercourse; the prohibition of male homosexual acts; and the promotion of female chastity. The regulation of sexuality during and after the Yongzheng reign represented the application of a uniform standard of sexual morality and criminal liability to all social sectors.[26]

One example of Sommer's reliance on legal documents is his study on the prohibition of homosexual acts, which was based on thirty-nine central court cases received from various regions. Sommer finds that these records reveal "a pervasive, powerful stigma attached to the penetrated male," along with the fact that sex between women was not construed as a crime. This stigma reflects an increasing fear of the threat to vulnerable males, as well as concern about their possible enjoyment of roles that conflicted radically with the demands of order. To Qing jurists, "the degradation of masculinity" threatened the gendered hierarchy of the household, just as the pollution of female chastity did.[27]

In his 2013 article "The Gendered Body in the Qing Courtroom," Sommer further explores how adjudications of homicides, rapes, and marriage

PING YAO

disputes from eighteenth- and nineteenth-century China reflect the *performative* aspect of bodily gender, which blurred the distinction between the physical and social dimensions of being. Qing jurists perceived a general category of woman, defined by a shared vulnerability to penetration. Males who had been used in the "female" sexual role would be examined for evidence in the female way. Several documents Sommer examined closely were memorials sent to the central court by magistrates regarding stone maidens (*shinü*), women who had impenetrable vaginas. The magistrates' priority in these cases seemed to be whether or not—and in what ways—these women could perform a wife's role. Overall, Sommer finds that "Qing magistrates interpreted bodily evidence in order to enforce orthodox norms of gendered behavior."[28]

Ellen Cong Zhang's study of Hong Mai's (1123–1202) *Record of the Listener* (Yi jian zhi) examines how illicit affairs during the Song dynasty were perceived and policed. As she sees it, the *Record* shows that while law and local government clearly had a role in regulating sexual conduct, the punishments offenders received often differed from those specified in the penal codes; many illicit affairs, for example, were never reported or prosecuted. Meanwhile, elite and popular denunciations of sexual transgression—as well as fear of karmic retribution—played important roles in regulating sexual behaviors at this time. Zhang finds that Hong's stories "apply the harshest standards to ordinary women"; in these accounts, women are labeled "licentious," charged with bringing shame and humiliation to their husbands and sons, and blamed for the downfall of families and disorder in communities. Such tales reflect the fear and suspicion that sexualized women would upset familial and gender order. Issues such as female chastity, proper gender roles, and family and gender hierarchy would continue to occupy center stage in political and intellectual discourses of late imperial China, long after the Song era.[29]

FEMININITY, MASCULINITY, AND EROTICISM IN CHINESE LITERATURE

Literature has evolved consistently throughout Chinese history. Poetry has been a popular genre since *The Book of Songs* (Shijing), exhibiting extremely diverse trends over time; other genres, such as the novel and play, developed considerably later. Probably because of that, research on sexuality using Chinese literature as source material takes a more focused approach and somewhat lacks broad and comparative studies. Nevertheless, scholarship in this area is probably the most vibrant compared to the previously discussed two areas, as both Chinese literature and late imperial China have long been established fields of study.

How Chinese literature represents/portrays femininity and masculinity is an extremely popular topic in studies of Chinese sexuality, and various types of source materials are abundant throughout Chinese history. In her study of feminine representations in *The Book of Songs,* for example, Eva Kit Wah Man finds that the earliest collection of Chinese poetry contains "a large range of adjectives relating to beauty and praise of femininity . . . projected onto female historical characters and figures." Certain physical appeals are considered feminine: majestic physical size, whiteness, slenderness, and attainableness. The collection also offers a distinctive description of beauty in the presence of water and the feminine space. Man suggests that ideal masculinity is best represented in "Shu Is Away in the Hunting-Fields" (Shu yu tian), in "The Airs of Zheng" (Zhengfeng): Shu is pleasant, kind, good-looking, and martial, and "the key to this ideal is a strong body that can ride, shoot, and play games excellently, and which possesses moral courage."[30]

Another study on sexual attractions in early Chinese literature, Paul Goldin's *Culture of Sex in Ancient China,* explores sexual imagery and sexual attractions in early Chinese literature (such as, for instance, *The Zuo Commentary* (Zuozhuan) and Qu Yuan's poetry). Goldin argues that many scenes in *The Book of Songs* evoke eroticism; the collection repeatedly employs sexual imagery—for instance, copulating birds (*jiaojiao huangniao*)—for metaphoric effect.[31]

The theme of feminine beauty continued to prosper in poetry during and after the Han. Many of the works in *New Songs from a Jade Terrace* (Yutai xin yong), a collection of 769 poems dating from the Han dynasty to the mid-sixth century, express an intense desire to physically reach the so-called "fine lady" (*jiaren*), who always resides on the other side of the river (*zai shui yi fang*). Using conventional terms for describing women's features—beautiful eyes (*meimu*), white teeth (*haochi*), red lips (*zhuchun*), slender waist (*xianyao*), and jadelike fingers (*yuzhi*)—poems in *New Songs from a Jade Terrace* also stress the fragrance of the female body, mostly indicated by a woman's fragrant dress (*xunyi*). Several poems in the collection might imply sexual encounters, but their descriptions are rather indirect and metaphorical. A few poems in the collection—"Song of Joyful Sound: One" (Huanwen ge yi), for instance, written by Xiao Yan (464–549), Emperor Wu (r. 502–549) of the Liang dynasty (502–557)—are interpreted by scholars as erotic descriptions of lovemaking.[32]

Entering the golden age of Chinese poetry, the Tang dynasty witnessed a much broader and more nuanced poetic representation of femininity, masculinity, and eroticism. Poetry was by then competing with the newly developed genre of fiction. In his monograph on Tang *chuanqi* (tales of marvels), Daniel Hsieh argues that the drastic rise of fantastical fiction during the Tang dynasty's second half did not simply result from the literati's desire to escape from the decline of the dynasty—rather, it reflected a literary fascination for the "other" in its various forms. As such, fictions of the period became much more elaborate and sexual. Interestingly, Hsieh finds these stories often reflect a paradox of the Confucian literati: The heroines of the stories are often the most erotic beings. And "having created a division between correct, everyday, respectable women and the creatures of their fantasies," Tang literati imagined that they could possibly "unite and harmonize these two poles."[33]

Other scholars suggest that the drastic change in writing about sexual attraction was somewhat parallel to the rise of the new elite: civil service examination graduates, who were eager to flaunt their association with courtesans[34] and their knowledge of Daoist and Buddhist sexology. The earliest erotica in Chinese literary history, the Tang dynasty "Poetic Essay on the Great Bliss of the Sexual Union of Heaven and Earth and Yin and Yang" (Tiandi yinyang jiaohuan dale fu) and "Merry-Making in a Transcendent Dwelling" (You xianku), bears several interesting characteristics—among them an emphasis on propriety, etiquette, erudition, and refinement, and the assertion that sexual pleasure can be amplified by the enjoyment of nature, music, scent, color, words, and mutual affection. These two texts reflected how the Tang elite interpreted sexuality and gender relations. Both masculinity and femininity were defined by literary knowledge, learned etiquette, sophisticated tastes, and spiritual intuition. Such qualities were also described as indispensable to achieving sexual bliss.[35]

Relatively speaking, studies solely focused on sexuality in Song literature are rare, but scholars have made progress in this area. Beverly Bossler, for example, examined the Song literati's attitude toward and writings about courtesans in her 2002 article on the identities of Song courtesans.[36] In her recent book *Courtesans, Concubines, and the Cult of Female Fidelity*, she argues that in various cases, Song poetry valorizes a literary identity that embraces erotic and emotional sensitivity: "A true literatus, we are told, is not only a creative genius who can compose a brilliant poem on a moment's notice; he is also a man who enjoys an aesthetic appreciation for women (or perhaps girls) as objects of erotic desire, and a man of high sensibility who feels profoundly the sorrow of parting from his lover."[37]

Most scholarship on sexuality in Chinese history, however, has focused on late imperial China, as available sources are abundant. This is especially true when studies draw on fictional works, many of which are erotica. Interestingly, by the Ming dynasty, sexuality was generally regulated and, as Martin Huang points out, the literati were quite ambivalent about publicly celebrating sexual desire.[38] Therefore, while erotic literature may have been produced by prominent literati, it was often published anonymously. The most well-known work of Chinese erotic literature, *The Plum in the Golden Vase* (Jin ping mei), for example, was authored by the Scoffing Scholar from Lanling (Lanling Xiaoxiao Sheng), clearly a pseudonym.[39] And as scholar Charles R. Stone shows, *The Lord of Perfect Satisfaction* (Ruyijun zhuan) is probably authored by Huang Xun (1490–1540), a prominent Confucian scholar and a *jinshi* ("advanced scholar") degree holder.[40]

Many fictions produced in the later periods of imperial Chinese history are quite erotic in nature. As Keith McMahon points out in his pioneering study on the subject, literary eroticism is an excellent source for understanding "the structure of social power, the limits of masculine and feminine, the scope and regulation of pleasure, [and] the containment of the body."[41] Ka F. Wong, meanwhile, asserts in his 2007 study that the Ming dynasty novel *The Wild History of the Embroidered Couch* (Xiuta yeshi) demonstrates a new style of pornographic writing: its material world, filled with objects, ingredients, technical know-how, obscene words, and numbers, represents an erotic world in which the notion of the human body is redefined. Wong explains, "To the late Ming audience, the fascination with pornography derives not only from its explicit portrayal of sex but also the production of 'true' sexual knowledge that is intricately knitted into the social fabric of the material conditions, the lifestyle of the libertine, and the anatomical understanding of the human body." Wong also finds that *The Wild History of the Embroidered Couch* "upholds traditional male supremacy, as the promiscuous men, after a series of licentious escapades, find enlightenment at the end. In contrast, women are the victims of physical violation and bearers of the stigma of the sexual misconduct."[42]

Keith McMahon's *Misers, Shrews, and Polygamists*, a major work on fictional sexuality, investigates the portrayal of male sexual privilege in the Qing novel *The Dream of the Red Chamber* (Honglou meng) and other eighteenth-century Chinese erotic fictions; McMahon finds that polygamy was a defining feature of eighteenth-century China's sexual economy.[43] In his more recent *Polygamy and Sublime Passion*, McMahon expands his research to include fictional sources from the eighteenth century to the twentieth century, investigating polygamy practiced both by men and women. Here,

McMahon notes that even though perhaps only 10 percent of Chinese males could afford multiple sexual partners, the cultural-sexual ideal of polygamy nevertheless defined successful Chinese manhood. As such, the practice became indicative of a decaying civilization under assault from a powerful West. Consequently, as Chinese modernizers embraced Western culture, they strove to explore "the right path for the modern Chinese man" that in one way or another legitimized such practice.[44]

McMahon's recent work represents scholars' attention to the so-called "blue pavilions literature" (*qinglou wenxue*), erotic fictions that often involve prostitution. In her book *Lost Bodies*, Paola Zamperini pores through an impressive list of *qinglou wenxue*; she argues that representations of courtesans and prostitutes in these fictions tell us not only about perceptions of femininity, but also a great deal about men and ideas of masculinity. For late Qing men, reading and writing the courtesan was "a very important moment in understanding their gendered identity as the Old and New Men of China."[45]

Finally, Ming-Qing fictions provide a great source for understanding homosexuality in Chinese history.[46] Tellingly, the first sourcebook on sexuality in Chinese history was *Homoeroticism in Imperial China*, coedited by Mark Stevenson and Cuncun Wu; both have published on homosexuality in Ming-Qing China.[47] The sourcebook contains five types of sources—history and philosophers, poetry, drama, fiction, and miscellanies—but the genre of fiction constitutes more than one hundred pages (and nearly half) of the book.[48]

Martin Huang has also relied on Ming-Qing fictions in his study of sexuality and masculinity.[49] Recently, Huang has examined the theme of chastity in fictional stories on male-male sexual relations, which he characterizes as hierarchical in nature and different from male friendship. In his 2013 article "Male-Male Sexual Bonding and Male Friendship in Late Imperial China," Huang argues that although male friendships and male-male sexual relationships in late imperial China were not necessarily mutually exclusive, there were tensions between the two, and resultant complications when they coincided: "Sexual passion tended either to hierarchize a friendship or accentuate the hierarchy already existing in a friendship by introducing elements of traditional gender inequality and their complex social ramifications." Still, he cautions, the overall picture is complicated.[50]

Research on sexuality in Chinese history has been closely linked to the availability of sources. From its beginning barely half a century ago, this field has grown immensely and produced some very fine scholarship. What to do from here on? What are the sources that remain largely untapped? Is it possible (or meaningful) to break the link between sources and topics? What comparative tools can we use to approach these topics?

One type of source that has been underexplored is visual art—especially painting and sculpture from early eras. We know, for example, that by at least the Han dynasty objects had become very much part of the sexual culture: quite a few male-organ-shaped objects, made of bronze or animal bones, have been excavated from early Han tombs.[51] Tang divination texts discovered in Dunhuang also point to ritual objects that claimed to help or destroy one's sexual attractiveness. Many paintings and drawings that served as sex handbooks (or inserts of such manuals) have survived; they are yet to be studied systematically and comparatively. Another type of source we can use is biography—including biographies in standard histories, epitaphs (*muzhi*), and records of conduct (*xingzhuang*). Most of these have been collected in the China Biographical Database and can be extracted easily.[52] Careful computations of these biographies can provide a variety of information—the average age of marriage consummation, patterns of interethnic marriages, sexual attractions among relatives of the same generation, rates of childbirth, information about fertility cycles, perceptions of sexuality. Numerous topics remain to be investigated in greater depth, such as lesbianism, adolescence and sexual desire, transmission of sexual knowledge within the family, childhood sexual abuse, sex trafficking, bisexuality, masturbation, and abstinence. Study of these topics will contribute to a better understanding of the history of sexuality in China.

NOTES

Some discussions on sexuality in Chinese history have been published in my coauthored essay "Discourses on Gender and Sexuality" (with Scott Wells) and my journal article "Changing Views on Sexuality in Early and Medieval China."

1   For a brief overview of the field, see Lu, "Introduction," 201–206.
2   According to Paul Goldin, who tracks and updates publications on gender and sexuality in premodern China, as of May 2017, the number of publications was approximately 1,350. See Goldin, "Gender and Sexuality in Pre-Modern China."
3   Harper, "The Sexual Arts of Ancient China as Described in a Manuscript of the Second Century BC."
4   Harper, *Early Chinese Medical Literature*.
5   In addition to Harper's works, other major publications on the Mawangdui medical manuscripts include Li and McMahon, "The Contents and Terminology of the Mawangdui Texts on the Arts of the Bedchamber"; Pfister,

"The Production of Special Mental States within the Framework of Sexual Body Techniques"; and Leo, *Sex in the Yellow Emperor's Basic Questions.*

6   Goldin, *The Culture of Sex in Ancient China,* 6–7.

7   Van Gulick, *Sexual Life in Ancient China,* 78. Van Gulick translated title to "The Handbook of Sex of the Plain Girl."

8   For an overview of the Daoist concept of uniting *yin* and *yang* through intercourse and sexuality in post-Han literature, see Despeux, *Immortelles de la Chine ancienne.*

9   For a detailed analysis on perception of sexuality as seen in the text, see Goldin, "The Cultural and Religious Background," 285–307.

10   According to Harper's study, this text is also referred to as the so-called *Outer Scripture of the Yellow Court* (*Huangting waijing yujing*). Composed around the second or third century, it was the oldest scripture to discuss sexual cultivation in Daoism. *The Inner Scripture of the Yellow Court* (Huangting neijing yujing) was composed within the Shangqing school of Daoism around the fourth to fifth centuries (1987, 541n4). For a study of the outer scripture, see Schipper, *The Taoist Body,* 130–59.

11   For studies of these texts, see Robinet, *La Révélation du Shangqing dans l'histoire du taoïsme*; and Raz, "The Way of the Yellow and the Red," 86–120.

12   See Goldin, *The Culture of Sex in Ancient China,* 6–7.

13   See Raz, "The Way of the Yellow and the Red."

14   See Despeux and Kohn, *Women in Daoism,* 14–15.

15   See Jia et al., *Gendering Chinese Religion,* 183–200.

16   *Sunüjing,* an important source for understanding early Daoist influence on China's perception of sexuality and sexual practice, was lost to China after the Tang dynasty. Its text, however, was preserved in the Japanese medieval medical anthology *Ishimpō*—along with, among other texts, *Secret Instructions of the Jade Bedchamber* (Yufang mijue) and *Master Dongxuan* (Dongxuanzi). For an annotated translation of *Ishimpō,* see Yasuyori et al., *The Essentials of Medicine in Ancient China and Japan.*

17   Wile, *Art of the Bedchamber.*

18   Ibid., 5–8.

19   Schipper, "Science, magie et mystique du corps," 11–42.

20   Lu, *True to Her Word,* 3–5.

21   See T'ien, *Male Anxiety and Female Chastity*; Carlitz, "Shrines, Governing-Class Identity, and the Cult of Widow Fidelity in Mid-Ming Jianan"; Furth, "The Patriarch's Legacy"; Mann, *Precious Records*; Theiss, "Managing Martyrdom"; and Theiss, *Disgraceful Matters.*

22   See, for example, Holmgren, "The Economic Foundations of Virtue"; Birge, "Levirate Marriage"; Birge, *Women, Property, and Confucian Reaction in Sung and Yüan China (960–1368)*; Bossler, *Faithful Wives and Heroic Martyrs*; and Bossler, "Faith Wives and Heroic Maidens."

23   Lu, "Abstaining from Sex," 232–38.

24 Ibid.; and Lu, "The Chaste and the Licentious."

25 See Birge, "Levirate Marriage and the Revival of Widow Chastity in Yuan China." Birge's recent article on sexual misconduct during the Yuan dynasty, "Sexual Misconduct in Mongol-Yuan Law, with Some Observations on Chinggis Khan's Jasagh," also reflects this approach.

26 Sommer, *Sex, Law, and Society in Late Imperial China*, 6, 9–11.

27 Ibid., 148, 163–65.

28 Sommer, "The Gendered Body," 307–8, 281–311.

29 Zhang, "Anecdotal Writing on Illicit Sex in Song China (960–1279)," 278–79.

30 Man, "Discourses on Female Bodily Aesthetics and Its Early Revelations in *The Book of Songs*," 113–30, 122.

31 Goldin, *The Culture of Sex in Ancient China*, 23–26.

32 Birrell, *New Songs from a Jade Terrace*, 285. The poem reads:
 Sleek, sleek girl in a golden house, 艷艷金樓女
 Her heart like a jade pool lotus. 心如玉池蓮
 With what to repay her lover's favor? 持底報郎恩
 A promise to roam with him in the Buddhist paradise. 俱期遊梵天
The "jade pool lotus" (*yuchi lian*) was often used in Chinese literature as an analogy for the female sex organ, while "roaming in Buddhist paradise" (*you fantian*) may imply reaching Buddhahood, or Great Bliss, through sexual intercourse. See (among other scholarly interpretations) Fu, "*Tiandi yinyang jiaohuan dale fu* chutan," 80.

33 Hsieh, *Love and Women in Early Chinese Fiction*, 108. Hsieh's sources include nearly two hundred *zhiguai* (records of anomalies) and *chuanqi* that appeared prior to and during the Song dynasty. (See also Tsai, "Ritual and Gender," for a discussion of Tang-era erotic fiction's role in supporting the social order.)

34 For a study of the Tang literati's relationship with courtesans and their public displays of pleasure, see Yao, "The Status of Pleasure."

35 For a study of Daoist and Buddhist influence on the Tang literati's writing about sexuality, see Yao, "Historicizing Great Bliss."

36 Bossler, "Shifting Identities."

37 Bossler, *Courtesans, Concubines, and the Cult of Female Fidelity*, 37.

38 Huang, *Desire and Fictional Narrative in Late Imperial China*, 5–22.

39 See Hanan, *The Invention of Li Yu*, 23.

40 See Stone, *The Fountainhead of Chinese Erotica*, 55–73. Another study on this fiction is Mark Stevenson's "Sound, Space and Moral Soundscapes in *Ruyijun zhuan* and *Chipozi zhuan*."

41 McMahon, "Eroticism in Late Ming, Early Qing Fiction," 217–24, 263–64.

42 Wong, "The Anatomy of Eroticism," 284–329, 325, 326.

43 McMahon, *Misers, Shrews, and Polygamists*, 2.

44 McMahon, *Polygamy and Sublime Passion*, 14.

45 Zamperini, *Lost Bodies*, 185. The *qinglou wenxue* she examines are *Chuan-yinglou huiyilü* (by Bao Tianxiao); *Honglou meng* (by Cao Xueqin); *Huitu*

   PING YAO

Haishang mingji si da jingang qishu (by Wu Jianren); *Jingshi tongyan, Xingshi hengyan,* and *Yushi mingyan* (by Feng Menglong); *Haishanghua* (by Han Ziyun); *Fengyue meng* (by Hanshang Mengren); *Sai Jinhua gushi* (by Hong Yuan); *Jinpingmei cihua* and *Rouputuan* (by Li Yu); *Xingshi yinyuan* (by Pu Songling); *Saijinhua benshi* (by Liu Bannong); *Mudan ting* (by Tang Xianzu); *Qinglou meng* (by Yu Da); and *Qinglou yunyu* (by Zhang Mengwei).

46   It is noteworthy that the earliest major scholarship on homosexuality in Chinese history was conducted by Bret Hinsch, whose *Passions of the Cut Sleeve* has also examined Ming-Qing erotic fictions (chapters 6 and 7).

47   See Wu and Stevenson, "Karmic Retribution and Moral Didacticism in Erotic Fiction from the Late Ming and Early Qing"; Wu and Stevenson, "Speaking of Flowers"; Wu, *Homoerotic Sensibilities in Late Imperial China*; and Stevenson, "Sound, Space and Moral Soundscapes in *Ruyijun zhuan* and *Chipozi zhuan.*"

48   Stevenson and Wu, *Homoeroticism in Imperial China.* The book includes an excellent bibliography on both primary and secondary sources on sexuality in Chinese history.

49   See Huang, "Male Friendship in Ming China"; Huang, *Negotiating Masculinities in Late Imperial China*; and Huang, *Desire and Fictional Narrative in Late Imperial China.*

50   Huang, "Male-Male Sexual Bonding and Male Friendship in Late Imperial China," 330.

51   See Xiao, "Xi Han shiqi de xing guannian."

52   The China Biographical Database is an online relational database containing biographical information, primarily from the seventh through nineteenth centuries, for about approximately 360,000 individuals as of April 2015. https://projects.iq.harvard.edu/cbdb.

CHAPTER 3

THE PORNOGRAPHIC DOCTRINE OF A LOYALIST MING NOVEL

Social Decline and Sexual Disorder in Preposterous Words *(Guwangyan)*

KEITH MCMAHON

A RECURRENT THEME IN THE RHETORIC OF SOCIAL DECLINE IN CHINA was its link with sexual disorder. Dynasties fell because of bad last emperors, one of whose most telling signs of corruption was sexual profligacy. This was also the case for the basic unit of social order, the household, in which the conduct of self and family was said to radiate to the realm at large. As pronounced in the *Great Learning* (Daxue), order and disorder took shape at the most intimate level and worked their way out from one sphere to the next.

By the sixteenth century, self and family had entered new territory; fictional narratives had begun to portray sexual activity in graphic detail, translating the terms of family and social order into explicit sexual imagery. The new form of portrayal carried an underlying sexual logic, which went something as follows: First, social disorder was fundamentally a case of sexual disorder, the foundation of which was the imbalance between the sexual energies of man and woman. Second, as warned in the ancient art of the bedchamber, the imbalance was one in which women dominated men in their capacity to excite and enjoy sexual pleasure.

Writers who engaged in pornographic detail varied in terms of how far they took this logic, but the eighteenth-century novel *Preposterous Words* (Guwangyan) was an extreme, unabashed in its portrayal of sexual ecstasy, especially the woman's, and extravagantly committed to the logic of sexual imbalance, in which it invested deep social and historical meaning. In the author's view, when men did not live up to women, the result was the unbridled explosion of female sexual energy. Translated into historical terms, such an imbalance explained the chaos at the end of the Ming dynasty, characterized by sexual anarchy at all levels of society. If men had been potent and dutiful husbands, then social harmony would have prevailed and the dynasty would not have fallen. *Preposterous Words* used pornography to convey this message, and it did so in two main ways: as a weapon of invective against late Ming decadence, and as a vehicle for imagining an alternate world of social and sexual harmony.

Preposterous Words is an anomalous work: unsung, long, bizarre in its contents. It presents large questions—the first of which is, simply, "Who would write this, and why?" The novel survived, unknown and unpublished, for more than two centuries after being written. The author is flagrant in his use of pornography. *Preposterous Words* is easily among the most extreme of novels from the Ming and Qing dynasties, but it is serious in its moral message, which is brutally simplistic. Modern readers—even those used to the sixteenth-century *Plum in the Golden Vase* (Jin ping mei) or the seventeenth-century *Carnal Prayer Mat* (Rouputuan)—would find the book deeply misogynistic, riddled with repetition, and even mad. It relentlessly portrays a sexual drive that often has little relation to its moral message, and at other times it so overstates its moral message that readers suspect another kind of enjoyment to be going on—namely, the enjoyment of pornographic portrayal.

The novel takes place in the last two reigns of the Ming dynasty, the Tianqi (1620–27) and Chongzhen (1628–44) periods; it also includes the brief reign of the Hongguang emperor (1644–45) of the Southern Ming dynasty. The "great Qing army" (*da Qing bing*) is the final victor, finally referred to in respectful terms in the last chapter, though not portrayed. *Preposterous Words* describes the period by re-creating these emperors and other historical figures, but it mainly focuses on fictional characters recurrently consisting of old men who take young wives who, naturally unsatisfied, have affairs with stepsons, brothers-in-law, slaves, and monks; widows and wanton wives who, craving outlet, have affairs with man after man and even animals; henpecked husbands whose fear of their wives makes them lose their virility; girls who become wanton at young ages because of their parents' failure to understand young women's sexuality; and soft, blockheaded boys who have to be shown how to have sex by older women, but who turn into debauched adults. The most prominent historical figures, apart from the emperors, include the corrupt official Ruan Dacheng (1587–1646) and the late Ming rebel Li Zicheng (approximately 1605–45); all of them, except for the Chongzhen emperor, are portrayed in sexual terms.

As a rule, the novel takes sexual aptitude as the core measure of a man's worth. The narrative's most worthy man is Zhong Qing; he and the blind prostitute Qian Gui make up the ideal romantic couple that stands at the center, never portrayed pornographically. They eventually inspire a small group of venal men to reform themselves—first by improving sex with their wives, and then by performing social good deeds (though it is too late to save the dynasty). The novel ends with the demise of the Ming dynasty and all its villains—including a group of elderly widows who, as bosses of their homes, indulge in wantonness until they die. The final scenes portray male Ming loyalists, including Zhong Qing, who retires to live in hermetic seclusion, leaving his wife Qian Gui and their sons to serve the new dynasty.

Like other novels both before and after, *Preposterous Words* draws on centuries of sexual lore to portray debauchery in men and women. Sex as a battle is a common metaphor, deriving from Daoist themes and terminology that frequently appear. The analogy between social and sexual disorder is nothing new. What is new is what had happened in Chinese literature since the mid-Ming: the growth of both the writing of vernacular fiction and the publishing industry; and, concurrently, the intense and explicit portrayal of sexual bodies and acts. The author of *Preposterous Words* is steeped in this new tradition, already over two centuries old by his time; the novel refers to its predecessors, and imitates their language, character types, episodes, and plot patterns.[1] But *Preposterous Words* goes further in its portrayal of sexual anarchy, which culminates in a woman so lascivious that she couples with a monkey and gives birth to a half-monkey son, whose concubine couples with a fox demon to give birth to Qijie, "Strange Sister," who is female half the month and male the other half. Challenged by his own extremes, the author counters these characters with yet another tour de force: the man of supreme potency, whose penis is like a miniature person with mouth and movement, able to pulse on its own, to suck, and to bite. All at once, the man satisfies his wife and becomes a model member of society—the implication being that, were all men possessed of such an organ, universal harmony would ensue. The theme is both universal and historical in scope, emerging with a voice that is all the more adamant because of the author's use of pornography.

With a preface dated 1730, *Preposterous Words* has led a strange existence; it lay hidden for centuries and was never fully published until 1997.[2] At over a million characters in twenty-four lengthy chapters, it is a serious

KEITH MCMAHON

and ambitious work, both for its grand-scale staging of sexual orgy and for its simultaneous framing of that depiction in an "anti-libertine" rhetoric, to use Giovanni Vitiello's words, that takes as its central hero a man who is a "shining example of political and romantic loyalty."[3] Next to nothing is known about the author, Cao Qujing, and little is known about the context for his writing. With its relentless and untrammeled focus on sex, *Preposterous Words* was unpublishable at a time when government censorship prohibited works with pornographic content and was suspicious of literature expressing loyalism to the Ming. Although works with comparable levels of explicitness existed in the Qing, they were in general lighter and more playful. An exception was the mid-eighteenth-century novel *The Humble Words of an Old Rustic* (Yesou puyan), which was occasionally pornographic and serious in moral intent, but not published until 1881.

Like many of its predecessors, *Preposterous Words* stages a tumbling series of sexual events, one leading contagiously to the next, with characters and actions described in as obscene and raucous a way as possible. Episodes advance at a feverish pace, with an endless spreading of sexual frenzy. The sexually voracious woman is an object of obsessive fascination; the author cannot stop describing her various modes of craving and arousal. In all this, however, Cao Qujing accomplishes the feat of writing pornographically while in effect denying that *Preposterous Words* is pornographic. He performs this sleight of hand by using pornography in order to demonstrate the thorough, shameless decadence of an entire society, while at the same time projecting a society in which none of the behavior he describes so graphically and defiantly would ever appear again.

The use of the word *pornography* deserves brief qualification, as well as comparison with its use in Europe of approximately the same period as *Preposterous Words*. Pornographic literature in France and England was similarly loaded with political and historical meaning and was subject to suppression because of its threat to ideological authority. Pornography was linked with "attacks on absolutist political authority," in historian Lynn Hunt's words, and the push for democratic values and revolutionary change. It is in fact taken for granted among scholars of pornography in the United States that the rise of pornography significantly coincided with the rise of modern democracy.[4] Although this was hardly the case in *Preposterous Words* or China in general, enough points exist in common between China and Europe to make using the word still viable and comparison still fruitful.

The explicit description of sexual bodies and acts is the first level of commonality, where such description violates social norms. The ease with which characters meet and have sex is inherent to this level and, whether in

China or France, is a matter of the erasure of conditions that normally apply in terms of what is likely or permissible. A man desires sex with a woman he does not know and she is automatically receptive; a desiring woman chances upon a naked man, not her husband, and invites him to have sex.[5] A second level of commonality is the reduction of sexual acts to a matter of "repetition and enumeration." Pornography in China and Europe likes lists and scores. It likes to compare and rank sexual organs and their capacities. People possess gargantuan sexual appetites, having sex for hours and days at a time. Penises are huge—though they can also be pathetically small, or in the Chinese case, retracted, only appearing at a moment when least expected. Vaginas are wide, or tight; they flow copiously; women are sexually ravenous.[6]

A third level has to do with the link between pornography and social and political criticism—or social and political invective. Although pornography may be mainly or solely about sexual pleasure (though what counts as pleasure is debatable, as will be seen), when it is loaded with political intent and social meaning it is generally the case that "sexual disorder [is] a sign of a breakdown in public order."[7] A bad ruler is a debauched one—though in seventeenth- and eighteenth-century Europe, the bad ruler is in particular a tyrant opposed to democratic values. But similarly in both realms, "sexual events . . . explain political events."[8] Pornographic satire is about figures who abuse privilege and exemplify corrupt authority.

Finally, in both Europe and China, "production of both novels and pornography seems to be related," which conforms with the notion of the novel as "an oppositional genre," to use Hunt's words. "In early modern Europe," as she writes, "that is, between 1500 and 1800, pornography was most often a vehicle for using the shock of sex to criticize religious and political authorities."[9] In that period, pornography in the novel played a key role in calling "for the type of revolutionary change that Foucault terms the creation of an episteme."[10]

The impossibility of *Preposterous Words* being published in its time is alone a sign of the extremity of its boundary-testing. It would be going too far to say that its pornography was "revolutionary" in the sense of creating a new episteme—in particular if the words "revolutionary change" mean overturning a monarchy in favor of a democracy, or a similar type of radical political change. Some would say that its pornography is merely shocking and provocative, or even gratuitously and randomly obscene. The meanness of *Preposterous Words*' portrayal of sensuousness, whether in men or women; its denigrating depiction of women's sexual arousal; and its leering fascination with scene after scene of adultery, incest, and bestiality endow

     KEITH MCMAHON

it with a kind of megalomania (which is common, though far from universal, to pornography in general) that sets the novel apart from other works addressing the catastrophe of the fall of the Ming, especially works that do so in the aesthetic-romantic mode of authors such as Wu Weiye, Qian Qianyi, and Liu Rushi.[11]

But *Preposterous Words'* pornography nevertheless conveys a consistent thematic message. The translation of the ancient analogy between self, family, and body politic into explicit and grotesque sexual imagery is a radical move, which conveys both affirmation and negation. The affirmation promotes the notion that good marriage is fundamental to society and must be grounded in romantic (and especially sexual) fulfillment. The negation portrays a society plagued with sexual debauchery on the part of both profligate men and wanton women. These were not broadly proclaimed messages at the time, nor could they be except in the mode of provocation and defiance. Shock and provocation were inherent to the novel's enraged and even gloating way of condemning people from all levels of society. The Ming deserved to collapse, *Preposterous Words* seems to say. People were so debased that using pornography to describe their debasement was the only way truly to illustrate what happened.

The above deals with what pornography conveys in terms of its contents, themes, and ideology. According to some, the radical potential of pornography, its positive subversiveness, has to do with how it describes a utopian world featuring the free rein of desire, however constructed and fantasized that world may be.[12] *Preposterous Words*, for example, portrays a twenty-day sexual orgy, with poetry unabashedly describing the beauty of the characters' pleasure, though the author finally deals them a deadly ending (15.1798–99, 15.1811, 1812–13). Some also say that pornography serves as a vehicle of provocation that is critical or satirical of some segment of society. As cultural historian Robert Darnton wrote, pornographic books censored by the *ancien régime* in France threatened the state not merely because of their obscenity but because their publication constituted a denial of the state's control over their contents.[13] It was the same in China, where the publication of pornography challenged the state's desire to guarantee unity between its moral and political agendas, on the one hand, and the contents of literature, on the other.

But an inevitable point in the discussion of pornography has to do with its alleged reality effect—particularly, the charge that it exerts a "negative effect" on society. Even if authors claimed that their use of licentious language was merely a way of leading people to enlightenment, as in the saying "using lewdness to preach the dharma" (*jie yin shuo fa*), they had no way of preventing readers from reading only the lewd parts of a book and disregarding the message of enlightenment.[14] Works like *The Plum in the Golden Vase* were said to degrade public morals. In twentieth-century America, feminist scholars Catharine MacKinnon and Andrea Dworkin argued that pornography contributed to the degradation and exploitation of women and played a role in "creating and maintaining a system of civil inequality." As a stereotypically gendered discourse, pornography's sexual subordination of women both produced and enforced misogynistic beliefs about women.[15]

In *Preposterous Words* such a bias comes down to the way in which its pornography promotes the triumphant virility of not just the man, but especially the polygynous man. Even though MacKinnon and Dworkin have since been criticized for too narrow a definition of pornography, and even though some works do not go as far as *Preposterous Words* in promoting triumphant virility or portraying sexual aberration, it is still the case that pornography produces and upholds systems of value and ranking—of sexual organs, of capacities for fulfillment, and of what constitutes pleasure and satisfaction.[16] The questions include: who gets to experience enjoyment, who has the most intense pleasure, and who deserves the most partners? *Preposterous Words* effectively presents a contest in which participants are measured and ranked—evident in the novel's feverish pace of portrayal, frequent use of battle metaphors, and competitive scenes of orgy.

The idea of pornography's reality effect relates to the way in which it is read, which some advocate as a preferable approach to begin with because of the difficulty in defining pornography in terms of contents, especially in legal contexts.[17] Here, "reality effect" refers to pornography as it becomes an object of desire and a form of sex in itself, to be consumed as such; it is an inherently "interactive" discourse.[18] It tries to persuade the reader that it is a reality—or that there is somewhere such a reality—that can be experienced and consumed, then and there, in an enclosed moment, divorced from external considerations and conditions of possibility. Hence the constant repetition of scenes with nearly identical, slightly varied elements in works such as *The Plum in the Golden Vase* and *Preposterous Words*, as if attempting to arrive at a scene of not only complete satisfaction but complete rendition of that satisfaction—that is, the perfect portrait that captures the state of sexual ecstasy. Sheer repetition belongs to the same scheme, as in counting (thrusts) and switching (positions or partners), as do portrayals of the failure to arrive at a state of fulfillment. A space and time emerge in which the reader approaches a sheer sense of presence, freed from social relations and critical considerations about those relations— though it is obviously the case that not all readers feel such a way, and that

     KEITH MCMAHON

such a sense of suspension still involves measures of value and ranking that stretch in multiple directions.[19]

What is most useful in this brief consideration of the word *pornography* is the opportunity to define it in a comparative context—especially in the cases of coincidence, or lack of coincidence, between the history and the phenomenon of pornography in China and Europe. What follows returns to a narrower treatment of *Preposterous Words* in the attempt to describe its themes and contents in light of its didactic platform (what can be called its pornographic doctrine) and its contextualization within its period—as difficult as that may be due to the lack of information about the author and the dating and history of the text. It is an anomalous work because of the extremes of its portrayals, its great length, and its underground existence (remarkably similar to that of the Marquis de Sade's *120 Days of Sodom*).[20] Little critical discussion exists that can be used to evaluate the novel, unlike European works that were published in their time and read and discussed for centuries. But it also needs to be said that *Preposterous Words* is not simply a work of pornography. Beginning in chapter 21, long passages consist of scenes of turmoil at the end of the Ming, with the novel ending in scenes of loyalist hermits who withdraw from both family and society and refuse to join the new world of the next dynasty. The sexually explicit descriptions in *Preposterous Words* are part of the same narrative agenda, which can be fruitfully articulated once better understood against the backdrop of the period it portrays and the period in which it was written. There is still a long way to go in examining and understanding this text.

SEXUAL ANARCHY

The narrative eye of *Preposterous Words* sees sexual anarchy everywhere it looks. As Vitiello says, the novel "displays sexual indulgence as the most meaningful sign of political and moral degeneration," seeing "disorder on a national scale."[21] It is a topsy-turvy world that has lost its sense of decency, beginning in the first chapter with a wanton woman who invites men to have sex for free, but charges them if the sex is no good. She engages in "intermittent marriage," "leaving the door half-open" (*lingsui jia, bankai men,* 1.159)—the latter being a term for operating a covert brothel. Women have sex with slaves, filthy beggars, and animals, bestiality being an extreme that retrospectively colors all aberrant sex with the same brush. Incest is a particularly strong sign of topsy-turviness. Sons have sex with stepmothers (whether a father's second wife or concubine), brothers have sex with sisters-in-law, and—the farthest the novel goes—a father is fooled into sodomizing his son (10.1664), and two brothers have sex with a stepmother who is a reincarnation of their mother (24.2854–55). Ruan Dacheng's family is a center of incestuous activity. One woman has affairs with Ruan and both his sons, the latter two of whom have sex with her at the same time, with the author irresistibly adding the flourish that their penises rub inside (8.984). There is rampant buggery, with husbands using their wives and concubines to lure boys whom they desire as catamites. Strange sexual beings include the lustful half-man, half-monkey, Yi Yuren (whose name puns with "unlike a human," 14), the intermittently male and female Qijie (14), and the real-life eunuch Wei Zhongxian (1568–1627), who regrows a penis and has an affair with the emperor's wet nurse, Madam Ke—like Wei, a historical figure, who furthermore is the Tianqi emperor's first sexual partner in what amounts to a shadowy form of mother-son incest (8).

Preposterous Words' exceptional couple is made up of the student Zhong Qing and the blind prostitute Qian Gui. They are the novel's version of an already well-established pair, the literatus and the courtesan, whose union centers on the kindred nature of their souls, their meeting outside the confines of arranged marriage, their resistance against corruption and all types of meanness and vulgarity, and the connoisseurship they share of literature and the arts. The author of *Preposterous Words* could not fail to have known of the most famous of these couples in the late Ming, who wrote in a literary environment that for the most part eschewed the pornography that the novel now surrounds them with. *Preposterous Words* appropriates elements of courtesan culture from fiction, drama, and biography, endowing Qian Gui with familiar traits such as independence of spirit, defiance of norms and expectations, and generosity with her earnings from the brothel. Other works label the courtesan of this type with the term *xia*—"valiant" or "chivalrous"—which in the strongest sense refers to women who fight for the cause of justice and dynastic loyalism, doing such things as organizing or advocating resistance and remonstrating with men for their weakness in the cause.[22]

The couple first establish their bond in a brothel, but when Zhong passes his exams, he frees Qian from the brothel with money she gives him and marries her (14). Theirs is a monogamous marriage—as it should be, based on the model that the novel likewise appropriates from literature of the period about the idealized union of the brilliant and handsome man and the talented and beautiful woman, commonly known as "the scholar and the beauty," *caizi jiaren*.[23] The presence of other wives would destroy the exclusive nature of their love, which is furthermore perfect in its sexual aspect, which the novel describes poetically and adumbratively (4.439–40), thus

     KEITH MCMAHON

conforming to another standard of Ming and Qing literature, the rarefied description of sublime love. But *Preposterous Words* adds another element to the formula: that of Qian Gui's blindness, which is a metaphor for the recognition of the man's true worth. As the novel's commentator puts it, the world is too blind to recognize talented and virtuous men like Zhong Qing. In decadent times, it takes a blind prostitute to do so. Another mark of Zhong's superiority is that he takes as a concubine Qian's virginal maid, Daimu, but only after being pressured to do so. As in other works of the period, the monogamous nature of the marriage is not destroyed if the man *reluctantly* takes one more wife, whom according to formula the first wife welcomes and loves as much as the man.[24]

Preposterous Words' linkage of social disorder and sexual and gender anarchy is not unusual in Ming and Qing fiction,[25] nor is the combination of pornography and moral message.[26] Even the most libertine of pornographic works generally punish or somehow discipline the characters whom they otherwise so explicitly describe.[27] The difference among these works has to do with the gravity and complexity of theme. *The Carnal Prayer Mat* is a case of pornographic folly, hardly serious compared to *The Plum in the Golden Vase* or *Preposterous Words.* The male hero has an operation to enlarge his penis and, with his new prowess, skips from one illicit affair to the next, in which all of the women enjoy him as he enjoys them all. In the end he realizes the vanity of desire, cuts off his penis, and withdraws into Buddhist asceticism. But the novel's tone is farcical—its enlightenment is hardly profound, though not meaningless. The enlarged penis is a parody of the male fantasy of super-potency; the cutting off of the penis is part of the same joke on that overblown fantasy.

The Carnal Prayer Mat is an example of witty and urbane pornography; it features a sexual anarchy of sorts, but not one that is a sign of social chaos—merely a norm that has gone off-kilter. Each episode is its own tour de force, reaching a crescendo of frenzy and ecstasy before linking with the next episode in a clever transition. Scenes focus on quantity and rhythm: the number of thrusts or partners, the size of organs, and the quality, sight, and sound of arousal. In *The Carnal Prayer Mat*, as in other Ming and Qing works, the female characters divide between the beautiful and delicate main wife, with whom sex is exquisite but who cannot be made love with too often; the sex-crazed woman who either dies in the end or becomes a nun; and finally the playful, sexy, and always-ready concubine. Characters engage in varieties of sexual positions, games (as in who can fill the most cups with their fluids), and acrobatics, which mainly comprise the choreography of sex between one man and multiple women on the same bed (or, in other works, partners of the same sex of either gender, or one woman and multiple men). The narrator's asides in *The Carnal Prayer Mat* amount to lessons about how to enjoy sex, or how to know what is enough or too much. He leaves no doubt that sex is a pleasure that one should enjoy, that the tendency is to go to extremes, and that the extremes are something that an urbane and rational person should be able to avoid.

Preposterous Words follows many of the same patterns, but compared to *The Carnal Prayer Mat* and *The Plum in the Golden Vase*, it has a perverse and caustic edge. Its repeated portrayal of rampant, grotesque sexuality is all in the name of promoting the pure and exalted. It is callous and derisive in its portrayal of wanton women and licentious men, but at the same time it describes them enjoying heights of ecstasy. Sex is like a fever that turns people into animals, with the narrator grinning and leering as he displays his thorough knowledge of the human sexual machine. Characters are like toys that he winds up and spins into delirium, then casts aside as he moves to another variation. The woman in particular is capable of stupendous pleasure; unless she meets an able man, she is a shameless, mindless force. The definition of the able man is where the novel tries to make its most convincing argument about the virtue of pornography in bettering the world. His pulsing, sucking, super-mobile penis will not only bring the wanton woman under control, but embody the moral and energetic force that will reform the chaotic world.[28]

THE MALADY OF MALE IMPOTENCE

The literatus and romantic hero, Zhong Qing, is surrounded by constitutionally inferior men who join the sexually voracious woman in the book's extravagant parade of social decay. The image of the deficient man pervades late Ming and early Qing literature by both men and women.[29] He is corrupt, or fails to stand up to corruption when he should. He engages in self-castigation. He vacillates, especially during the tense times before and after the fall of the dynasty, when he should have taken part in loyalist resistance. *Preposterous Words* takes part in the same kind of portrayal, telling for example of a "heroic woman" (*liefu*) who commits suicide rather than submit to abduction by invading bandits (21.2512–13). The official Shi Kefa (1601–45) praises her in contrast to the cowardly men employed by the Ming court, who join the bandits rather than oppose them to the death.[30] The Hongguang emperor, meanwhile, is more worried about his lack of good opera singers than the fate of the dynasty (23.2778–79).

But the focus of *Preposterous Words* is primarily on male sexual inferiority. One set of men displays grotesque sexual appetite. The Hongguang emperor has a penis like a donkey's, while another man's is shaped like a bell (6.649–50); they have indiscriminate, abusive sex, unless they meet the sexually strong woman, when both find their match. Such men and women are the quintessence of the monstrous chaos threatening the world at the end of the Ming.

Another set of men exemplifies sexual deficiency, as seen in the recurrent portrayal of impotent, henpecked husbands married to domineering, sexually unsatisfied wives. The men's problems begin in childhood: as boys, they are so soft-witted and infantile that their fathers have to ask older women to introduce them to sex. The first of three such men is Huan E, whose parents delegate a forty-year-old widowed servant to get in bed with him, for "he hasn't the slightest idea of the facts of life" (5.528–29). In the same chapter another young master, "delicate and tender" (*jiaopi nenrou*), still sleeps at age ten in the same room with his wet nurse, where he wakes at night to see her having sex with her husband. After she dies, a twenty-year-old maid takes over and, sleeping naked one summer morning, finds him on top of her, lets him continue, and likes him more than her husband. The boy is still too young to ejaculate (5.557–59). A third young man from a later chapter is newly married, but mentally deficient and likewise ignorant about sex. He watches as his wet nurse and her husband demonstrate how to have sex, pointing out their organs and going through the steps of intercourse, preparing him for his wedding night with his wife—though when he is shown the nurse's vagina, he is afraid of its mouthlike appearance and worried that his wife will bite him on his "peepee" (*jiji*). The young man succeeds after all with his wife, likes sex, and can now be said to be the father of the bastard child his wife is already pregnant with (12.1327–28). Boys and girls witnessing parents or other elders having sex in front of them is another recurrent scene in *Preposterous Words* and is a sort of example in passing of the novel's underlying premise that pornography is everywhere in the world—that is, the act, discussion, and demonstration of sex.[31]

Although the figure of the deficient man had particular resonance in the late Ming, the relationship of the sexually weak man and wanton, domineering woman had already formed as an archetype in early history. The *Jinshu* (History of the Jin) reports that, as a youth being prepared for royal marriage, the young Jin dynasty emperor Hui (who reigned from 290 to 306) "still knew nothing of the affairs of the marriage chamber." Because of the boy's mental deficiency, his father, Emperor Wu (236–90), had one of his own consorts "attend [the boy] in the bedroom" (*shiqin*). Hui later married Jia Nanfeng (257–300), who became notorious for allegedly smuggling men into the palace for sex, after which she had them murdered; later, she and her family launched a coup and took control of government.[32] An author did not have to refer directly to Emperor Hui or Jia Nanfeng—nor did all the details of their case have to apply. The outline of a sexually political pornographic story had already long existed, which an author like *Preposterous Words'* could readily adapt to his own purposes.

Whether or not the author had Emperor Hui in mind, he was no doubt thinking of the two Ming emperors who bonded for years with older, dominating women—in both cases nurses, not wives. The first was Xianzong (1447–87), the Chenghua emperor, whose first sexual partner was his nursemaid and honored consort Wan Guifei (1430–87), seventeen years his senior and his sexual favorite when he assumed the throne at age fifteen. The second was the Tianqi emperor (1605–27), who for his entire short life was attached to his wet nurse, Madam Ke (ca. 1588–1627). Both the Tianqi emperor and Ke are characters in *Preposterous Words*; the former loses his virginity to the latter. In the obscene-burlesque language the author often employs, he writes, "They went from her giving him the milk of her little nipple to put in his upper mouth to drink, to her now taking the 'milk' of his 'big nipple' and giving it to her 'lower mouth' to eat," adding that "once he tasted that delicacy, nothing from the imperial pantry could ever again compare" (8.910).

Historically, it was the Ming emperor Xianzong who coupled with his nursemaid (but not wet nurse), while the Tianqi emperor did not have sexual relations with Ke, though he was so attached to her that he could not tolerate her banishment from the palace. Engaging in a kind of pornographic lèse-majesté, *Preposterous Words* refers to Tianqi's penis as his "royal schlong" (*yudiao*), which was "never to begin with very endowed" (8.911)—the word "royal," *yu*, being an honorific reserved for emperors, as in expressions such as the "imperial pantry" just quoted. A respectable writer would not refer directly to an emperor's organ and would only refer to his intercourse at a dignified remove—using, for instance, the word *xing*, for when the emperor "favored" an imperial wife. The author carries the insult to a further extreme by having the eunuch Wei Zhongxian regrow a penis and sleep with Madam Ke, who is more satisfied with him than with the useless emperor.[33]

The malady of male impotence extends as well to the rebel Li Zicheng, likewise pathetically underendowed. He is cuckolded by all three of his wives—the second of whom, Lady Xing, is valiant in both sex and war and

KEITH MCMAHON

joins the Ming to fight alongside it (22.2586–87, 22.2595). Li was an ubiquitous object of scorn in Qing literature, in particular because he was a safer such object than the Manchu invaders, maligning reference to whom was dangerous under the conditions of Qing censorship. One should not refer to the fall of the Ming as anything but a necessary and successful transition— in *Preposterous Words*, as elsewhere, presumed to be caused by internal forces of destruction.[34] In real life, Li Zicheng launched a rebellion that resulted in the invasion of Beijing and the suicide of the last emperor. He was defeated by a combination of Ming and Manchu forces, the latter of which *Preposterous Words* finally refers to in its last chapter.[35]

As with Ruan Dacheng and Wei Zhongxian, the novel goes into Li's family background to show the extent of sexual decadence and its ramifications throughout families and generations. Li Zicheng's father marries a thirty-year-old prostitute, who at forty still has no son, but finally begets Li Zicheng, who grows into a young man who runs with prostitutes, though his penis is "infinitesimally small." When the prostitutes create a sarcastic ditty about him, saying his erection is "only as big as a thumb" (21.2449), he determines to marry a virgin, but he fails with one woman after another until someone tricks him with a prostitute who pretends she is ignorant of what a penis is and acts as if in pain at their first sex (21.2450–54). A common feature of *Preposterous Words'* pornography appears again in this scene: demonstration, in passing, of the supposed knowledge of female sexuality. In other words, the author demonstrates his expertise, further supporting the logic and effectiveness of his use of what would otherwise be thought of as obscene and shameful language.

Rampant buggery is another sign of male impotence and is the common pastime of men who fail to satisfy their wives (6, 7, 10). As Vitiello says, the novel reads the "craze for boys . . . as the symptom of a fundamental literati weakness [and] a mark of the inadequacy of . . . Confucian virility"—though, as he also demonstrates, the novel does not present homoerotic relations in a purely negative light.[36] Sodomy is a way for boys and men to survive and advance by becoming sexual retainers of men above them, as in the case of the poorly endowed Li Zicheng. Once he gains power, he suddenly experiences both young and old Ming officials offering him their buttocks (18.2151–52). In Vitiello's words, "receptive sodomy" comes to signify wholesale "imperial capitulation."[37] The explicit and farcical nature of Li Zicheng's portrayal is all the more effective in driving such a point home. Wei Zhongxian is a parallel case of sexual aberration throughout families and generations. His father is a county magistrate's catamite who marries a woman already pregnant by a monk with Wei Zhongxian; Wei eventually marries a woman who sleeps with other men and whose son becomes a catamite. When first married, Wei presents his buttocks to his wife until he realizes that he is marrying a woman, not "servicing a patron" (*ban gulao*, 8.904–5). He sells her, castrates himself, and becomes a favorite of the Tianqi emperor (though not a sexual favorite). Once in that position, Wei uses a drug to grow a new penis, turning from passive to active partner and, in effect, from eunuch-slave to de facto emperor.

The eunuch who regrows a penis—or, in some stories, who was never castrated to begin with—belongs to a set of motifs that since at least the Han dynasty has been part of the myth of eunuch potency, a myth that especially comes alive in times of political disorder and imperial weakness. Wei Zhongxian became an object of vilification in fiction and drama beginning immediately after he died; authors at times mixed stories about different eunuchs together, as in the case of growing the new penis, which perhaps derived from a historical account of an earlier Ming eunuch who was fooled into thinking he could do so by eating the brains of young boys, as Wei does in *Preposterous Words* (8.910).[38] In the world of *Preposterous Words*, it is as if the knowledge and technology exist to turn anyone into a potent man, even the ultimate nonman, the eunuch. He was a type notoriously prone to the abuse of power—Wei being one of four so-called eunuch dictators in the Ming. Along with figures such as Li Zicheng and Ruan Dacheng, Wei was an example of the depths to which humanity sunk in the Ming, leading inevitably to its invasion and defeat.

PREPOSTEROUS WORDS' SUPERIOR WOMAN

A common motif in Ming and Qing fiction is that when men are inferior or absent, the superior woman appears and does what needs to be done. She is superior in talent, courage, and moral fiber. A story tells of a man, for example, who fails to have sons or whose sons are incompetent and whose daughter, in some instances raised as a man, performs as well as or better than men.[39] It is especially in times of dynastic crisis that such women either outshine the men responsible for the crisis or together with male heroes represent bastions of cultural excellence in times of decay—as in the case of *Preposterous Words*' Zhong Qing and Qian Gui. In general, as said in *Preposterous Words*, "many are the so-called imposing men who are inferior to the sequestered gentlewoman," to which the commentator responds, "This is the main theme of the book!" (16.1905). Versions of the same statement appear in other Qing texts.[40] The blind prostitute, Qian Gui, is *Preposterous*

KEITH MCMAHON

Words' version of the superior, talented woman, whose heroic qualities emerge in her moral character, literary talent, and courageous resolve. She refuses, for example, to serve villainous clients—such a courtesan being an idealized figure in Ming-Qing literature, as noted above.[41]

In contrast with such figures portrayed elsewhere, both real and fictional, Qian does not engage in actual loyalist activity or resistance to invasion, though other women briefly referred to do.[42] But the author links her indirectly to the cause of Ming loyalism when her maid, Daimu, reads to her from *Biographies of Exemplary Women* (Lienü zhuan), referring to Du Xiaoying, a young woman who committed suicide after being abducted by renegade Ming troops. Du berates the general who is about to rape her, accusing him of perverting his imperial mission to fight "bandits" and becoming no more than a bandit himself (3.338–39). As Li Wai-yee writes, earlier versions of Du's story had her confronting Qing troops, but later versions, including *Preposterous Words'*, changed the story in fear of Qing censorship. In Qian Gui's eyes, Du is heroic because of her chastity. Reference to the theme of Ming loyalism has disappeared. But against the backdrop of *Preposterous Words'* description of late Ming decadence, Du Xiaoying's story in effect reinscribes itself with the overtones of Ming loyalism, even if it is impossible to know whether the author knew of the earlier versions of the story and its overt link with that theme. In the early Qing, chastity alone could be allegorized as loyalism, without having to refer to historical or political realities.[43]

But Qian Gui is not the typical superior woman in the novel. It is instead the sexually dominant woman who performs the role of superior woman— that is, Qian Gui's obscene obverse.[44] The wanton woman was both a long-existing character type and a particular focus of Qing writers, who turned her into an emblem of late Ming depravity. As a long-existing character type, she was someone capable of taking one man after another, exhausting them (but never herself).[45] *Preposterous Words* endows her with an animal quality that the novel explains through a dream of Zhong Qing's, in which he learns that three of the novel's wanton women were men in previous lives who committed bad deeds and, as punishment, were reincarnated as animals. After serving their karmic terms as animals, they are reborn as women; they still retain the animal qualities (*shouxin*) of their former incarnations, but because their husbands have voluntarily turned virtuous, the judge of hell now transforms the three wives into virtuous women (17.1946–47). As an emblem of late Ming depravity, the shameless, wanton woman appears in both fictional and historical texts of the Qing; instead of resisting invaders, she brazenly throws herself upon them. She has no concept of loyalty to the Ming, nor any sense of chastity, but easily succumbs to the pleasure of sex with her abductors and only cares about surviving.[46]

In *Preposterous Words*, the wanton woman drives the novel's relentless depictions of licentiousness—which, however, also include unabashed portraits of ecstasy. She is condemned as an emblem of late Ming debasement, but at the same time acknowledged for her sexual formidability. The character type includes both the girl who, improperly raised, becomes wanton at an early age, and the widow or unsatisfied wife, who craves sexual outlet into advanced age. Both choose their men freely, a blaring sign of their leading role in the drama of sexual anarchy.

If young men show an initial stupidity in sex, young women open up naturally. A husband and wife, surnamed Yin, run a small variety store and put their daughter in a local boys' school, thinking that, given her intelligence, she will become a "well-formed person" if she learns to read (*quanren*, 6.670). But temptation takes over as she overhears the boys' sexual banter, spies them masturbating, and soon begins having sex with them (6.675–76). Her superiority continues to manifest itself when she becomes a famous actress, but because of her past, she can only marry a lowly man—in her case, a former catamite—with whom she has a daughter, Jiaojiao, who continues in her mother's footsteps after observing her parents having sex (6.717). Jiaojiao similarly marries a deficient man, Wu He, a so-called "natural eunuch" (*tian'an*, 10.1108), but nevertheless a kindly person who rescues her from abduction by an evil monk.[47]

Yet another girl, Duoyin, whose name puns with "Full of Lust," also has parents who have sex in the presence of their children (Duoyin, nine, and her brother, thirteen). The exceptionally ugly Duoyin soon wants to try it herself and begins in an open space in back of the house where men go to urinate. Years go by; she becomes pregnant several times; her mother buries the babies. As with others, she finally marries the only man who will have her, You Xialiu, whose name puns with the word for "lowly and obscene," the son of a beggar chief's daughter and a rascally *xiucai* ("budding scholar"). You Xialiu is the man referred to earlier whose father was tricked into sodomizing him. He takes a wanton catamite as a lover and is clumsy at sex with Duoyin, who threatens to hang herself because he is ruining her youth, but by chance they discover his skill at cunnilingus (10.1191–92). In *Preposterous Words'* ribaldry, "He is far better at licking her than the most shameless licker of a rich man's crack" (10.1193). A case of utter male submission, he obeys her every wish, sweeping the floor, making the bed, and fixing her food (10.1194).

The other type of sexually voracious woman besides the girl is embodied by wives and widows, including elderly women. The recurrent theme in language and literature of the obscene is that women are more voracious the older they become, the fictional versions of the elderly widow-empress Wu Zetian being their prototype. *Preposterous Words*' wives and widows have sex with servants, filthy beggars, and potent monks with large penises (1, 5, 8, 11, 12), dogs (2, 12), donkeys (12), and monkeys (14). They prostitute themselves and exhaust one man after another, sometimes with their husbands openly knowing it (6); they are polyandrous (8, 17, 24); they pay men money to have sex with them (10); or they teach their maids to please them sexually and have no need for husbands anymore (13). They crave sex even when they are wrinkled and grey; one woman at the end of the book dies from sex with a dildo (24). Unless they die from their deeds (like, for example, the young Bao'er, 8, or the elderly ladies Hao and Mao, 24), women only cease being this way when their husbands finally become competent at sex (15, 17).

The novelist's eye is that of an obsessive analyst; he details every aspect of how the woman feels, looks, and sounds, accounting for her every phase of arousal. She is already like an animal before she actually copulates with one, as when she sounds like a "snorting" pig (*heng*, 15.1738) or a sow calling its young (19.2296). Her fluids flow with a sound like crashing waves (6.717, 17.2010). The noise beneath the bed is like people tramping in muck so loudly that it drowns out the woman's moans (11.1262). As in other novels, *Preposterous Words* uses the word *sao* to describe her—meaning swinish, randy, or rutty. Sometimes she is ugly, as if to imply that the uglier she is, the more *sao* (1.171). The descriptions combine hyperbole with pornographic cliché: scenes of sex being spied upon, of a virginal maid becoming aroused listening to others having sex, or of such a maid's eagerness to take the place of her tired mistress, who gladly gives the maid to the husband, all recur in Ming and Qing literature.[48]

If we render the story of the wanton woman in terms of a progression to the novel's climactic portrayal of aberrant sexual beings, we should begin with Duoyin, mentioned earlier, who pays men to have sex with her—including beggars, with whom she enjoys an ecstasy that "no amount of words can express" (10.1188). Later, referred to as Lady Bu, she resorts to sex with a dog and gives birth to pups, including half pups and half humans, though she does not think it odd (12.1375). Next is Lady Rong, who generates a chain of sexual beings who depart even further from normal human heredity. Since her husband is too old to satisfy her, she has sex with a monkey and gives birth to a boy who is like a human but has a monkey-like head—the above-mentioned Yi Yuren (14.1580–82). Yi has a huge sexual appetite, but is infertile.

Attracted by the wanton aura surrounding the house, a fox infiltrates Yi's family and impregnates one of the monkey-man's concubines, who gives birth to a baby with a penis above its vagina. Once grown up, this character, named Qijie, "Strange Sister," has erections during the first half of the month and uses her vagina the other half (14.1598). Qijie is infertile and marries a man who only likes anal intercourse; when Qijie is a man, the couple have anal sex and share eight female concubines. Qijie also obtains eight male concubines for the half of the month during which she is a woman.

In the novel's allegorical scheme, Qijie is the culmination of the world-wide wantonness that leads to the fall of the Ming. The woman who is also a man is the "licentious monster" (*yinyao*) that results from universal sexual anarchy (14.1596)—the underlying message being that the voracious woman, once let loose, will necessarily replace the man and do his sexual job as well or better, whether the job is homosexual or heterosexual. Doing that job means not only having her own penis, which is an organic sort of replacement (as it was in the case of Wei Zhongxian), but also assuming the role of polygamist, a social form of replacement, which two polyandrous women do in the final chapter, including Ruan Dacheng's wife.[49] For the primary badge of the superior man, the truest sign of his potency, is his possession of multiple wives. Even the genteel Zhong Qing, though hesitant at first, is persuaded to take a concubine, while his male allies eventually all take concubines as soon as they shed their henpecked ways and become sexual adepts. It is, moreover, their formerly shrewish wives who insist that they do so.

THE PORNOGRAPHIC DOCTRINE OF THE POTENT PENIS

Preposterous Words ends with the hero Zhong Qing and other hermits withdrawing from the world in loyalty to the fallen Ming. One of them performs a ritual in which he weeps and calls out for the Chongzhen emperor (24.2914). Other works about the fall of the Ming end with heroes similarly withdrawing, because they know the fall is inevitable, and refusing to serve the new dynasty.[50]

But the author submits another type of hero who (by implication) in better times might have come to the rescue: the man with the triumphant penis. He appears in several versions; the most exemplary one is Zhong Qing, who is never subjected to pornographic scrutiny. Zhong is the handsome literatus who possesses the innate talent and virility needed in an upright society, for whom pornographic detail would be superfluous and degrading. Zhong is joined by three gentry men, Huan E, Jia Wenwu, and Tong Zida, and Daoist and Buddhist monks, all of whom possess virile potency, which *Preposterous*

KEITH MCMAHON

Words describes pornographically and with ideological undertones. In other words, pornography is put to good use with these men, for when pornography applies to a good man's body, it is not obscene and inflammatory, but doctrinally effective as a positive example. The pornography of negative example is about men who possess giant penises and huge sexual appetites—including the Hongguang emperor mentioned above, whose penis is like a donkey's, who has sex with a donkey, and who takes palace women roughly and randomly (23.2778, 23.2783–84). The positive portrayal is about wholesomely virile men and their robustly lustful wives, whose sex the novel presents in as affirmative a way as possible, given its deference to the rule of shielding the most virtuous characters from pornographic description. The novel promotes potent sexual virility according to the three doctrines of Confucianism, Daoism, and Buddhism, with the Confucian Zhong Qing joined by Daoist and Buddhist monks who instruct Jia Wenwu and Tong Zida. The portrayals of these men culminate *Preposterous Words'* positive pornographic doctrine, which amounts to a sexualized version of the syncretic teaching of the "unity of the three religions" (*sanjiao gui yi*).

The portrayals emerge in the second half of the book, when the sworn brothers Huan E, Jia Wenwu, and Tong Zida experience a sudden moral turnaround, one after the other—each described in pornographic detail that focuses on their mastery of sex with their wives. All three begin as henpecked husbands and sexual impotents, vulgar and ill-educated, pretentiously trying to pass as men of high culture. The episode about Tong Zida is the pièce de résistance of the portrait of male potency. A Buddhist monk teaches him the Daoist art of the "battle of absorption" (*caizhan*, 17.2027), gives him aphrodisiacs, and has him undergo an operation that turns the opening of his penis into "a little mouth" that can open and close (17.2026–27). He delights his wife: "Inside her it bit a little here and nibbled a little there, giving her a tingling, buttery sensation, more exciting than she could stand . . . until finally it chomped on her flower heart like a baby sucking at the breast, sucking so hard that she nearly died of delight." She shakes like someone with "the shivers of malarial fever" (17.2031). It is a scene of ultimate male conquest, one of the author's most concentrated attempts at portraying sexual bliss.

PREPOSTEROUS WORDS AS A WORK OF MING LOYALISM

A preview of the orally mobile phallus already appears in the first chapter of *Preposterous Words*, emerging full-blown in Tong Zida after more than half of the novel's exposition and allowing us to make some concluding points about *Preposterous Words'* use of pornography and its mission as a work of Ming loyalism. The phallus that pulsates on its own appears elsewhere in Ming-Qing fiction and was undoubtedly part of widely shared sexual lore.[51] To characterize the "male thing" (*yangwu*) in this way is to endow it with a self-mastery that allows the man unchallengeable control over the woman. She "dies" of pleasure, becomes "paralyzed," and is so overcome that she asks her husband to take concubines because he is too much for her alone. A key detail in *Preposterous Words'* description of the super-penis is the reference to the baby sucking at the breast. The description of the Daoist's phallus in the first chapter makes the same reference. It is "now like a snake bobbing its head and fluttering its tongue, now like a baby sucking at the nipple" (1.172). The image recalls chapter 45 of *The Classic of the Way* (Daode jing), in which the infant erection is a symbol of innate potency, representing the height of *yang* energy—which in the Daoist scheme is subject to loss through the wear and tear of life.[52] In other words, the babylike phallus is anything but helpless and dependent. *Preposterous Words* expands upon that image by imagining the adult man recapturing the original, innate potency of the male babe and harnessing that potency in order to satisfy the appetite of his wife. It is only in this way that the man can reverse and correct what the novel presents as the dangerous rise of *yin* energy in the woman, whom *Preposterous Words* portrays as being entirely consumed by her sexuality and the demand to be satisfied.[53]

Preposterous Words' adherence to the theme of male potency links both to the centuries-long tradition of the analogy between self, family, and body politic, on the one hand, and to the similarly ancient tradition of sexual absorption in the Daoist alchemical arts, on the other. The novel applies both traditions to the cause of Ming loyalism, for *Preposterous Words* must be added to the long list of works devoted to that subject, which carried through the entire span of the Qing in spite of its inherent risks. Beginning in chapter 21, the novel devotes pages of narrative to the battles between Li Zicheng's "bandits" (*zei*) and Ming forces, describing rape, abduction, mass devastation, starving people eating the dead, and fields filled with rotting corpses. These scenes intersperse with the idyllic pastimes of Zhong and friends, with the author spending his last pages solely on Zhong and other loyalist hermits in remote southern Zhejiang. It is as if the novel had never contained a single pornographic scene.[54]

Other writings devoted to Ming loyalism and reacting to the trauma of dynastic collapse were by authors who experienced the fall; some (including *Preposterous Words,* if we believe the date of its preface) came a generation or two afterward. Some works take place in the late Ming, such as

     KEITH MCMAHON

Preposterous Words; others reflect the late Ming through another period.[55] Among these, *Preposterous Words* is not alone in portraying the period in the polarized terms of good *yang* versus evil *yin*. What singles it out is its use of pornography, which was a choice on the part of the author that carried specific historical meaning. Who made such a choice and why is a subject for another study. For present purposes, the most important factor has to do with the time in which the novel appeared.

By the time of *Preposterous Words*, the choice to speak in the language of pornography meant something different from what it meant in Ming works such as *The Plum in the Golden Vase*. The practice of pornography was thought by many to be an inherent part of Ming decadence and disorder—even, to a degree, the cause of it. Censorship in the Qing was categorically stronger than in the Ming, targeting what it thought was emblematic of the Ming failure. But *Preposterous Words* took the approach that the only way to describe the extent of the shame and blame for the Ming collapse was to portray it pornographically. Doing so made it such that its pornography had to be read for its political and historical meanings. In the relentless drive to portray the extremes of licentiousness, *Preposterous Words* embodied unbridled excess in itself, the same monstrous chaos threatening the world at the end of the Ming. By simultaneously being what it condemned and condemning it, the novel demonstrated what was fatal for the Ming and affirmed a better version of the Ming. In so doing, it spoke in a voice that defied the censoring authority of the Qing empire and that dared to affirm the wholesome pleasure of an activity for which there was no easy label and that was risky to talk about—namely, sex that was not licentious.

NOTES

1   See Huang, *Desire and Fictional Narrative in Late Imperial China*, 253–54, for references to *Ruyijun zhuan* (The lord of perfect satisfaction), *Dengcao heshang* (The candlewick monk), and *Rouputuan* (The carnal prayer mat).

2   Except for partial publication in the 1930s, the novel survived as a handwritten manuscript that sometime during the 1840s or 1850s was taken to Russia, where it stayed until it was published in Taiwan in 1997. Giovanni Vitiello translates the title as "Nonsense"; Martin Huang translates it as "Presumptuous Words." "Preposterous Words" comes from Qing Ye's paper "The Private, Metaphor, and Masculinity." I use the 1997 Taipei edition of Cao Qujing's *Guwangyan*. Studies I have consulted in addition to Qing Ye's are: Vitiello, *The Libertine's Friend*, 134–38, 142–53, and elsewhere; Huang, *Desire and Fictional Narrative in Late Imperial China*, 251–70, 251–52; Chen, "*Guwangyan* sucai laiyuan chukao," and "*Guwangyan* sucai laiyuan erkao"; and Xu, "Ethics of Form."

3   See Vitiello, *The Libertine's Friend*, 135.

4   See Hunt, "Introduction," 12–13; Hunt, "Pornography and the French Revolution," 303; DeJean, "The Politics of Pornography," 109–23, 117–18; and Ferguson, *Pornography, the Theory*, xii.

5   See Hunt, "Introduction," 39.

6   See DeJean, "The Politics of Pornography," 114; Hunt, "Introduction," 39; Norberg, "The Libertine Whore," 225–52, 239; and Weil, "Sometimes a Scepter Is Only a Scepter," 125–53, 131, 148.

7   See Hunt, "Pornography and the French Revolution," 309.

8   See Weil, "Sometimes a Scepter Is Only a Scepter," 140.

9   See Hunt, "Introduction," 10, 23, 36; and Darnton, *The Forbidden Bestsellers of Pre-Revolutionary France*.

10   See DeJean, "The Politics of Pornography," 120, 122–23.

11   See these authors and others, such as Yu Huai and Mao Xiang, as discussed in Li, *Women and National Trauma in Late Imperial Chinese Literature*.

12   See Williams, *Hardcore*; Williams, *Porn Studies*; and Kipnis, *Bound and Gagged*. These books introduced a less condemnatory view of pornography, especially after the era of Catharine MacKinnon and Andrea Dworkin.

13   See Darnton, *The Forbidden Bestsellers of Pre-Revolutionary France*.

14   See, for example, Li, *Rouputuan*, chapter 1; and Ding Yaokang, *Xu jin ping mei* (Sequel to *Jin ping mei*), chapter 23.

15   See Ferguson, *Pornography, the Theory*, xiv; Brennan, "*Pornography, the Theory*," 155–56; and Williams, "Porn Studies," 11.

16   MacKinnon and Dworkin belong to an earlier phase of porn studies grounded in the assumption that "pornography expressed the power and the pleasure of heterosexual men." See Williams, "Porn Studies," 7.

17   See Ferguson, *Pornography, the Theory*, 7–8.

18   See Ullén, "Pornography and Its Critical Reception."

19   Ullén talks about "the emergence of a new kind of cognitive space," "marked by a supreme sense of presence." See "Pornography and Its Critical Reception."

20   Sade had hidden his manuscript of *The 120 Days of Sodom* in the wall of his Bastille cell, which he had to hastily abandon, but the manuscript was found and survived through three generations of a French family before being bought and published in 1904 by a German sexologist.

21   Vitiello, *The Libertine's Friend*, 135, 145.

22   See Li, *Women and National Trauma in Late Imperial Chinese Literature*, 304–6.

23   As the story goes, in a former life the woman's family refused to let them marry because of his ugliness (16). In their current life, the woman is punished by being reborn as a blind prostitute. See Huang, *Desire and Fictional Narrative in Late Imperial China*, 268, for a lengthier explanation.

24   According to the commentator (reportedly a friend of the author's), the author creates a blind prostitute in order to shame the men who fail to recognize

KEITH MCMAHON

true talent and are thus the truly blind ones. See *Guwangyan*, 2.192; and Huang, *Desire and Fictional Narrative in Late Imperial China*, 251–70, especially 258. On the phenomenon of two-wife marriage, see McMahon, *Polygamy and Sublime Passion*, 44–47.

25   See, for example, the anonymously written novel *Xingshi yinyuan zhuan* (Marriage destinies to awaken the world).

26   See, for example, Anonymous, *Jin ping mei* (The plum in the golden vase); Anonymous, *Ruyijun zhuan* (The story of Ruyi); Fang Ruhao, *Chan zhen yishi* (The tale of Buddhists and Daoists); Fang Ruhao, *Chan zhen houshi* (Sequel to the tale of Buddhists and Daoists); and Anonymous, *Lüye xianzong* (Trails of immortals in the green wilds).

27   Huang engages the topic of pornography and moral message at length; see *Desire and Fictional Narrative in Late Imperial China*, 138–44.

28   As Vitiello writes, the woman was "the ultimate embodiment of sexual desire and cause of social disorder"; see "Family Affairs," 249.

29   The poet Wang Duanshu, among others, "indicts the collective failure of men"; see also regarding Wu Weiye and Qian Qianyi, in Li, *Women and National Trauma in Late Imperial Chinese Literature*, 120, 242–50, and 266. Maram Epstein explores the theme of male deficiency and the "making of the shrew" in *Competing Discourses*, 120–49.

30   See also 21.2475–78 for a woman who resists Li Zicheng to the death; and 21.2552 for a woman who participates in defense against the "bandits from the northeast" (*dongbei zei*).

31   The author was perhaps inspired by the reference to childhood sex in the Ming novel *Hailing yishi*, or *Hailing yishi*'s shorter version in Feng Menglong's *Xingshi hengyan* (23.8a); see Ling, "Yilu yindu zhi can."

32   See Fang, *Jinshu*, 31.968, 31.963–965.

33   On the Tianqi reign, Wei Zhongxian, and Madam Ke, see Dardess, *Blood and History*. For fictional variations on the story of Wei Zhongxian and the theme of eunuch potency, see McMahon, "The Potent Eunuch."

34   See Li, *Women and National Trauma in Late Imperial Chinese Literature*, 540–43.

35   *Guwangyan* uses respectful terms to refer to the Qing—e.g., "the Great Qing army," *da Qing bing*; "the Great Qing Heavenly army," *da Qing tianbing*; "our army," *wo bing*; and "our dynasty," *wo chao* (24.2858, 24.2900–91, and elsewhere).

36   See Vitiello, *The Libertine's Friend*, 141, 152–53, and 145–53.

37   See Vitiello, *The Libertine's Friend*, 143–44.

38   In a later Qing novel, the Ming eunuch Liu Jin (ca. 1452–1510) uses the same method to regrow a penis. The source is probably an account by Shen Defu (1578–1642); a similar tale appears in the late Ming novel *Chanzhen houshi*. See the 1842 novel *Zhengde you Jiangnan* (The Zhengde emperor roams in the south) in Wengshan and He, *Baimudan* (White peony), 5.191 (Liu Jin);

Shen, *Wanli yehuo bian buyi*, 6.158 (brains); and Fang Ruhao, *Chan zhen houshi*, 37.280.

39 See a brief and comprehensive example in Feng Menglong, *Gujin xiaoshuo* (Stories old and new), story 28.

40 See poetry by Wang Duanshu and the line from Qian Qianyi, quoted by Li, *Women and National Trauma in Late Imperial Chinese Literature*, 120, 266.

41 See Li, "The Late Ming Courtesan"; and McMahon, *Polygamy and Sublime Passion*, chapter 3.

42 See 21.2475–2478; 21.2512–2513; and for a woman expert in the "art of war," 21.2552.

43 See *Guwangyan*, 3.337–44 (the maid obviously purchased an expanded version of this book, which includes stories of Ming women); Li, *Women and National Trauma in Late Imperial Chinese Literature*, 405–29, 426–27, and 462; Grace Fong, "Signifying Bodies"; Huang, *Desire and Fictional Narrative in Late Imperial China*, 259; and Chen, *Cong "Jiaohong ji" dao "Honglou meng,"* 306–7.

44 On the superior woman and her wanton obverse, see McMahon, *Polygamy and Sublime Passion*, 18–19.

45 For a brief history of early examples, see McMahon, "The Polyandrous Empress."

46 See Wang Xiuchu, *Yangzhou shiri ji* (Rape of Yangzhou), about women "shamelessly pander[ing]" to the enemy; and Ding, *Xu jin ping mei*, about abducted women happy to be captured by Qing forces, as cited in Li, *Women and National Trauma in Late Imperial Chinese Literature*, 392, 450, 481, 492. *Guwangyan* portrays abducted women who enjoy sex with their abductors (22.2640–43, 22.2647–50).

47 See Huang, *Desire and Fictional Narrative*, 263–64, about the rebalancing of *qing* and *yu* in this case (*Guwangyan*, 7.793).

48 *Xingshi yinyuan zhuan* comes close to *Guwangyan* in its lurid focus on the shrew as "the epitome of uncontrollable destructive energy," though not in sexually explicit detail; see Epstein, *Competing Discourses*, 125. On the reality of polyandry in the Qing, see Sommer, *Polyandry and Wife-Selling in Qing Dynasty China*.

49 See 24.2905 (Ruan Dacheng's wife).

50 See Li, *Women and National Trauma in Late Imperial Chinese Literature*, 217, 255–58, and 526–53; and Vitiello, *The Libertine's Friend*, 137.

51 See also Anonymous, *Xinghua tian* (The paradise of the apricot blossom), chapter 3; and Anonymous, *Taohua ying* (In the shadow of the peach blossom), chapter 5.

52 See Lagerwey, *Taoist Ritual in Chinese Society and History*, 6–7.

53 I am borrowing from Slavoj Žižek's critique of Otto Weininger's caricature of the woman as being "entirely dominated by sexuality"—that is, entirely motivated by the desire to seduce the man and keep him perpetually in the sexual

realm. She does not exist except for this goal, which diverts the man from his pure and spiritual pursuits. See Žižek, *The Metastases of Enjoyment*, 137.

54 Passages about loyalist heroes and hermits are taken from another source, as explained in Chen, "*Guwangyan* sucai laiyuan erkao," 127–36.

55 Anonymous, *Tianyu hua* (Heaven rains flowers), and Kong Shangren, *Taohua shan* (Peach blossom fan), for example, take place in the period, while *Xu jin ping mei* approaches the late Ming via the Song-Yuan transition.

CHAPTER 4

BERTRAND RUSSELL AND ELLEN KEY IN CHINA

Individualism, Free Love, and Eugenics in the May Fourth Era

MIRELA DAVID

IN 1923, THE *LADIES' JOURNAL* (FUNÜ ZAZHI) PUBLISHED A TRANS-lation of the Swedish feminist Ellen Key's writing on free love, spotlighting Key's argument that "love originates in the force of racial preservation between the two sexes." The translated passage continued, "True love includes both factors: soul and carnality. What one needs are not only sensual sexual desires, or feelings of friendship, but also emotional longings."[1] A firm believer in evolution and eugenics, Key had depicted women as key agents in defining the future of human race.[2] Conveyed in Chinese by the feminist writer YD—the pen name for a man named Wu Juenong—the above statement elegantly illustrates the way Key combined love and eugenics in a symbiotic framework.[3]

YD had internalized Key's understanding of racial preservation as a basic human instinct, achievable through the convergence of body and soul. Despite the apparent contradiction between eugenics and the ideals of individualism/humanism, Key had been able to gloss over that philosophical tension, and to argue in a way that bridged those contentions; relying on eugenic considerations, for instance, Key had firmly attached a racial significance to monogamy by turning it into an instrument of the larger project of racial engineering.[4] Key's writing stimulated the editors of the *Ladies' Journal* to publish special themed issues debating topics she had addressed in her book *Love and Marriage*, such as free love, free divorce, and a new sexual morality.

During the first half of the 1920s, male liberal intellectuals, witnessing the real-life romance between British philosopher Bertrand Russell and feminist writer Dora Black, engaged in what can be called an ontology of love—an existential quest to define humanity as rooted in love, and split between the needs of the individual and systemic categories such as society or race. Spurred by Russell's ideas of "social reconstruction," they looked to the promise of eugenics to account for these larger social structures in a time of political upheaval. Meanwhile, Russell's cross-country lectures—delivered in places such as Shanghai, Hangzhou, Changsha, and Beijing—repeatedly raised the need for science and individuality in China's quest for modernity.

Promoted as a set of scientific practices and ideologies, eugenics quickly became foundational for any conversation about love and sexuality. Of interest here is the eugenic version of a "robust" individual, envisioned by both Chinese intellectuals and Russell. Individualism had emerged as a "translingual practice" during the New Culture Movement of the mid-1910s and 1920s, when the opposition of individualism/humanism and tradition led to the state being taken for granted as a category.[5] In this context, "the individual," "humanism," and "the state" can be interpreted as flexible and historically contingent categories, best seen as mutually constitutive and sometimes in tension with each other.

What can be inferred from the grounding of identity in the unity of a robust, sexual body and a soul that has the freedom to love? This was a major question in the May Fourth period (1915–1921), during which liberal intellectuals sought to do away with Confucian marriage values. Feminists, however, shifted from this familiar juxtaposition to focus instead on the growing awareness of the need for individuals to shape social change. This conceptual reorientation guaranteed not only self-centered development, but also wider social benefits. Enlightenment thought became the modus operandi of propagating the discourse on individual choice. Sentiment and sexuality represented one way to self-discovery, along with self-cultivation, political participation, economic emancipation, and divorce.

The May Fourth debate over the ontology of love was imbricated with the questions of individualism, the meaning of science, and racial fitness from the start. Yet this debate also marked men's response to feminism with a growing contradiction. On the one hand, they sought to subvert the arranged marriage system by rethinking the role of sensuality and sentiment in free marriage choice and, by extension, reconsidering how women's gender roles should be refashioned. On the other hand, once male feminists began to liberate women sexually and socially from the confines of traditional gender conventions, they faced the difficulty of reconciling not only the social and racial implications of sexual liberation, but also their own anxieties of emasculation.

Debates around individual free will can serve as a window into the articulation of more radical stances on divorce, birth control, and sexuality in the early to mid-1920s. The appeal of Ellen Key to Chinese (male) intellectuals was rooted in the way she conceptualized a "new sexual morality"—a eugenic blending of individualism, race, and a distinctively modern form of love. As male editors of China's most widely circulated feminist magazine, the *Ladies' Journal*, Zhang Xichen and Zhou Jianren declared that eugenics constituted a new sexual ethics to replace China's old, Confucian morality. British sexologist Havelock Ellis, Ellen Key, and Bertrand Russell offered them a way to reconcile the idea of sexual freedom with eugenics. For the editors, sex was not just for procreation; like Russell, they considered reproduction a qualitative racial and social issue. They also took significant cues from the writings of European feminist sex reformers to rebut cultural conservatives—such as the Beijing University professor Chen Bainian, who disparaged Zhang's sexual ethics, and the biologist Chen Jianshan, who criticized Zhang's liberal understanding of eugenics.

BERTRAND RUSSELL AND DORA BLACK IN CHINA:
FREE LOVE AND FREE DIVORCE IN REEL TIME

Bertrand Russell's 1920 ten-month stay in China, where he had been invited to give lectures at Peking University, sparked debates on free love and free divorce. This was a case of personal experience being transformed into cultural discourse, as he was accompanied by his lover Dora Black.[6]

Russell's lived experience embodied his belief in free love. Thus, at the time of his stay in China, he was also openly exchanging romantic letters with the actress Constance Malleson, informing her of his arrival in Beijing.[7] Meanwhile, Russell and his wife Alys were in divorce proceedings, at which evidence of adultery was being raised.[8] Frowned upon by missionaries, Russell and Black spent most of their time in the company of Chinese students and intellectuals, such as the philosopher and liberal scholar Hu Shi. According to Black, "Our doings were so much the talk of the town that curiosity to meet us would overcome the stern duty of ostracizing us."[9] One *Shenbao* contributor, Ms. Wang, initially assumed that Dora was Mrs. Russell, but apologized to Russell and promised to rectify the "serious mistake" in the next day's edition.[10]

Upon arriving in China, Russell had some difficulty relating to local intellectuals because they were less interested in philosophy than in his opinions on "social reconstruction"; the latter was essential to their refashioning of key domains of human experience, such as love and marriage.[11]

　　　　　　　　　　MIRELA DAVID

Following the sensational publication of a letter by Russell on October 16, 1920, revealing the nature of his relationship to Black, a commentary appeared in the *Republican Daily* (Minguo ribao), restating Russell's skepticism toward the "corrupt and useless" British marriage law. The author referred to Russell's criticism of marriage as a legal and economic system that degraded humanity; according to Russell in *The Principles of Reconstruction*, the writer asserted, only children, and not what was between a man and a woman, could constitute the basis of social concern.[12]

Two years later, in 1922, birth-control activist Margaret Sanger would visit China; during her stay, Hu Shi would inform her of the growing discontent with the marriage system in China and comment on the new fashion for young couples to live together without marriage. Sanger would respond, "It seems that Mr. Bertrand Russell and Ms. Black are blamed or credited for this great move; it is on the increase, or so it is said."[13]

Indeed, in 1920 the Russell-Black affair ignited a reconsideration of the system of arranged marriage, because it symbolized the crystallization of individual free will—to love or to split. But Russell's ideas also put Chinese intellectuals at odds, since he was criticizing monogamy at the very moment when free marriage was being celebrated as a sign of modernity. The freedom to divorce, then, occupied an important role in the way Chinese intellectuals reconciled these tensions. The romantic poet Xu Zhimo, for example, asked Russell for advice on the dissolution of his loveless marriage to the educator and banker Zhang Youyi;[14] Xu's was the first modern divorce in China, and as reasons he cited the nascent notions of love and freedom championed by the New Culture critics.[15]

Authors such as Se Lu (aka *Ladies' Journal* editor Zhang Xichen) argued that Russell's opposition to the arranged marriage system was based on his reverence for liberty. Zhang-as-Se described Russell as a leading figure in social change, someone possessing an abiding respect for individual freedom. According to Se, Russell had attacked marriage laws as shameful "cultural relics" that hindered the development of "socially harmonious partners." Quoting from *The Principles of Reconstruction*, Se also called attention to Russell's attack on the way religion lent support to arranged marriage.[16]

Yet Se's feminism also led him to be critical of Russell. He pointed out the tension between Russell's advocacy of individuality and his eugenic understandings. Russell had advocated for the reproduction of intelligent families and cautioned against birth-control practices among mentally fit couples; according to Se, "Russell supposes [that practicing birth control] can cause intelligent families to degenerate, leading to the decline of people's spiritual value. If this situation does not change within two or three generations, the character of men of culture will deteriorate into nothingness."[17] Whereas Russell attributed the deterioration of the intellectual class to economic and legal constraints, Se looked to women's lack of individual freedom for explanation. On a more personal level, Russell's anxiety about mental illness in his own family had led him to decide not to have children with his first wife, Alys.[18]

Se translated the following passage from Russell's writings in order to challenge it:

> From a racial standpoint, the most urgent need is to eliminate
> the economic burden that falls on physically able men and women,
> give them legally a greater freedom of reproduction, and openly
> name the father of illegitimate children. For society to maintain
> the life of children and mothers, there is only one condition: the
> physical and mental health of both parents is related to the health
> of the children, and has to be robust. As for people whose bodies
> and minds are not vigorous, there is no need to restrict their
> reproduction, but let them assume the economic responsibility
> of caring for their children on their own.[19]

Se, considering this a weak argument, wanted to improve the lives of those less healthy, instead of burdening them with the responsibility to give or prevent birth. While Russell argued for privileging the more robust members of society, Se thought it unfair to put social and economic responsibility entirely on the frail.[20]

Still, Se found inspiration in Russell's positions on other related matters. For example, Russell believed that the state should financially support "desirable" mothers; he also found value in British polymath and eugenicist Francis Galton's work preaching socialism as a method of upholding the breed. Inspired by Russell's lived experience, Se also argued that free divorce was at the core of the polemic between the new morality and the old morality.

Meanwhile, after being invited to express her views on love, marriage, and women's rights in a piece for the *Ladies' Journal*,[21] Dora Black confessed that she admired the radical pursuit of social reform and personal freedom among Chinese feminists, who unlike their Western counterparts did not shy away from asking bold questions about love and marriage.[22] In a different forum, Black suggested that science had taught man a new sexual ethic, which entailed respecting women's individuality by placing it on a

     MIRELA DAVID

similar sexual playing field as that of men (an idea that Chinese intellectuals also endorsed).[23]

Russell's stance on sexual mores had inspired young Chinese thinkers to fight for severance from arranged marriages; the most courageous who married for love called it a "Russell marriage."[24] Inspired by Black and Russell's relationship, Chao Yuanren, a linguist who had been living in the same house as the couple's translator, became critical of old marriage traditions. Having fallen in love with Yang Buwei, a gynecologist, Chao broke his arranged engagement of fifteen years; Yang also backed out of her arranged engagement of twenty years,[25] against the wishes of her family. Russell lent Chao one hundred pounds to settle the annulment of his previous engagement; Chao repaid this loan almost twenty years later.[26] Eschewing a traditional engagement and wedding, they merely changed addresses. Their "no-ceremony wedding" caused quite a stir; one outlet published an article on the union, titled "New-Style Wedding of New-Style People." Other young couples also imitated their actions.[27] These young intellectuals were living their commitment to love-based marriage, a symbol of individual free will.

Black depicted Chao and Yang as "new thinking people." She described Yang, who had established the first nonmissionary hospital in Beijing and become the first person in China to impart birth control advice, as "fabulous and indomitable."[28] Black's close friendship with Yang, as well as her admiration for her professional achievements and courage, also influenced Black's future advocacy of contraception. Black found no use in only addressing childcare and education in China, if one did not also address "the problem of teaching limitation of families."[29] Russell, similarly, believed that large-scale birth control was needed to combat famine.[30]

EUGENICS AS A SCIENCE OF FREE LOVE: TRANSLATING ELLEN KEY IN THE *LADIES' JOURNAL*

In 1921 Zhang Xichen[31] became the editor-in-chief of the *Ladies' Journal*; he invited Zhou Jianren, influential writer Lu Xun's youngest brother, to join his editorial team.[32] Zhou's background in science and biology contributed to the broad dissemination of eugenic ideas in the journal. Together, they revolutionized the journal's content, culminating in what historian Wang Zheng has labeled a "feminist mental revolution"—one that constructed a new cultural order by altering the psychological understandings of men and women.[33] When Zhang took over the editorship of the *Ladies' Journal*, he introduced the problematic of the "new woman," drawing on gender equality, liberalism, and individualism.[34]

Circulation of the *Ladies' Journal* increased under Zhang's inclusive editorial style, especially his inclusion of the *tongxun* column, which featured readers' letters to the editors.[35] In response to criticisms of his predilection for Ellen Key, Zhang named two reasons for privileging her insights over those of other authors: her idea that human nature could be improved; and her notion of a "love morality" that upheld "the sacredness of reproduction."[36] For Zhang, social reproduction and women's reproduction coincided, and society in its most basic form was always gendered.

Zhang and Zhou extolled Key's feminist visions as the most advanced in the world. Zhang particularly admired her theoretical approach, as well as her ideas on the new sexual morality. Nonetheless, Key's praise of motherhood did not extend to people with "inherited physical or psychic diseases," who she felt should "not transmit [their ailments] to an offspring."[37] This argument appealed to many Chinese intellectuals.[38]

Key essentially promoted a scientific view of humanity; her eugenic ideas had emerged in many ways as a reaction to Friedrich Nietzsche's philosophical arguments, which positioned man as a transitional being, between animal and Übermensch, and as an agent carrying the responsibility for "the amelioration of race." Key found that Nietzsche was quite serious about eugenics, but his approach was more poetic in nature than Galton's scientific method.[39] Whereas Nietzsche alleged that the superhuman led humankind to evolution, Key believed evolution occurred for a reason intrinsic to humanity itself. She stressed "humanism in the form of evolution," and "the monistic belief of the unity of body and soul as two forms of the same existence."[40] She underscored the centrality of humans in evolution—an argument especially appealing to Chinese intellectuals, and compatible with the political climate following China's various defeats to European and Japanese powers. Consequently, Zhang believed that humanity was formed by the two sexes, whose procreative union was salient for the continuation of the race.[41] YD, similarly, emphasized the humanistic/eugenic fusion of Key's argument from *The Evolution of Love*: "Humankind has the instinct to preserve the race, and the instinct to preserve the sex."[42]

Key was critical of religious conservatives who demanded that the individual "serve the community with his love" at the expense of his own individuality. At the same time, she believed in "the extension of the instinct of love through the racial sense." Key's eugenics relied upon her organic view of society as a human organism; she connected individual well-being with social and racial well-being.[43] Key based her fascination with the body in natural science, emphasizing in particular "the whole antique love of bodily

 MIRELA DAVID

strength and beauty." Part of the new enlightenment thought was also a return to the ideals of antiquity, and Key admired Sparta's cult of physical strength,[44] which also fascinated Chinese intellectuals.

In China, a special issue of the *Ladies' Journal* titled "Free Love and the Freedom of Love" (Ziyou lianai yu lianai ziyou) published a contentious debate between Miss Feng Zi, the female pen name employed by Zhou Jianren,[45] YD (aka Wu Juenong, as noted earlier), and the editor Zhang Xichen. The range of views presented in the issue destabilized earlier configurations of gender norms by highlighting the racial and social underpinnings of a romantic view of sex and marriage. Assuming Feng's female voice, Zhou Jianren advocated for a woman's right to dictate her relationship status, including the decision to stay single and enjoy platonic love. Zhou-as-Feng observed that, given modern progress in human relationships, singlehood did not necessarily entail celibacy. Feng also drew attention to the problem of women's oppression through the arranged marriage system: the system was seen as an exchange of goods, wherein women were reduced to the status of men's property.[46]

Feng did not want to degrade freedom of love by reducing it to sexual fulfillment, believing that doing so would only demean female experience. Here, Feng's critique was informed by Key's criticism of the degrading "low sensualism"—sensualism being low in the sense that "it did not mean the elevation of mankind."[47] Feng upheld individual awakening, embraced singlehood, and promoted self-realization on the basis of a liberal ideal.

Feng discussed the constraints of the marriage system through the lens of "her" experience as a divorcee: "I do not advocate marriage, because men want to use the law to restrain us. . . . Free divorce is quite an insightful approach to this problem. I write this as a proud divorcee who understands the marriage system."[48] Zhou Jianren's textual impersonation of a divorced woman was meant to make divorce more acceptable for women; he envisioned his pretense as a subversive means of contesting the rigidity of the marriage system, and he sought to reconfigure the performance of traditional gender roles to allow more expression of individuality. Like Russell, Zhou-as-Feng viewed legal restrictions on divorce as a source of women's oppression.

YD, better known for his interest in tea and peasant economy, replied that freedom of love was a guarantor of equality—a new form of morality that could also impact political participation and education. YD's emphasis on free love above other issues in the women's movement, as well as his view of love as a fundamental problem of humanity, was also in conversation with

Key. "Humanity has to deal with three main issues," he wrote. "Fundamental humanity, livelihood, and love." YD appreciated Key's radical anarchist ideas on love and livelihood, but his assessment of the relationship between social pressures and love was grim: "The oppression of the household, the shackles of the Confucian morality, economic panic, legal restrictions—all these lead to love's disconnection."[49] YD's contribution to the dialogue can be inscribed in the moral revolution of the May Fourth movement, with its critique of patriarchy and Confucian morality. Yet his fascination with Key's humanism was also a way to turn an established Confucian category, *ren* (a virtue, sometimes translated as "humanity," denoting the good feeling a virtuous human experiences when being altruistic), on its head and to infuse it with evolutionary meanings drawn from natural life.

"For love to develop," YD wrote, "one must obtain freedom of love, freedom of will, lack of restrictions, and mutual union in the body and soul."[50] His argument insisted on attaining humanity; it also reflected the European dualism that had prompted Chinese writers to consider the elevation of the spirit over the body.[51] "If young people do not display self-control toward love, and do not understand love is for humanity," YD continued, "for sons and daughters, for social and global relations, and only concern themselves with appeasing carnal desires; if they borrow the name of love to engage in the habit of free sexual relations, we have to call it libidinal use of free love."[52]

In a piece analyzing the debate between Wu-as-YD and Zhou-as-Feng, Zhang Xichen also employed translations from Key's work to criticize unrestrained sexuality: "According to Ellen Key, irrespective of what kind of love it is, it can be free. The meaning for Ellen Key is that one can marry or not; one can live together or separately; one can love multiple people simultaneously, or have the freedom to love only one; one can take or not take responsibility for one's children; one can have sex or not. One should not unleash this kind of libidinal love because it gives one too much freedom, so Ellen Key is against it."[53]

Zhang drew from Key that love entailed social responsibility—at least, if it had reproductive consequences. Zhang was at the forefront of considering the spiritual value of love; meanwhile, Zhou Zuoren—Zhou Jianren's other older brother, and an essayist in his own right—was the first writer to criticize what he considered to be a crude dualism of soul and sex coming from a puritanical tradition.[54] Ultimately, given their beliefs in eugenics and reproductive social accountability, all of these thinkers contested unrestrained, irresponsible sexuality resulting from libidinal behavior. Despite the radicalness of discussing sexuality, these liberal writers and others struggled with both subverting existing gender roles and making new ideas about femininity and masculinity acceptable to a wider public.

Inspired by Key's *Love and Marriage*, a special issue on free divorce appeared in the *Ladies' Journal* in 1922.[55] Divorce had become widely debated in China, following Hu Shi's translation of Norwegian playwright Henrik Ibsen's *A Doll's House* and its publication in the New Culture Movement journal *New Youth* (Xin qingnian) in 1918.[56] Russell's impending split from his wife reignited debates around divorce's social and moral merits. Wu Juenong included an abridged translation of chapter 8, on "free divorce," from Key's book *Love and Marriage*,[57] advocating "the necessity of divorce, individualism's affirmation, reconsideration of chastity, and of issues regarding children."[58]

In abbreviating the translation, Wu made a conscious effort to highlight Key's individualism. He began his translation by skipping the introductory paragraph, where Key argued that love's freedom was a means of wiping away prostitution and that free divorce was a way of lessening adultery cases. Instead, he introduced Key's emphasis on individualism and opted for a more general, less radical foreword.[59]

By starting his translation with the second paragraph from Key's chapter, Wu addressed the critics of free love head on. He inverted the order of the sentences in this paragraph, so that in Chinese "polygamy" comes at the end of the paragraph instead of the second line, thus taming its critical potential: "People who advocate monogamy attack the advocates of 'the new immorality'; whether in magazines, at the pulpit, or in schools, they express their worry. They consider that freedom of love and freedom of divorce brazenly opens the way for polygamy."[60]

Subsequently, Wu modified the text slightly to bypass the problematic of religion and sin, placing an emphasis on the discussion of whether in cases of extramarital sexuality one could still talk about monogamy. To give the text local urgency and make it speak to the indigenous Chinese practice of concubinage, Wu inserted a passage in italics that did not appear in the original text. Here, he introduced Key's defense of illegitimate children from *The Century of the Child*. "Some unmarried couples have children before marriage. *Despite the secrecy, society does not ostracize them. Were it not for divorce, manifold detrimental social behaviors would occur: for instance, another concubine apart from the wife, or a lover apart from the husband. Can one really say this is a monogamic system?* But today is not the ideal time, if we consider it is the transition from the traditional to the new era. Then freedom of divorce is a good way of improving and assuring the monogamous system."[61]

Key, like Russell, exposed the limitations imposed by law, religion, and family on the individual. Most radical liberal intellectuals approved of these criticisms. The debates over free love and divorce in the pages of the *Ladies' Journal* reveal the dynamic ways in which anarcho-feminists and liberals discussed the fraught relationship between social change and the rapidly evolving gender and social mores of the time.

THE SCIENTISM AND HUMANISM OF EUGENICS

Zhang Xichen continued debating the convergence of love and eugenics with the culturally conservative scientist Chen Jianshan in the *People's Tocsin* (Minduo zazhi). Zhang disagreed with Chen's prediction of rising divorce rates as a result of free love; conservatives like Chen had launched a trenchant critique of free love's antisocial potential.[62]

What was at stake here was the relation of love to society and the individual, and the question of whether science alone could explain the totality of social relations. Despite Chen and Zhang's shared belief in eugenics, they had conflicting views about the modern sensibility embodied in free love ideas, and about free love's compatibility with eugenic thought. In early twentieth-century China, as elsewhere, the flexible traction of eugenics discourses provided an entrenched platform from which competing ideas about the relationship between the biological and social body could be inferred. Chen, a biologist interested in heredity, criticized free love advocates from a eugenic perspective. For Chen social relations, marriage, and sex were filtered through the lenses of science—in this case, eugenics, which functioned as a modern standard for optimal social relations. Zhang, however, believed that "modernity" also nested nonscientific elements, and he expressed skepticism toward Chen's rejection of free love on purely scientific grounds.[63]

Chen clearly differentiated between sexual desire, as espoused by "primitive" men, and platonic love devoid of sexual desire.[64] Zhang, on the other hand, maintained that the rejection of sexual desire in platonic love was very different from the modern conception of the unity of body and soul. And he did not consider sexual desire purely a matter of the flesh in the way that Chen was inclined to believe. Chen deemed sex an animal instinct,[65] and approached free love from a strictly eugenic vantage point: "Speaking from a eugenic point of view, wherein lie the terrible results? The so-called love from the catchphrase 'free love'—there are many who assert it. Discussing this from an individualist point of view, even if the partner has tuberculosis or leprosy, and although there are inadequacies, loving each other is also happiness. However, this does not benefit the nation and the future of mankind. Family is not merely for satisfying individual love."[66]

Chen saw in individual desires a hindrance to larger eugenic social goals, and considered individualism to be incompatible with eugenics: "No matter how highly we praise modern individualism, eugenics is difficult to implement."[67] From Chen's eugenic perspective, free love was in conflict with national interests. For Chen, love transgressed and displayed the limitations of modern rationality and eugenics: "Love is blind, love is outside of rationality, and cannot be built upon eugenic reasoning," and "people do not love for eugenic reasons."[68]

Puzzled by such diverging standpoints, and yet also drawing on overlapping eugenic principles, Zhang responded to Chen by emphasizing the modernity and progressiveness of free love as well as the salience of the individual for modern civilization. Zhang highlighted the ways in which certain ideas in Key's *Century of the Child* and *Love and Marriage* were rooted in Galtonian and Darwinian thought. Zhang also cited Zhou Zuoren, Zhou Jianren's brother, to show that "the fluctuating heart is normal, and the static heart is in fact pathological: if the heart does not change in adolescence, it is believed to be puerile and slow-witted, and in old age a sign of deterioration." Zhang associated the changing heart with progress and the stagnant heart with regression.[69]

Zhang based this scathing critique on his humanistic and liberal beliefs, pointing out the limitations of purely natural scientific comprehensions of human behavior. But he also rejected the idea—shared by Chen and some fellow intellectuals—of returning to antiquity as a means of achieving modern tasks: "Chen wants to use ancient Spartan methods to implement eugenics—to categorize people like domestic animals. To even contemplate man as the task of botanists and zoologists, even if one wants to apply this kind of eugenic goal, one would have to turn mankind into an animal deprived of feelings. In this sense eugenics cannot be applied. If one thinks one can, one cannot proclaim the eugenic goal."[70]

According to Zhang, botanists and zoologists' views were only relevant to plants and animals; people could not be confined to a reductive view of "shallow social value." Zhang emphasized that Spartan people's "importance assigned to the physique, aimed at strengthening society, as well as the extolling of superhumans . . . left no room for missteps." Therefore, "they were appealing to nonhumanism to deal with mankind that did not conform to their standards." Zhang was able to recognize the privation of humanism in Spartan eugenic exaltations of vigor; to him, this kind of eugenic view should not be extended to "the entire mankind's eugenics."[71] The selective reception of Key's ideas is apparent here: Despite Zhang's commitment to Key, he implicitly disagreed with the more problematic aspects of her thinking. Similarly, while Chen disavowed Key's symbiosis of love and eugenics, he was nonetheless attracted by Key's fascination with Spartan physical potency.

Zhang, continuing his argument, declared mental abilities to be more germane than bodily prowess. He recommended Zhou Jianren's account on sexual selection in animals and its compatibility with eugenics. Chen, like Zhou, had drawn parallels between human copulation and animal mating, but when combined with the prospect of obtaining better offspring, this argument disturbed Zhang: "What I find most strange is that Mr. Chen used the paradigm of animal copulation to illustrate that parents who are not in love cannot give birth to good children. Animal choices are not necessarily equivalent to people's selections. When he employed animal mating to suggest love can produce good children, he was right. But using a similar logic to insinuate that people who are not in love give birth to no good children is a big scientific inaccuracy."[72] Here, Zhang's critique of biological science based on humanism differed from that of Key, who had grounded humanism in evolutionary science.[73]

In introducing Key's writings in subtle and at times contradicting ways, Chinese intellectuals ultimately left many of her ideas open for debate. While some more biologically inclined authors—such as Zhou Zuoren, Zhou Jianren, or even Wu Juenong—saw the individual as part of evolutionary humanism, others, such as Zhang Xichen, presented different versions of humanism as a critique of science.

In Zhang's view money and family status constituted noneugenic elements for spousal selection, so he militated against them. Zhang criticized Chen's skepticism regarding the progressive character of free marriage choice, asking, "Since when is free marriage choice a regression?" Zhang then interrogated Chen's understanding of individuality and arranged marriage: "When he talks of individuality, does he know the difference between choosing partners for one's children and letting the children pick their own partners?"[74] Chen, in disagreement with Havelock Ellis's perspective, had opined that "enlightened parents" selected the most eugenically sound partners for their children.[75]

Selection in love and marriage posed an intriguing eugenic dilemma in regard to the incidence of venereal disease. Zhang, unlike Chen, was mostly interested in disclosure and modern methods to cope with the reality of venereal disease. Rejecting invasive measures to forbid unions of people afflicted with venereal disease, Zhang displayed respect for individualism: "If young people are aware that their partners have a genetically transmitted disease, and despite that are still profoundly enamored, and still want to wed, to respect individual choices we cannot use autocratic means to forbid them. To prevent social detriment, one can use the means of surgery to interrupt pregnancies, to allow couples to still live happily together and not reproduce."[76] Zhang concurred with Havelock Ellis that people suffering from venereal disease should be permitted to marry; he had also derived the idea of social and racial responsibility regarding reproduction from Ellis's book *The Problem of Race-Regeneration*.[77]

Zhang's belief in individual freedom was inhibited by his conviction that descendants plagued with hereditary diseases constituted a social problem, to be solved through consensual sterilization or abortion. For Zhang, like for Bertrand Russell, individual freedom extended to love selection, but not necessarily to procreative liberties. Nonetheless, he was able to show that conservative eugenic measures that prohibited unions of people afflicted with venereal diseases were dehumanizing. Despite his critiques of some of the field's particulars, Zhang did not disavow eugenics. Eugenics was, in China as it was elsewhere in the world, transcending the conservative/liberal divide.

TOWARD A MODERN SEXUAL ETHICS

In *The Collected Debates on the New Sexual Morality* (Xin xing daode taolunji), Zhang Xichen and Zhou Jianren tried to rearticulate the moral dimension of sexual desire. Initially published in a special edition of the *Ladies' Journal* titled "The New Sexual Morality" in 1925, this volume (subsequently compiled by Zhang) included the pair's repeated responses to criticism from Chen Bainian, the conservative Beijing University professor.

Although these debates were seen simply in terms of sexuality versus morality and as conveying repressive sexuality,[78] Zhang and Zhou's positions were in line both with Bertrand Russell's view on the private dimensions of sex and with the new, eugenic sexual ethic they were enunciating. Their position of viewing sexuality as a private matter even allowed for extramarital affairs and explorations of women's sexuality. The sexual content in Zhang and Zhou's formulations deflected attention from the type of eugenic sexual morality they were trying to present. Zhang and Zhou's feminism, informed by equality between men and women, formed the basis of their nonoppressive sexual ethic.

Zhang and Zhou's discussion on eugenic ethics was, first and foremost, derived from and in conversation with Havelock Ellis's *Problem of Race-Regeneration* and the discussion of sexual morality in Ellen Key's *Love and Marriage*. (Despite acknowledging Ellis's influence, they did not cite the respective paragraphs that will be pointed out below.)

Ellis offered the editors a way out of the quandary of reconciling the ideas of freedom and eugenics, in particular through his "garden of life" metaphor. Ellis did not see an incompatibility between social order and freedom: "If in our efforts to better social conditions and to raise the level of the race we seek to cultivate the sense of order, to encourage sympathy and foresight, to pull up racial weeds by the roots, " he wrote, "it is not that we may kill freedom and joy, but rather that we may introduce the conditions for securing and increasing freedom and joy." In his chapter on eugenics, Ellis held that the means to achieve "freedom and joy for all" was to "repress the license of those who . . . gratify their own childish or perverted desires." These categories of people infringed upon the "garden of life," as they would "pluck up the shrubs and trample on the flowers."[79]

Ellis further identified "the extirpation of the feeble-minded class," whom he classified as "the defective" and "the very defective," as the biggest social issue. Environmental improvement in the conditions of life had not been sufficient, according to Ellis, and as a result the fit were shackled with providing for the unfit. Social accountability required "voluntary control of the number of offspring." Ellis conceptually linked social improvement with racial duty, expressing the need for humanity to develop and nurture "social instincts." According to Ellis, "the new social feeling which has been generated by the task of improving the social conditions of life and of caring for those who are unable to care for themselves has made possible a new conception of responsibility to the race." He framed social duty with eugenic connotations, in the phrase "We generate the race; we alone can regenerate the race."[80] The interplay between race "generation" and race "regeneration" established the ideological link between women's reproduction and ideas of racial improvement.

Zhang Xichen laid out the foundations of his eugenic view of society: "Having a strong mankind requires the sacrifice of the frail; otherwise the feeble mankind will lead to the diminution of robust people." Zhang opposed privileging "the benefits of this 'minority of weak people,'" as in his view this would lead to a "big evil." He outlined the two opposing categories of a strong majority and a weak minority to form the basis of what he phrased as "the correct definition of morality." For Zhang, this new

　　　MIRELA DAVID

morality "depended entirely on enhancing individual happiness and the happiness of the majority," "leading to its evolution."[81] This was because Zhang did not consider the individual alone, but as part of a "universal collectivity."[82]

By the time of this debate, in 1925, Zhang had moved away from his previous, more conciliatory position toward nonrobust people, expressed earlier in his criticism of Russell. As eugenics insinuated itself into his ideas, he came to privilege the healthy majority in a dualistic, reductive worldview. Zhang's castigation of the "evil" of benefiting a minority, as well as the implication that only the advancement of the majority ensured individual freedom, was in complete agreement with Ellis's vilification of dysgenic behavior.[83]

In the following passage, Zhang engaged with Key's eugenic views of society, and with her postulations of individual and social happiness.[84] Zhang's fusion between love, the individual, and society was condensed in his statement: "There is no big difference between altruism and egoism."[85] Zhang's conception of love was also informed by Sigmund Freud's idea of the narcissistic origins of love, and Ellis's assertion that even altruistic love sprang from an egotistical impulse.[86] By relativizing morality, Zhang could ground it in both humanism and eugenics; by obliterating the altruism/egoism binary, he could root morality in love while preserving its private aspect.[87] This differed from YD's previous rejection of selfish love.

Zhang further identified several "errors" in the new sexual morality guided by eugenic concerns: "Most people acknowledge people suffering from transmittable venereal diseases can marry and have children. Otherwise, they would not be considered filial to the clan. . . . If they reproduce the race, surely it will turn the entire mankind into diseased people. As a result, the amoral race cannot diminish, and the immoral ones in society will be unsurpassable."[88]

Zhang was concerned with the dysgenic effects of traditional family obligations to marry and provide descendants. The danger of venereal disease had led to changing perspectives on family morality, geared toward maintaining healthy bodies. Zhang identified people suffering from venereal diseases as "amoral"; he was also urging legal changes to forbid women from marrying diseased men. Here, Zhang's image of woman as "reproducer of the race" was endowed with a social responsibility and a sexual ethic, ideas also emphasized by Ellis.

Chinese intellectuals' readings of evolutionist and eugenic attacks on religion also spurred the New Culture Movement's attack on Confucian family values such as the importance of kinship and parentally arranged marriages. Zhou's liberal views were inspired by Russell's critique of oppressive religious morality in the West. "People are not good because they are afraid of morality," Zhou wrote. "If you teach people to respect 'the moral quality, or human dignity' and freedom, there is no need to take concubines and prostitutes." The new morality was not seen as oppressive, since it was "based on the principle of gender equality."[89] Following Bertrand Russell's attack on religion and his advocacy of science, Zhang, like Ellis, was now rooting the new morality in eugenics, which he considered scientific; Zhang eventually succumbed to the scientific view of life most likely also as a result of his association with Zhou. On an evolutionary scale, science was placed above religion, and, by implication, it could potentially replace religion. Even for Key, religion had never succeeded in merging the needs of the individual with those of the race.[90]

The moral dimension of love, for Zhang, was also related to love's assistance (or damage) to society: only when "diligent, intelligent, and bodily healthy young men" found "a similar partner" would a relationship be considered "the right love." Zhang considered unwed mothers amoral because of their "illiterate children, despised by society, diseased, that ended up being beggars, robbers, and prostitutes." Here, Zhang's association of eugenic views of heritable criminality with motherhood outside of marriage was tenuous at best, conflating the perceived social damage of two seemingly social deviant categories. With respect to men, Zhang believed "it was not moral" to fulfill solely their sexual needs during marriage, and Zhang's feminism also informed his view on female sexuality: "Men should not force women to fulfill their sexual desires, but also please their partner."[91] Zhou, too, believed women possessed the same desires as men, and therefore should enjoy similar freedom.[92]

In formulating a modern sexual ethic, Zhang drew on the writings of other European sexologists too. For example, with respect to the idea of repressing sexual desires, advocated by Swedish psychiatrist and eugenicist Auguste-Henri Forel, Zhang supported it only "when a man of dubious quality indulged in temporary inferior carnal feelings, and seduced a virgin," as this resulted in a "negative" social effect. Sex was considered "inferior" by Zhang, whose utopic and eugenic ideas, informed by Key, led him to privilege sex infused with feelings. Zhang dismissed Forel's suggestion of repressing marital sexuality, and acknowledged the innate nature of sexual desire. Like Key, Zhang felt that one could control sexual desire via this new morality, but also believed that sexual desire was the basic foundation of any kind of moral value.[93]

     MIRELA DAVID

According to the new May Fourth sexual morality, sexual behavior should not be detrimental to society.[94] Zhang and Zhou aligned with Russell's view that the relationship between men and women—"superior, mature people," in Zhou's words—was a "private matter," and that it only became a social problem when it concerned children.[95] Zhang wrote, "According to genetics and eugenics, the superior and the inferior are transmitted genetically from the parents. Socially, to give birth to superior children, and to avoid the birth of weak and inferior children, is mankind's highest morality; birth control is a necessary part of the new sexual morality."[96] Here, Mendelian eugenic thought was apparent, and Zhang favored eugenic birth control. Zhang's humanism-based, antiscientific critique of eugenics had turned, in the span of a few years, into a view similar to Key's that even acknowledged hereditary scientific theories. For Key, "the life, the individual, and the race suffers" when "mature and fit" people "are not in a position to produce and rear an offspring."[97]

Resonating with Zhang's eugenics, Zhou Jianren's view of sexual morality unambiguously centered on ideas of racial rejuvenation and concerns about the nation's future well-being. "The results of sexual behavior concern the future of the nation, and must take into consideration racial betterment," Zhou wrote. "Epileptics, the feeble-minded, the insane, and the handicapped cannot marry," he continued, "but they can have a sexual life, and their offspring is not suitable for the future of the nation. One cannot separate reproduction from marriage. Eugenicists advocate detention and forced sterilization. One cannot use such strict methods."[98] Despite viewing reproduction of eugenic categories of diseased people as problematic, Zhou could not condone coercive measures of curtailing their reproduction, on account of his liberal and humanist convictions. For Zhou and Zhang, the offspring belonged to "society," "the nation," or "the race," and women's reproduction was regarded as a matter of public concern. In this sense, their liberal ideas were restricted by what they considered social obligation to the nation or the race.

Zhang's most controversial statement came out of his belief in the sanctity of sexual privacy: "If one has the approval of both partners, even if you have one husband and two wives, or two husbands and one wife, if it does not harm society, one cannot say it is amoral."[99] Zhang suggested that even polyandry was conceivable, with consent. When Beijing University professor Chen Bainian attacked Zhang for resurrecting the polygamous system by promoting free love, Zhou came to Zhang's defense, suggesting that one could love multiple people if the partners involved were in agreement.[100] To strengthen the credibility and authority of his argument, Zhou cited

German socialist August Bebel, French philosopher Henri-Louis Bergson, and Sigmund Freud's nonjudgmental writings on extramarital sexuality.[101] As a result of Chen's criticism of their open praise of female sexual desire, Zhang and Zhou were eventually dismissed from the editorship of the *Ladies' Journal*.[102] They subsequently founded an audacious journal, *Xin nüxing* (The new woman), which dealt extensively with sexuality.[103]

The primacy of the individual is evident in Zhou's promotion of "self-love." From an individualist perspective Zhou found the institution of widows' chastity damaging and unreasonable—a "sign of an inferior nation and society" and of women's oppression. From a scientific point of view, he averred, widows' chastity was an offense, because it was not in accordance to women's natural desire.[104] Here, he echoed an earlier essay by his eldest brother, Lu Xun, "My Views on Chastity," published in 1918, in which Lu also contested the tradition.[105] Both Zhou and Lu critiqued widow chastity based on their belief in gender equality, and took into consideration women's voices on this issue.

Despite his wishes to overcome "taboos and sexual prejudices," Zhou conceded that this was not his and Zhang's primary concern. They were more interested in employing a scientific view to explain sexual relations, and combining that perspective with a respect for the freedom of mature, healthy individuals.[106] Even when Zhou's liberalism clamped down on the coercive aspects of eugenics, a eugenic framework concerning only "the healthy" still narrowed Zhou's notion of freedom.

Russell's and Key's ideas informed May Fourth debates on the merits of love, individual freedom, divorce, sexual morality, science, and eugenics. Russell's notion of the privacy of romance enlightened Chinese intellectuals' commitment to individuality, while his ideas extolling the potential of love for improving humanity offered them hope for advancing society. However, considerations of these larger issues ultimately limited their support for individual freedom, because it extended only partially to certain groups of people, such as those suffering from mental illness or sexually transmitted disease. In the name of preventing detrimental social repercussions, individuals who were considered dysgenic were granted approval to love, but not to procreate. Liberal intellectuals also drew inspiration from Key, whose symbiotic understanding of these issues formed the matrix for their delineation of the different facets of free love, free divorce, and the new sexual morality that served as the linchpin of a strong and healthy modern nation. Questions pertaining to the individual subject were thus constantly

 MIRELA DAVID

deliberated in relation to larger categories such as race or humanity. These debates revealed the tendencies of male feminists to both subvert and reinforce gender roles, marking the beginning of an ecumenical shift in the Chinese conceptualizations of marriage, intimacy, and kin relations. They also revealed the inherent contradictions in evolutionary humanism, which sometimes critiqued eugenics and at other times appeared to reinforce it. Last but not least, these discourses exposed opposing views of the social function of women's reproduction, which evoked both oppressive racial ideologies and the modernist pledge of free love and free divorce.

NOTES

1   YD, "Ziyou lianai yu lianai ziyou," 16,288.

2   Nyström, *Ellen Key*, xii.

3   Hiroko Sakamoto identifies YD as a pen name for the feminist and agrarian writer Wu Juenong in footnote 71 of "The Cult of Love and Eugenics in May Fourth Movement Discourse," 355.

4   Key, *Love and Marriage*, 289.

5   Liu, *Translingual Practice*, 94.

6   Fu to Muirhead, 0000575 048256A, BRA.

7   Russell to Malleson, BRA.

8   Sanger to Russell, 0080498 055413, BRA.

9   Russell, *The Tamarisk Tree*, 118.

10   Wang to Russell, letter forwarded to the Shun Pao, 0000579 048261 048261, BRA.

11   Wang, *John Dewey in China*, 26.

12   Ming, "Luosuo he nannü guanxi."

13   Sanger, *World Trip Journal 1922*, MSPP.

14   Laurence, *Lily Briscoe's Chinese Eyes*, 143.

15   Pan, *When True Love Came to China*, 211.

16   Se, "Luosuo yu funü wenti."

17   Ibid.

18   Heathorn, "Explaining Russell's Eugenic Discourse in the 1920s," 112.

19   Se, "Luosuo yu Funü wenti," 3.

20   Ibid.

21   Russell, *The Tamarisk Tree*, 124.

22   Black, "Zhongguo de nüquanzhuyi yu nüxing gaizao," 51.

23   Black, "Young China," 10.

24   Russell, *The Tamarisk Tree*, 118.

25   Chao and Chao, *Autobiography of a Chinese Woman*, 185.

26   Russell, *The Tamarisk Tree*, 132.

27   Chao and Chao, *Autobiography of a Chinese Woman*, 185, 193.

28   Russell, *The Tamarisk Tree*, 132.

29   Black, "Young China," 10.

30   Russell, *The Tamarisk Tree*, 210.

31   Zhang Xichen (1889–1969) initially coedited *Dongfang zazhi* (Eastern miscellany) until he took over the editorship of *Funü zazhi* (Ladies' journal) in 1921. In 1922, he began editing the supplement *Xiandai funü* (Modern woman) of *Shishi xinbao* (Current events daily), as well as the supplement *Funü zhoubao* (Women's periodical) for *Minguo ribao* (Republican daily). Wang, "*Funü zazhi* yanjiu," 55–58.

32   Zhou Jianren, a biologist and an editor at the renowned Commercial Press, wrote articles on democracy and science, the woman problem, family reform, love, divorce, prostitution, and Darwin's evolutionary theories. During the May Fourth Movement, he studied philosophy at Beijing University, but also took courses in science. Xie, *Zhou Jianren Pinzhuan*, 80–85.

33   Wang, *Women in the Chinese Enlightenment*, 85.

34   Nivard, "L'évolution de la presse féminine chinoise de 1898 à 1949," 167–68.

35   Ma, "Male Feminism and Women's Subjectivities," 3.

36   Zhang, "Tongxun," 15,403.

37   Key, *The Century of the Child*, 46.

38   Key's book *The Century of the Child* had been translated into eight languages, and enjoyed popularity abroad. Her romantic individualism, meanwhile, stirred up broad controversy. Nyström and Fries, *Ellen Key*, xii, 102.

39   Key, *The Century of the Child*, 5, 25.

40   Key, *Love and Marriage*, 5, 51.

41   Se, "Wenming yu dushen."

42   YD, "Ziyou lianai yu lianai ziyou," 16,288.

43   Key, *Love and Marriage*, 50, 143, 254. Key's humanism influenced prominent Chinese writers.

44   Key, *The Century of the Child*, 12–13.

45   Zhou used Feng Zi as a pseudonym, and also received mail under this name. Xie, *Zhou Jianren pinzhuan*, 3.

46   Feng, "Lianai ziyou jie ji pian," 16,289.

47   Key, *The Century of the Child*, 12.

48   Feng Zi, "Lianai ziyou jieda kewen di si,"16,286.

49   YD, "Ziyou lianai yu lianai ziyou," 16,287–88.

50   Ibid.

51   Pan, *When True Love Came to China*, 155.

52   YD, "Ziyou lianai yu lianai ziyou," 16,288.

53   Zhang, "Du Feng Zi Nüshi he YD Xiansheng de taolun," 16,294.

54   Pan, *When True Love Came to China*, 158–59, 162, 154.

55   Articles in the issue included Zhou Jianren's "Lihun wenti shiyi" (Dispelling doubts on divorce problems) and "Lihun wenti de jiujinguan" (The whys and

    MIRELA DAVID

wherefores of the problems of divorce). *Funü zazhi* (Ladies' journal) 8, no. 4, coll. vol. 32 (1922): 14,481–702.

56   Chien, "Feminism and China's New 'Nora': Ibsen, Hu Shi, and Lu Xun," 98.

57   Key, *Love and Marriage*, 287–359.

58   Wu, "Ai Lunkai de ziyou lihun lun," 14,481.

59   Key, *The Century of the Child*, 20.

60   Wu, "Ai Lunkai de ziyou lihun lun," 14,481.

61   Ibid.

62   Zhang, "Du Chen Jianshan Xiansheng 'Youshengxue he ji ge xing de wenti,'" 6.

63   Ibid.

64   Chen, "Youshengxue he ji ge xing de wenti," 53.

65   Zhang, "Du Chen Jianshan Xiansheng 'Youshengxue he ji ge xing de wenti,'" 4.

66   Chen, "Youshengxue he ji ge xing de wenti," 54.

67   Zhang, "Du Chen Jianshan Xiansheng 'Youshengxue he ji ge xing de wenti,'" 1.

68   Ibid.

69   Ibid., 8, 2, 4.

70   Ibid., 4.

71   Ibid.

72   Ibid, 2, 5, 6.

73   Ellen Key, *The Century of the Child*, 5.

74   Zhang, "Du Chen Jianshan Xiansheng 'Youshengxue he ji ge xing de wenti,'" 5, 6.

75   Lee, *Revolution of the Heart*, 175.

76   Zhang, "Du Chen Jianshan Xiansheng 'Youshengxue he ji ge xing de wenti,'" 5.

77   Ellis, *The Problem of Race-Regeneration*, 66.

78   Chung, *Struggle for National Survival*, 112.

79   Ellis, *The Problem of Race-Regeneration*, 60, 67.

80   Ibid, 65, 38–40, 45–48. Ellis also associates "hereditary feeble-mindedness" with criminality.

81   Zhang, "Xin xing daode shi shenme," in *Xin xing daode taolunji*, ed. Zhang, 3.

82   Lee, *Revolution of the Heart*, 177.

83   Ellis suggested that freedom of the few categories of people could be nefarious, if it endangered society and the race. Ellis, *The Problem of Race-Regeneration*, 67.

84   Despite her commitment to individualism, Key had to acknowledge the restrictions demanded by eugenics for the well-being of society. Key, *Love and Marriage*, 254.

85   Zhang, "Xin xing daode shi shenme," 4.

86   Ellis, *Psychology of Sex*, 324.

87   Lee, *Revolution of the Heart*, 176.

88   Zhang, "Xin xing daode shi shenme," 5.

89 Zhou, "Lianai ziyou yu yi fu duo qi," in *Xin xing daode taolunji*, ed. Zhang, 44–45.

90 Zhang, "Xin xing daode shi shenme," 20.

91 Ibid., 9, 6, 11.

92 Zhou, "Xin daode zhi kexue de biaozhun," in *Xin xing daode taolunji*, ed. Zhang, 22.

93 Zhang, "Xin xing daode shi shenme," 9, 4–5.

94 Ibid., 10.

95 Zhou, "Xin daode zhi kexue de biaozhun," 22.

96 Zhang, "Xin xing daode shi shenme," 12.

97 Key, *Love and Marriage*, 44.

98 Zhou, "Xin daode zhi kexue de biaozhun," 21–22.

99 Zhang, "Xin xing daode shi shenme," 11.

100 Zhou, "Lianai ziyou yu yi fu duo qi," 42.

101 Zhou, "Da 'Yi fu duo qi de xin hu fu,'" in *Xin xing daode taolunji*, ed. Zhang, 64.

102 Wang, *Women in the Chinese Enlightenment*, 111.

103 Nivard, "L'évolution de la presse féminine chinoise de 1898 à 1949," 169.

104 Zhou, "Xin daode zhi kexue de biaozhun," 23, 21.

105 Lu, "My Views on Chastity," in *Women in Republican China*, eds. Fong and Fong, 10–16.

106 Zhou, "Da 'Yi fu duo qi de xin hu fu,'" 69.

MIRELA DAVID

CHAPTER 5

"A PROBLEM OF GLANDS AND SECRETIONS"

Female Criminality, Murder, and Sexuality in Republican China

PETER J. CARROLL

"WHAT TYPE OF CRAZY AM I? I WILL NEVER FORGET LAST NIGHT. . . . When I undid the frog buttons on her [Chinese-style] jacket, being next to her body made me feel intoxicated . . . we kissed and kissed until drunk, and I embraced her tightly. Heaven . . . made us enjoy such sacred love." This sensual diary entry was read aloud to an almost empty courtroom at the Hangzhou district court in May 1932, after the judge dismissed the spectators overflowing the gallery due to the remarks' "lewdness." The occasion was the spectacular homicide trial of the diarist, Tao Sijin, a twenty-two-year-old female art student specializing in Western-style painting and art criticism at the National Hangzhou Art Academy. Tao was charged with the February 11, 1932, murder of the woman whose jacket she had removed and whose body she had caressed. That woman, twenty-year-old Liu Mengying, had been her girlfriend for more than three years and had also been an art academy student, a prodigy who excelled at all media: sculpture, Chinese ink and Western oil painting, and printmaking. Liu had also gained local renown as a published writer. The killing and the resulting series of trials—the case was appealed twice and eventually tried in China's highest court—earned headlines such as "Savage Murder Produced by Same-Sex Love" and "The Untoward Result of Girl Student Same-Sex Love."[1]

Christened "the murdering miss" and, more trenchantly, "a typical Salomé" (after the 1891 Oscar Wilde play, a contemporary cultural sensation performed three years previous in Shanghai and Nanjing), Tao was portrayed in the media as a debauched, mentally ill incarnation of Wilde's princess: one contemporary illustration depicted her in the guise of Salomé with Liu's head on a platter leaking blood. Tao had, in fact, mirrored this allusion in her diary, imagining Liu as Salomé and herself as her hapless prey. Nonetheless, Tao's savage act and her seemingly reckless abandonment to illicit sensuality reversed the roles in the public realm.

Wilde's aestheticism famously critiqued social conventions and aimed to "transform art into life." Yet the liberatory potential of realizing art as life—represented by *Salomé* and Tao, the art student—was counterbalanced by the violence of sexuality and desire, with actual lived experience outstripping theater: whereas Salomé had desired John the Baptist and had him killed, Tao had loved and lived with Liu and had killed her by her own hand.[2]

For the next several years, the Tao-Liu affair remained a touchstone for discussions of same-sex love between women, the particular menace it posed to schools and the greater nation, and theories of its origins—including the possible relationship same-sex love, along with criminality and various mental illnesses, bore to female physiology. The murder and subsequent press coverage of the sequence of trials both helped corroborate existing prejudices and establish an ascendant popular perception of same-sex love relations as deviant, tinged with jealousy and insanity, and potentially violent and fatal. Throughout this period, public discussions of same-sex relations often focused more on those between women than those between men. This pattern may be due to the belief that same-sex love was somewhat more prevalent among women due to various physiological and psychological factors, but it also reflects more general social anxieties provoked by the expansion of women's presence, and sphere of autonomous action, in civil society.

LOVE AND MURDER

Tao Sijin and Liu Mengying were unusual in several senses. In addition to being artistically gifted, Liu had graduated from high school at an early age and came from a moneyed, politically prominent Hunan family. Her physician father had served as the head of a Guomindang army hospital and was killed in a 1930 Communist attack on Changsha. Tao came from a less socially prominent Zhejiang family from Shaoxing. Nonetheless, she was familiar with leading artists and writers through her deceased elder brother, Tao Yuanqing. A renowned oil painter and graphic designer best known for his striking abstract modernist designs for the cover of Lu Xun's *Call to Arms* and assorted other books—he is now celebrated as one of the founders of modern Chinese graphic design—Yuanqing had taught at the National Hangzhou Art Academy.

     PETER J. CARROLL

Tao and Liu met in the fall of 1928 at Shanghai's Lida Academy, a modernist alternative school that boasted a veritable who's-who of prominent intellectuals and artists, including Tao Yuanqing, as faculty. Yuanqing subsequently moved to the National Hangzhou Art Academy, and his sister and Liu Mengying followed. Tragically, Yuanqing died of typhoid shortly thereafter, on August 6, 1929. His death was one of several personal losses—including the execution of Liu's father by Communist forces—that both tested and sustained the women's relationship, which proved romantically passionate and emotionally tempestuous.[3]

From the spring of 1929 to the summer of 1931, the women lived as dormitory roommates. A court judgment on the case stated, "Their relations were very close, such that they had taken naps together under a quilt, leading them to develop same-sex love relations" and to commence a "sort of long-term association." In order to preserve their romantic attachment, they resolved to not marry men; they swore to refuse any offer of engagement and to remain together their entire lives.[4]

In addition to Tao Yuanqing, whom both women adulated as an elder brother figure, artistic mentor, and teacher, Tao and Liu were extremely close with another resident of Hangzhou, Xu Qinwen. A celebrated fiction writer and essayist, Xu taught high school literature and lived near the art academy. He and Tao Yuanqing, both thirty-something bachelors (Xu was thirty-four, and Tao died at thirty-seven), had been roommates for many years. The men's affective bond led to Tao Sijin and Liu Mengying both being on intimate terms with Xu, who became a surrogate elder brother and paid Sijin's tuition anonymously when she was short of funds. Following Yuanqing's death, Xu's constancy to his deceased friend materialized in a building that regularly drew comment in the press as "curious" and "unusual," if not "queer" (the latter term used in its original sense as "odd"—though also, perhaps, as a label for same-sex intimacy): a small shrine/memorial gallery space exhibiting Xu's collection of Tao Yuanqing's art.

Bereft of his companion, Xu asked Tao Sijin to marry him. When she refused, he moved on to Liu, who also rejected him. His alacrity in pursuing both women, one after the other, is intriguing, because Xu accurately understood the nature of their relationship. In an interview during the initial trial, he characterized their same-sex love as "developed to an extraordinary degree." In fact, he noted, the ardency of their affection exceeded that normally found between a husband and wife. He knew these things from his friendship with both. He had also read Tao Sijin's diary, which he declared to be so fine and ingenious in describing the women's emotional and carnal intimacy that it surpassed the celebrated book *A Young Girl's Diary*, which recorded the adolescent longings of a heterosexual Viennese girl. (The 1919 German original was praised by Freud, who thought it provided evidence for his theory of the transition from infantile to adult sexuality. It was translated into many languages—including, in 1927, Chinese—and read widely.)[5]

Xu was not alone in recognizing the passionate attachment. Tao and Liu's same-sex love was acknowledged widely by their fellow students and teachers, even if they did not condone it. Tao's description of Liu's habitual jealousy suggests that their amorous bond was hard to ignore: "Whenever I had warm feelings toward classmates or friends, she became crazy and quarreled, especially when I would go outside with classmates to sketch from nature. Because of this, classmates avoided becoming friendly with me so as to prevent us from fighting." Both felt pangs of jealousy over suspected infidelity. At the time of the murder, Liu's chronic suspicion had cause. Tao had developed a close relationship with a female painting teacher, Liu Wenru, and planned to later travel with her to Sichuan. Liu had become aware of Tao's intention, and complained that Tao's affections had grown cold. (Tao did want to end things.) In the immediate term, Tao was anxious to visit her ill mother in Shaoxing. Liu Mengying begged her to remain in Hangzhou for one or two more days, to settle matters. Feeling sorry for Liu, Tao maintained there was no cause for a scene because her relationship with Liu Wenru was merely that of student and teacher, and she agreed to stay. They sat down on a sofa to discuss their situation.

The conversation—and subsequent murder—took place at Xu Qinwen's house. Both had stayed there at various times. Liu was there at this juncture because the entire academy, including the dormitories, had been closed due to fighting between Chinese and Japanese troops in and around Shanghai, some 180 kilometers northeast. (The conflict, known as the January 28 Incident, lasted from January 28 to March 3, 1932, and resulted in the demilitarization of Shanghai.) The women were alone in the house. Tao had been accompanied by her servingwoman when she came to meet Liu; she had dispatched the woman on an errand to buy some cold cream in town when Liu went to take a shower. What happened next remains open to conjecture and was debated in court. What is incontrovertible is that soon Liu Mengying lay naked and dead on the ground, her body disfigured by knife wounds in some ten places; Tao Sijin, covered in Liu's blood and her own, lay near her lover in a semiconscious state. The gruesome scene was discovered by Tao's maid when she returned.[6] The two women and their relationship thus entered the public realm as a homicide case and same-sex love scandal that prompted widespread debate over the prevalence and harm of same-sex love and the peril of romantic love, in general.

    PETER J. CARROLL

The initial police investigation dragged on for almost two months before the state prosecutor filed criminal charges. Angered at the slow pace of the legal process, Liu Mengying's elder sister, Liu Qingxing, filed suit less than two weeks after the murder against Tao for the killing of her sister, and against Xu Qinwen as an accessory to murder. Her suit propounded a theory—which was adopted by much of the press and the public, not to mention the court—that, the women's longstanding same-sex love relationship notwithstanding, the murder was propelled by a love triangle composed of Tao, Liu, and Xu.[7] The state filed criminal charges in April. In May, the Hangzhou district court found Tao guilty and sentenced her to life in prison, while Xu was found guilty of seduction and sentenced to a year in prison. (The state judged the evidence insufficient to charge Xu; he was convicted as a result of the suit filed by Liu Qingxing.) The verdicts were appealed, and the Zhejiang provincial court upheld their guilt and imposed capital punishment on Tao and a two-year term of incarceration on Xu. A second appeal to the National Supreme Court in Beiping reinstated the original sentences: life imprisonment for Tao and one year in prison for Xu.

Liu Qingxing's contention that her sister's murder was the result of a triangular amorous conflict resonated with the commonly professed notion that love triangles were the most explosive, potentially lethal pitfall associated with love. One editorialist noted that love was inherently dangerous: mutual love, jealousy, and murder constituted a baleful yet common combination. Love triangles were especially fatal because they compounded the awesome power of jealousy. They were invariably heterosexual in nature; the same-sex love component made the Tao-Liu case unique and was greatly responsible for its prominence.[8] Men and women were both known to be capable of jealousy, but women were held to be especially so, for social reasons: given the restricted professional possibilities available to women, they could not help but make marriage, love, and sex the center of their lives. As such, marriage could not be totally free; it was not easy for a woman to snag a suitable man, and she must plot for a long time to land him.[9] The murder could thus be viewed as Tao's strategy (perhaps with Xu Qinwen's encouragement, if not outright assistance) to rid herself of her main rival for Xu. Some popular versions of the murder made Xu the prime instigator: desiring to possess Tao exclusively, he connived to have her kill his main rival for her affections.

Xu's ostensible role in the murder normalized it by introducing male agency into the equation. The murder thus ceased to be solely or even predominantly between two women. Instead, it could be redacted as a more conventional heterosexual crime of passion, or a mixture of same-sex and opposite-sex affection, jealousy, and hate. In fact, the purported love triangle between Tao, Liu, and Xu convinced some that the murder could not have been provoked by same-sex love. One woman from Hang-zhou, Xu Meiyu, put this case strongly in the popular women's magazine *Linglong*:

> We shocked people in Hangzhou can see that the ultimate
> cause behind this murder is sexual jealousy. We currently sus-
> pect that it was a love triangle because Xu had been close to
> Tao and previously proposed to her. Tao's family did not approve,
> for reasons that remain unclear. Xu then shifted his affections to
> Liu. It seems that Tao's jealousy and hate engendered this homi-
> cide case. His actions are inexcusable. If same-sex love were the
> cause, she would not have needed to act in this way. Same-sex
> love was not the cause. The danger here was not same-sex love but
> a more pedestrian and pervasive animus, jealousy.

Liu's death was therefore tragic but of no particular social significance: it was "lighter than a feather," just run-of-the-mill jealousy. Xu had two young women staying at his house. He was clearly up to no good, and bore some measure of blame along with Tao Sijin.[10]

During the Republican period, the movement to determine one's own marriage partner—and a more general amatory discourse that generally extolled love and romance as the supreme fulfillment of human life—pervaded newspapers, literature, journals, plays, and film. The definition(s) of love and discussions regarding whether it promoted or hindered social progress were so vexed that the social debate broke down into broad pro-love and anti-love parties. Whether pro or contra, conservative, progressive, communist, or anarchist, all participants in this societal discussion generally agreed with the maxim that "resolving the problem of love is the first step to solving the problems of women." Much of the scholarship on this "revolution of the heart" has justly emphasized the positive, potentially liberatory effects of this broad social movement. Indeed, these transformations, and the potential of love to effect them, were widely lauded at the time. The Tao-Liu case, by contrast, charts the often-ignored underbelly of this revolution, which bestirred deep and pervasive anxieties about the power of love and other passions to disrupt and harm society and individuals

     PETER J. CARROLL

alike.[11] The fact that Tao had eviscerated Liu was beyond doubt. Nonetheless, the murder provoked a societal inquest as to whether society or biology were partially or fully culpable for the murder.

Much of the social debate was stimulated by testimony from the two women themselves. Scholars have accurately noted that Republican era newspapers provide tantalizing, although often frustratingly brief, records of same-sex relations among men and women. The Tao-Liu affair is thus rather unique in that the public record preserves a large number of sources, in addition to their diaries, that contain the voices of the two women discussing their intense, fraught relationship.[12] In addition, Tao herself testified at length at the trials, gave interviews to the press, and wrote about the predicament of her love for Liu and her prison experience. The diary passages themselves, however, more than allow for other readings. Liu's diary, February 11, 1929: "Love is mysterious and great; same-sex love is especially pure in spirit. Sijin, you are a beautiful, pure girl; your open, enthusiastic character moves me so." Again, Liu's diary, November 22, 1929: "I often find this kind of love painful and I must reluctantly force myself to taste it. When I am more self-confident, however, I can order myself to seize and control it—yet this has no effect! The [incredible] power of emotions conquers me."[13] Press commentary emphasized such passages as clear proof of the destructiveness of same-sex love, especially since the diaries and letters made it plain that the two had carried on sexual relations. At the same time, the press and wider public stressed that the diary entries were evidence of the troublingly fearsome power of passion more generally.

Writing in 1932, shortly after the Zhejiang provincial court had resentenced Tao to death, one woman writer noted that the guilty verdict had not resolved the issue of responsibility. Neither the law nor popular social attitudes actually valued life, so why then such a fuss over one, albeit horrific, murder? Should society bear some blame, or was the burden Tao's alone? Tao and Liu, she declared, were members of a "chaotic generation" that ignored their national obligations: "Their prime fault was that they forgot that they are elements of society." Tao's plight could be related to her exultation of love as mysterious, and her lack of understanding regarding sexual matters. Such unknowing zeal characterized youth as a whole but was particularly pronounced among women: enamored of romance, they ignored its dark side. In this aspect, Tao and Liu were hardly exceptional, but emblematic of their cohort. This ordinariness was responsible for the social panic the case bestirred.[14]

The murder ignited longstanding concerns regarding the moral consequences of the growth of the educational system, especially the plethora of potential problems created by proliferation of educational institutions with same-sex dormitories. The implied naturalness, if not the inevitability, of Tao and Liu's progression from sororal naps to long-term sexual relations resonates with contemporary concerns regarding the ostensible "epidemic" of same-sex love in schools. For all of the descriptions of Tao and Liu as anomalous, diseased inverts, the anxieties provoked by their case partly stemmed from the uneasily acknowledged belief that such relations were potentially universally latent and could seemingly develop between any women at any time. The freight of same-sex love relations in education, girls' schools especially, in early-twentieth-century China is highlighted by the fact that one of the earliest articles to discuss "same-sex love" in the Chinese press is a 1911 article in the *Women's Newspaper* (Funüshibao).[15] The pseudonymous male author, "Shanzai" (an interjection meaning, "Good!"), issued a sharp note of concern that educators must craft means of preventing same-sex relations among young girl students, despite the fact that neither girls' schools nor, it would seem, same-sex love among female students were yet widespread in China. Rather, Shanzai wrote as an oracle. Although the extent of development of female same-sex educational institutions in China was less than in other countries, in light of foreign experience, it seemed likely that same-sex love in schools (and elsewhere) would emerge as a discrete social phenomenon—and for Shanzai, generally, a troublesome one—once the number of schools increased. In particular, for reasons of propinquity and cultural similarity, he expected that China would soon resemble neighboring Japan, where same-sex love among girls was said to be so rampant that "there is almost no student who does not partake in it." In making this comment, Shanzai was drawing upon a significant body of Japanese literature on the "problem" of same-sex love in girls' schools that had accumulated since the advent of widespread state and private girls' education in the latter nineteenth century.[16] In other nations, such as Spain and Italy, social conditions ostensibly made women less prone to the pursuit of same-sex love, while in Arab countries and China sex segregation increased the incidence. Shanzai did note that same-sex relations among adult women were legal according to the "current laws of civilized nations," yet same-sex love relations among minors remained a legitimate moral, if not legal, concern.[17]

     PETER J. CARROLL

The Japanese discourse on same-sex love in schools on which Shanzai drew was, like similar discussions elsewhere, strongly influenced by the analyses of the British social reformers Edward Carpenter and Havelock Ellis. Their writings helped inform prevailing attitudes toward sexuality in China, as well, with Ellis being the more influential. Their key works, especially Carpenter's "Affection in Education" (initial Chinese publication, 1923) and Ellis's "The School-Friendships of Girls" (initial Chinese publication, 1925), significantly shaped debates throughout the 1920s and beyond over single-sex schooling vs. coeducation and the content and importance of sex education.

Carpenter and Ellis both argued that same-sex love was a naturally occurring and (for the most part) harmless phenomenon among adolescents. Both spoke of "love" as constituting a broad sweep of affects. In Ellis's memorable words, "Passionate friendships among girls [varied] from the most innocent to the most elaborate excursions in the direction of Lesbos." He also spoke of school same-sex friendship/love as a "love-fiction, a play of sexual love," most often chaste, that prepared students to express affection in adult romantic and sexual relations with their opposite-sex spouses. Carpenter went further in his endorsement of same-sex love and suggested that it be used as a pedagogical tool for intellectual and general social and moral refinement and improvement. Although laudatory in his treatment of same-sex love in education, Carpenter largely treated same-sex love as a spiritual and/or intellectual orientation. His reluctance to praise or even discuss the physical aspects of same-sex love thus give his argument a surprisingly conservative cast: same-sex love in an educational setting was progressive and civilizing, only as long as it was noncarnal.[18] Any physical aspect, whether between student and teacher or even among students, could thus be labeled problematic. Ellis was famously tolerant of youthful same-sex relations, although he saw a continuing adherence to same-sex relations in later life as a sign of incipient mental disorders and asocial behavior. He and many he influenced, such as the sociologist Pan Guangdan, who is discussed below, emphatically identified adult "inversion" as a psychological deficiency.[19] Liberal acceptance of same-sex relations often contained a discordant note of censure.

SAME-SEX LOVE IN THE PRESS

"Our thinking is very juvenile. Previously we thought same-sex love was like 'mounting the clouds and riding the mists' [as immortals legendary for their swordsmanship would do], something concocted by novelists' pens.

Now, in the wake of the Tao-Liu case, we know it to be real."[20] This archly disingenuous comment was one of several similar remarks that attested to the clarion the case sounded in the public realm, accentuating a topic that had theretofore often been consigned to brief, sometimes cryptic social dispatches or lurid, hyperventilating reports. Histrionic claims to the contrary, same-sex love was not absent from the pages of newspapers, literary journals, or general interest magazines. The Tao-Liu case did, however, quite literally put "same-sex love" (*tongxinglian'ai* or *tongxing'ai*) in the headlines. In the summer of 1933, the mainstream weekly the *Eastern Miscellany* (Dongfang zazhi) declared that the Tao-Liu affair had made "the problem of same-sex love" a hot topic for the publishing industry and that authors had analyzed the murder and trial from all manner of legal, psychological, biological, and sociological perspectives.[21]

Tabloid (aka mosquito) newspapers often featured stories that promised to reveal the underbelly of modern urban life. Like their namesake insect, the gossip rags and scandal sheets of the mosquito press were notorious for being loud (but small), intrusive nuisances during their often short lives. They promised to give readers inside intelligence on various mysteries of big-city life, including advice on subletting rooms or avoiding fake medicines, though all things sexual—e.g., gigolos, concubines, massage, and free love—were more favored topics, with items on college assignations, student/teacher romances, and the lifestyle of college coeds being perennial features. Abetted by innuendo, writers detailed "unimaginable" situations, such as male brothels or men kept by other men, for readers presumed unfamiliar with such hidden realities. Female college students—as a recently constituted genus of young, privileged women able to live semi- or fully independent of family constraints in dorms or near their schools, leaving them free to interact with fellow students and others—were often the subject of breathless, prurient exposés. One correspondent for Shanghai's *Big Secret* (Damimi) tabloid reported learning of a Beiping female college student who had been living only who knew where while her parents and aunt thought she had been staying with the other. How shocking! A series of articles described female college students immersed in an existence of sybaritic license. Living and studying in gorgeously appointed surroundings, these women had the luxury of focusing exclusively on their studies. As a cohort, they were lovely, elegant, and attractive, yet the things they learned were anything but: Their studies often involved smutty books. They even indulged in romances with teachers and male students.[22]

The press treated homosexuality as so taboo that even generally staid popular press publications like the *Peiyang Pictorial News* (Beiyang huabao)

     PETER J. CARROLL

would declare a story about a public row (heated words, a thrown glass, and a slap) caused by a same-sex love "triangle" of four foreign women who met unexpectedly in the lobby of a Tianjin hotel a reporting triumph: "The unknowable is known!"[23] Given the cultural fascination with female students and their lives, magazines and newspapers were wont to ballyhoo any story involving same-sex love between late-adolescent and mature female students, especially if it involved tragedy or intrigue. One women's magazine trumpeted that the widely reported 1929 Hangzhou suicide of a female postsecondary student, Zhao Mengnan, was actually due to same-sex love. When Zhao committed suicide by taking opium, the mainstream press reported that family conflict and the demands of the school curriculum had shocked her nerves, causing her to twice attempt suicide previously by taking a sleeping draught before finally succeeding. However, "the newspaper reports were incomplete and because we feel this matter is extremely significant for women, we will report in depth and give you the left-out bits!" Zhao was involved with a classmate, Cao Bixia, whom she had met in secondary school. According to a classmate, Cao, "although a woman, had many male traits and was much like a man." The two were inseparable: "Otherwise, Mengnan would be despondent, like a cast-off lover." The two addressed one another in romantic speech characteristic of a love letter between a man and woman, with Zhao calling Cao "beloved" or "you" (addressed to a man, with honorific overtones) and Cao dubbing Zhao "little sister" or "my love." Cao Bixia, bowing to parental pressure, broke her promise to not marry. Fearing that Cao would be moved to divorce her husband if she herself did not die, Zhao Mengnan committed suicide to avoid harming her. "Zhao Mengnan's death was the norm for same-sex love," one report read. "From this example one can see that same-sex relations between classmates are more perilous than coeducational classmate relations!"[24]

Reflecting on the emblazoning effect of the Tao-Liu scandal, a *Social Daily News* (Shehui ribao) writer noted that by putting the term "same-sex love" in the air, people were far more attuned to see this thing that "in reality grows in the shadows, especially schools, barracks, factories, and churches, places where men and women are separated." As a recent murder-suicide of two American men in Shanghai, "intimate friends for several years," made clear, same-sex love was volatile and affected more youths and adults, men and women, and Chinese and foreigners than one would imagine. These two murders confirmed that same-sex love moved people to greater levels of obsession and disappointment than even ardent heterosexual romance: "Love is virulent, same-sex love especially so. This type of love causes both parties to give their entire lives, to bleed, to support it. This is especially common among women. To clarify, same-sex love is the result of nervous morbidity, often with very unfortunate results. . . . Same-sex love is a serious social problem. It not only affects the social order but can interfere with one's career. . . . As a society we need efficacious, extreme measures to save people from it."[25]

For Tao Sijin, it was too late, although the writer did advocate a reduced sentence: same-sex love was a mental illness, so sufferers could not be held 100 percent accountable for any illegal behavior they committed. Her life sentence was excessive. The more pressing challenge was devising means to save others.[26]

A MATTER OF NERVES

That Tao had slaughtered Liu in a gruesome fashion was not in question. Nonetheless, her lawyers argued, there were mitigating circumstances: Tao suffered from advanced neurasthenia (*shenjing shuairuobing*), a condition of weakened nerves due to excessive stimulation of the senses by the clamor of modern life. The syndrome left one physically and mentally weak. Symptoms included fatigue, anxiety, headaches, fainting, and depressed mood. It also had more serious potential consequences, such as sexual dysfunction and lack of sexual libido due to the exhaustion of the central nervous system's energy reserves. As a young woman pursuing higher education—and an art student, at that—she had almost inevitably developed neurasthenia. (Her gender, education, and career were presumed to make her less physically vigorous, more ponderous, and more intellectually and emotionally sensitive than the norm—hence her heightened risk.) Indeed, the press and medical specialists largely agreed that Tao and Liu both had the malady—and perhaps other illnesses—as would be expected of women engaged in same-sex relations. Tao's condition was clearly the more dire, as evidenced by the murder.

According to Tao's lawyers, her neurasthenia had left her nerves unable to cope with the strong emotions and mental and physical stress caused by her same-sex romance with Liu. Had she not been so afflicted, her nerves would not have acted in such a disordered fashion as to precipitate the murder. Tao, they argued, should therefore be found not guilty or held to a lower level of culpability and receive a reduced sentence. Evidence of Tao's long-standing physical weakness was abundant, they maintained. Old letters demonstrated that she had long been prone to colds. This susceptibility to sickness, her lawyers argued, was evidence of the weakened constitution associated with neurasthenia.

     PETER J. CARROLL

If her lawyers could establish that neurasthenia had made her "insane" (*xinshen shuaishi*), Tao would then, per article 31 of China's criminal code, not be liable for the murder, although she might still be subject to restrictions of her liberty. Were she found to have been "feeble-minded" (*xinshen haoruo*), she would be given a reduced sentence. Should her lawyers only be able to establish that neurasthenia had affected her "state of mind" (*xinshu*) she could, per article 76, be given a lighter punishment at the judge's discretion. Were the court to not accept her mental state as a mitigating factor, a homicide conviction would bring extremely severe punishment. The relevant articles of the criminal code addressed murder (article 282) and "taking the life of another . . . 1. As a result of a premeditated plan; [or] 2. By dismembering, disemboweling or any other cruel or ferocious act" (article 284). The specified penalties were death, life imprisonment, or incarceration for more than ten years (seven to twenty years, if a sentence were reduced).[27]

Having suggested that Tao be found not culpable or guilty but subject to a reduced sentence due to neurasthenia, her legal team changed tack and alleged that she was actually afflicted with psychasthenia (*jingshen shuairuobing*), a condition marked by weakness of mind and characterized by phobias, obsessions, or compulsions one knows to be irrational. This second diagnosis may have been genuine, or it may have been a tactical move to bolster her defense by claiming that she suffered from a less common, more virulent condition. At first glance, the two could be confused, but they were distinct, her lawyers noted. Tao therefore required immediate medical attention—first, to determine definitively the illness or combination of illnesses that left her physically and mentally susceptible to commit murder. Second, she needed immediate treatment—for psychasthenia, according to her lawyers.

Liu Qingxing dismissed as absurd the notion that either condition could be valid grounds for reduced culpability. Psychasthenia, she declared, was a common condition. According to medical science, it was not an illness that could produce insanity. Neurasthenia, she opined, should provide no better defense. "If one is able to kill someone and receive a lesser sentence due to neurasthenia," she declared, "then everyone is free to murder others and receive a lesser sentence."[28] Speaking for her family, Liu Qingxing suggested that Tao had developed neurasthenia in the two months since the attack and that she had not been so afflicted when she committed the murder. Liu Qingxing's skepticism undoubtedly sprang in part from her conviction that Tao's evident guilt deserved the severe punishment prescribed by the criminal code. (The court would, in the event, reject the neurasthenia/psychasthenia defense of Tao's lawyers.) Liu's sophisticated familiarity with psychiatric diagnoses of psychasthenia and neurasthenia may have reflected knowledge gleaned from her years spent studying in Japan, where psychiatry was far more developed and had permeated popular culture to a greater extent than in China. Neurasthenia had been prevalent there more than a decade before it had attracted widespread alarm in China. Japanese scientific authorities and the general public had recognized it as epidemic in same-sex schools and debated the appropriate means of redressing this "social problem" for more than two decades.[29]

The possible effects of neurasthenia were debated in the press and in court. Some doubted that neurasthenia itself could be the cause, as Tao seemed to suffer from a mental illness, not just a problem of nerves. Orthodox opinion held that the condition's effects were less pronounced and virulent than hysteria. Neurasthenia often developed over a long period, yet Tao had been a successful art student for several years. How could that be possible? Could an illness develop and manifest in a moment of passion? One could also argue that a confused, weak state of mind was distinct from neurasthenia. A report in the Shanghai *Eastern Times* (Shibao) explained, "There are many wasting illnesses of the mind and types of hysteria: neurasthenia, brutal debauchery, madness, severe anxiety, hereditary madness, slowly developing madness." To make sure that the "law was applied in accord with twentieth-century science" she would need to be examined by a forensic specialist.[30]

Neurasthenia was originally described in 1869 by the American neurologist George Beard as an ailment predominantly affecting middle-aged businessmen whose nerves were overwhelmed by the excessive stimulus of urban life and the rough-and-tumble world of US capitalism. As a result of the disease's etiology and Beard's publications, especially his 1881 book *American Nervousness*, in Chinese and other languages it was commonly known as the "American disease." (Indeed, a 1930 article maintained that Americans continued to suffer the highest incidence of the disease.) Despite its American pedigree, diagnoses of neurasthenia became commonplace throughout Western Europe during the 1880s and by the 1890s were frequent in Japan. Neurasthenia quickly became an index of the "level of civilizational progress," in the words of one Chinese science writer. "As sensations and desires the world over grow ever more complex, competition more virulent, daily there are more neurasthenics." It thus acquired an additional appellation: the "civilization disease."[31]

For many, Tao's case highlighted the menace neurasthenia posed to Chinese youth. During the course of its global spread, it had transformed into an especial danger for elite intellectual youth (i.e., people who had

PETER J. CARROLL

achieved puberty and continued with their studies). A 1935 analysis warned that some 53 percent of American upper-division students suffered from debilitating neurasthenia. While there were no authoritative statistics on its incidence in China, given the state of the environment, family, schools, nation, and society, its rate among Chinese students was thought likely to be greater. Indeed, a 1934 five-month Tianjin medical study concluded that 75 percent of students had neurasthenia. Of those afflicted, 95 percent were young students, seemingly middle school and high school age. Although not conclusive, these statistics gave a sense of the problem weakened nerves posed for China. Most discussions of neurasthenia focused on its reported harm to male sexual function—masturbation, seminal emissions, premature ejaculation, and erectile dysfunction were putative disorders and symptoms of "sexual neurasthenia"—and, hence, negative effect on human reproduction.[32]

During the Republican period, Chinese political and social elites—like their counterparts in Europe, North America, Japan, and elsewhere—were obsessed with improving the intelligence, health, and general fitness of the national population via eugenics. This scientific approach to managing human reproduction aimed to prevent national degeneration due to the noxious genetic and cultural influences of the uneducated, the infirm, and others deemed undesirable. The eugenic project therefore required that men and women, especially the healthy and highly educated, contribute to the refinement of "race-culture" by marrying and producing healthy children. Female neurasthenics could, like male sufferers, experience impotence and lack the energy sufficient to produce healthy children. They might also suffer pains in their uterus and be ill due to secretions from the womb, among a host of other maladies. Some authorities warned that women—wealthy young students, in particular—were especially vulnerable to the disease due to anemia linked to unregulated, heavy menses and the alleged feminine propensity for sentimentality, excitability, and excessive empathy with classmates and others. The intimacy of school-life, where all students studied and lived in close proximity, fostered the transmission of nervous contagion, and many, if not most, female secondary and postsecondary students were believed to suffer from neurasthenia.

By diminishing one's appetite for sex, neurasthenia was viewed as threatening a biological imperative. One physician observed, "The desire for food and sex are strong. The former preserves one's own life, the latter the species. Thus the imperative for heterosexual intercourse to produce children can be viewed as hardwired. . . . One can even see the loss of sexual desire as of greater significance than loss of appetite for food." Articulating a view that might not be uncommon today, he continued that even those afflicted with temporary sexual dysfunction were deeply affected. Reflecting contemporary truisms of evolutionary biology and psychology (including Freud's emphasis on the libido as life energy), he continued, sexual dysfunction was "akin to losing the 'light of human life.' It is as if one had committed suicide." He noted that purportedly more than 90 percent of the letters sent to the magazine *Youthful Health* (Qingnian weisheng) complained of neurasthenia.[33]

Genetic and environmental factors might increase one's risk of neurasthenia, but most cases were attributed to lifestyle. Youthful men and women the world over were prone to putting themselves at risk of overstimulating their nerves via thinking morbid or unusual thoughts, visiting prostitutes, taking opium, drinking too much tea, or, the most pernicious vice, excessively masturbating. Some social commentators argued that the Chinese population was particularly susceptible to developing both neurasthenia and same-sex love as a result of the isolation of men and women from one another in society, especially in schools—most of which were single-sex. Unable to interact with members of the opposite sex, young men and women were wont to become sexually frustrated. The consequent "blockage of the genitals" "caused even a happy life to acquire a gray layer" of psychic pain. Intemperate masturbation and neurasthenia were the almost inevitable result. In women, the two were strongly associated with strong fits of suspicion and jealousy, as present in the relationship between Tao Sijin and Liu Mengying.[34]

Chinese society had long enforced gender segregation—yet, according to one analyst, "Previously it was the custom in our country to marry early, which made this malady [of same-sex love] rare. Recently, for a variety of reasons, the age of marriage has been successively delayed and [same-sex] group living has increased greatly. If we wish to continue, under these conditions, preserving our traditional separation of the genders, this evil vice will become extremely prevalent." A popular advice columnist similarly maintained, "As for why same-sex love is so common in China and rarely seen abroad, we think that that this is due to the fact that in European and American countries social intercourse is open. Men and women are completely free in their romantic relations. As a result, same-sex love develops less commonly than in China."[35]

Schools, which were generally single-sex institutions, were believed to be the most significant milieu for the development of same-sex love relations. Although some might treat the phenomenon as a joke, the prolific commentator on women's issues Yan Shi wrote in the early 1920s, "we should

　　　PETER J. CARROLL

be concerned about the grave harm caused by same-sex love to young men and women." Those who developed it strongly purportedly felt revulsion toward heterosexual love and were unable to bear the prospect of "normal married life." Of course, same-sex relations could develop outside the school environment, as well. Guangdong was famous for "sworn sisterhoods" in which women "pledge to not marry [but rather live together, and work to support themselves in] a life of same-sex love," Yan explained. "If subjected to extreme pressure to marry, women sometimes kill themselves jointly. Although locals have promoted methods to prevent it, they have been unable to stamp out the practice." The potential of same-sex love in secondary schools and institutions of higher education to be similarly intractable demonstrated that "all parents and teachers cannot ignore this reality." Given that youth brought the stirrings of romance, it would be best to promote coeducation to prevent girls from developing "emotional girl friends" and boys "comrades."[36]

The sociologist Pan Guangdan noted that Tao Sijin demonstrated the intractable nature of same-sex love as a social problem. Coeducation was no panacea. Since Tao had continued in her same-sex love relations well after adolescence, when one might expect and permissively excuse such behavior, there was a good chance that her deviancy was congenital. The fact that society could allow a person not in full control of her faculties to decline mentally until she turned, seemingly in an instant, from being a loving partner to murdering her lover with ferocious violence demonstrated a lack of responsibility on society's part. Not her own. Thus, while the murder provided chilling evidence of the pathology of same-sex love in adults, its true relevance lay in exposing societal complicity in failing to avert the development of Tao's fall into murderous rage—and, via the extension of his logic, in allowing her to carry out adult same-sex relations.

The dormitories at the National Hangzhou Art Academy were single-sex, yet the institution was coeducational—as was the Shanghai school at which the women met. They nonetheless were drawn to "share the same pillow and coverlet." This basic fact refuted theorists who opined that coeducational environments would stem the development of same-sex love. Tao and Liu had studied in such "nondeviant" environments, so their inversion, Pan argued, was innate and worthy of greater social compassion. He, however—like his intellectual hero Havelock Ellis, the Austro-German psychiatrist Richard von Krafft-Ebing (author of the twelve-edition *Psychopathia Sexualis*, a foundational forensic study of sexual pathology), and others—still judged such behavior abnormal. Schools and society as a whole should provide better supervision of students to identify and arrest—or isolate—deviance before it led to murder. How many social problems might actually be avoided if authorities knew how many times a week students masturbated?[37] The formative power of sexuality over all aspects of human morphology thus necessitated that school authorities exercise panopticon-like surveillance over their pupils. Pan Guangdan's charge, at once permissive and patriarchal, if not benevolently authoritarian, revealed the level of social panic regarding the latent possibilities of female same-sex love in schools. Surveillance of students might prevent same-sex love relationships (like that between Tao and Liu) that occurred beyond early to middle adolescence, when they might be permitted as emotional preparation for male/female relations, and threatened to develop into pathological deviancy. If society had demonstrated a serious commitment to bettering itself and preventing its constituents from harming themselves or others, Tao Sijin and Liu Mengying would have been no more than classmates: any congenital tendencies for same-sex love would have remained latent. Pan's vision of the good society, which exercised custodial care toward all citizens, was at odds with the realities of Republican China.

FEMALE PHYSIOLOGY, SAME-SEX LOVE, AND CRIME

A complementary strain of medical commentary attributed Tao Sijin's same-sex love feelings and her murderous impulses to female physiology. As such, women in same-sex love relations and female criminals, including Tao herself, deserved greater societal understanding. At the same time, recognizing the physiological basis of "social problems" like crime and same-sex love could allow society to rid itself of them.

Dr. Gu Yin, a well-known commentator on mental and sexual health and a physician at Suzhou's mental and venereal disease asylum, used the Tao-Liu case to explicate how homosexuality was "a problem of glands and secretions" that began in utero. According to Gu, one begins life with male and female sex cells; "if, during puberty, the female cells within a boy's glands do not decrease, his male sex cells will atrophy. Although a male, his secondary sexual characteristics and libido will have some female aspects, and he will become a homosexual. The opposite is true for women whose male sex cells do not diminish." Advanced authorities, he noted, advocated removing the testicles or ovaries of homosexuals and replacing them with those of heterosexuals to cure "this abnormal sexual orientation." Physiology provided the solution for mental and physiological problems.

The direct link between female reproductive organs and criminality revealed that violence like Tao's slaying of Liu had physiological roots. "One

     PETER J. CARROLL

can see female sexuality as an appendage of the ovaries," Gu declared. "Indeed, everything that makes a woman a woman is found in her ovaries. Complexion, long beautiful hair, soft manner, light tinkling voice, purity, and more—these are all woman's beauty, and caused by the sexual hormones secreted by gonads"—as was a propensity for criminality. Drawing on the work of the Italian psychiatrist and criminologist Cesare Lombroso (1835–1909), whose writings on crime argued that criminality was inherited, Gu noted that famous female criminals were found to have unusual menses. It was no coincidence, Gu continued, that many had abnormal reproductive organs. Studies had established that women often committed crimes when they were menstruating: changes in body chemistry and blood pressure affected the brain. "Menstruation can negatively affect even normal women," Gu proclaimed. "It is especially deleterious to the undernourished and the mentally ill." Emotions are magnified; social disturbances, suicide, and theft—and, in the extreme case of Tao, murder—become more prevalent. Yet Tao's actions were not unprecedented. Gu noted that Richard von Krafft-Ebing told of "a woman with a strong genetic disposition for mental illness who became unusually concupiscent during her menses, inducing same-sex love. Rejected by her girlfriend, she then murdered her."

Women's physiology and mental outlook clearly differed from men, he concluded. In particular, the influence their reproductive organs worked on their minds made them relatively easily susceptible to criminal impulses. Should such scientific knowledge be part of the legal calculus when considering criminal culpability? In civil law women generally had an inferior legal status to men, and they possessed fewer property rights. Yet criminal law held them to the same standard as men. "Speaking from a medical perspective," Gu propounded, "this equality is inappropriate. Should they not be more protected?" Tao Sijin's sentence might merit reconsideration.[38]

Shortly after the initial trial, Tao's defense lawyers received a lengthy missive of more than ten pages that was subsequently published in the *Eastern Times*. The correspondent, an unnamed male "renowned doctor" from Anhui, wrote an impassioned apology. Tao deserved commiseration and a reduced sentence, if not exoneration, for she was a victim of both her physiology and the age—"a transitional state, caught between new and old mores and visions of society." He counseled the lawyers that she must be examined by a qualified physician like himself, who should be advised to scrutinize her menstrual cycle and hymen: female physiology provided the key to understanding female mentality.

Voicing a common refrain, the doctor characterized the murder and the women's same-sex love as unusual, even extreme, although their plight was commonplace. Physiological impulses, environmental influences, and psychological shocks caused by sexually suggestive messages prevalent in urban Chinese society left youth open to indulging in "illusory sexual encounters (such as same-sex love and fantasizing while masturbating)." Such practices were harmful, but anyone afflicted with a similar mental outlook would likely be unable to escape the fate of Liu and Tao. The case therefore deserved careful study, which might revolutionize understanding of psychology and crime and spur legal and/or medical reform.

The doctor justified the necessity of a medical exam by citing foreign forensic practice: "In Western civilized nations, when white female criminals are arrested for instances of arson, assault, and murder, a medical professional gives them a physical and psychiatric evaluation. Physicians' reports demonstrate that 80 to 90 percent are either menstruating or suffering from abnormal pathology associated with menopause." Such results helped clarify how Tao, a highly educated woman whom one would not associate with criminality, became a fearsome murderer: "She was unfortunately afflicted with these biological impulses and stimuli—pathological sexual ones that caused her criminal behavior." In fact, her elite education made her especially pitiful: Despite her learning and breadth of knowledge, she suffered from the lack of courage to jettison the traditional morality of female chastity. Why else would she have confided, "I have already become a broken criminal," in her diary? The doctor addressed an impassioned appeal to Tao herself: "Ah, Tao Sijin, sexual desire is a universal human trait. It is sacred and no bizarre object of shame. . . . However, old morality of human society and custom can make people, when they discover their sexuality, feel forced into enacting aberrant sexuality. . . . Your writings recognize that you both are victims sacrificed to the age, so why be so uncomprehending, so lacking in courage?" Although permissive, the doctor, one of Tao's most sympathetic defenders, assumed that her three-year relationship was aberrant. Given their educational attainment and artistic talent, Tao's and Liu's same-sex attachment ultimately could only be attributed to the dark force of traditional morality. Virginal shame had forced them on the path of same-sex love, which had depleted their bodies and minds, leading to murder.

The physical exam, he specified, must address several key factors. Was Tao's hymen whole, or had it deteriorated so that there was nothing left; or was there light scarring from tearing? Similarly, "do the lips of her vulva show the luster of a virgin, or are the veins somewhat pronounced and the color and luster liver-like? Or are they notably large and elongated, with the opening gaping?" A similar raft of questions followed, regarding the clitoris

     PETER J. CARROLL

and other genitals and menstruation, to establish whether excessive masturbation or her unique individual physiology had played a role: were her internal reproductive organs healthy, or might disease or other flaws have affected her state of mind, perhaps precipitating the murder? A similar inspection of Liu's fresh corpse might have provided physiological evidence of her physical and mental state. In the end, a physical exam might demonstrate that Tao's same-sex and murderous passions largely resulted from female hormones and menstruation. Despite his opinion of the aberrant, if not pathological, state of the women's attachment, this physician affirmed their affection as sacred. Tao's plight—that is, her sense of entrapment, shame, and mortal fury—were products of traditional morality. Physiology might provide the basis of human mentality, but social forces could profane even the sacred and make it toxic.[39]

Writing a couple of weeks after these two self-proclaimed experts, Pan Guangdan noted that Tao had yet to receive any of the urgent medical attention she had long required. Neither the legal system nor the collective of jurists understood their proper obligations. (Pan likely would not have accepted the above two physicians as medically qualified. The Suzhou insane asylum, he wrote, mainly offered palliative care and lacked scientific equipment.) His optimism that the case might spur a more scientifically accurate and humane treatment by the law and greater society of those with abnormal psychology seemed unrealized. Pan decried the fact that only two people in the entire country had the specialized foreign training to be "truly qualified" in the treatment of sexual psychology, let alone sexual criminal matters. Neither participated in the trial. Nor had experts in criminal psychology. Nor were prison authorities required to provide treatment to Tao while in prison. Worse yet, the case had inspired unenlightened pronouncements in the national legislature, the Legislative Yuan. Zhang Mojun, a female revolutionary and Legislative Yuan member (one of only two active women legislators), was offended by the violence of Liu's murder and the lesbian nature of the women's relationship. She proclaimed that she would have imposed death. (The Zhejiang provincial high court agreed with her when the case was appealed.) Pan ironized that Zhang seemed ideally qualified for the present legal system: unenlightened, bombastic, and illogical.[40]

The bankruptcy of the legal system notwithstanding, how should society as a whole attempt to deal with Tao's mental condition? There were several clear options: pronounce a lighter sentence; provide her with medical therapy in prison; or perhaps place her in isolation, so as to block out noxious stimuli. Pan favored vigorous therapy, although credentialed psychiatric medical treatment was unlikely. It was essential to prevent Tao from developing new same-sex love relations, since her previous liaison had helped precipitate her insanity. One must also consider whether Tao would be allowed to reenter society, reenroll in school, and frequent public places. "Who," he asked, "would prevent her from again developing same-sex love, engaging in lesbian sexual relations, and again committing murder?"[41] No one. The chance of her being found redeemable and able to live outside the Zhejiang prison seemed nil. In the meantime, she sat in her cell, awaiting her fate.

TAO SIJIN IN PRISON

By the time the Supreme Court in Beiping vacated the capital sentence imposed by the Zhejiang provincial high court and reimposed the original penalty of life imprisonment handed down by the Hangzhou district court, Tao had been in prison for over two years. She was by then a less public figure: her letters to the press and interviews with journalists had become rare. She applied for amnesty and was denied. After a significant period in prison, she started to express remorse. In late 1933, she adopted orthodox Buddhist precepts, abstaining from meat and becoming the disciple of a Buddhist master. She took to chanting Buddhist sutras morning and evening, for the merit of Liu Mengying and her own penance. She also began writing out sutras in a fine calligraphic hand on spirit paper, which she burned to benefit ghosts, release souls from Hell, and to expiate her sins. She became so devout that in early May 1936, she took initial vows as a nun. The Buddhist press reported her religious awakening and wrote that her seeming recovery revealed that her same-sex affection was not so pathological as to make her an incorrigible homosexual. She did not display the physiologically disordered brain that would afflict one permanently drawn to same-sex love. If she had, she would not have recovered her sanity. To Tao, the three-year-long episode of same-sex love and the murder seemed like a dream.

Not everyone admired her transformation or thought she might now qualify for amnesty. One popular education magazine editorialized that while her regret and improved mental outlook were laudable, "we hope that she might decide to pen some articles to help common people. Although she is locked up in prison, she could still endeavor to be a useful person. After all, what benefit does chanting sutras from morning until night offer people?" In the end, her supporters, Buddhist and otherwise, were unable to win her release. Nonetheless, she soon left prison.[42]

Shortly after Hangzhou fell to the Japanese army on December 24, 1937, Tao was freed, as part of a general amnesty. Following her discharge, she

    PETER J. CARROLL

worked as a teacher. A year and a half later, on June 28, 1939, she married a man, a county government official in Zhejiang.[43] At that point, she disappears from press accounts.

The final denouement of the Tao-Liu murder provides an opportune moment to compare the overall attitude of the courts and the public toward their tragic romance with that afforded Alice Mitchell. In 1892, in Memphis, Tennessee, the nineteen-year-old Mitchell attacked seventeen-year-old Freda Ward with a razor, eventually slitting her throat almost to the point of decapitation. According to the women's mutual understanding, they were affianced and planned to live as husband and wife. Mitchell explained that she butchered Ward because she loved her and feared that she would lose her to a man. Mitchell's trial generated lurid, spectacular press coverage, as did Tao's. The basic premise of the case, that Mitchell had stabbed Ward to death, was also not in doubt. Mitchell was found to be insane and sent to a state asylum. She reportedly died there six years later. Nuanced studies of the case by Lisa Duggan and Lisa J. Lindquist have made the incident a touchstone in the scholarship on the history of gender and sexuality in the United States at the turn of the twentieth century. Their respective arguments, which differ greatly and highlight complementary aspects of the case, are that 1) the press coverage of the case demonstrates that it served as a touchstone for medical experts and the public in the development of the lesbian as a social subject in the late nineteenth century (Duggan) and 2) that despite the same-sex romance at the heart of the case, Mitchell was judged guilty of violating gender roles and behavior, not sexual mores; as such, her act did not challenge Victorian notions of female sexuality and she was reintegrated discursively into society (Lindquist).[44]

Unlike in late-nineteenth-century America, in Republican Chinese society the "lesbian" (i.e., "female same-sex lover" who went beyond a school romance and permanently eschewed marriage to a man) was already established as a social type, perhaps partly due to the fact that Alice Mitchell became part of the scientific literature that influenced the development of medical, legal, and social opinion in China. Richard Krafft-Ebing incorporated Mitchell as an illustration of the typical invert in the tenth edition of *Psychopathia Sexualis*. In fact, the Mitchell-Ward case may be the one that Gu Yin referred to in his comment on Tao and Liu. Havelock Ellis also mentioned Mitchell as personifying "a typical invert of a very pronounced kind." People with exclusively same-sex sympathies, especially those for whom the condition was congenital and not acquired due to societal, physiological, and/or mental causes, were held to be very few, as well as being permanently physiologically and mentally abnormal. As discussed by Chinese medical authorities, social commentators, and journalists, the "lesbian" represented one extreme of a spectrum of women who engaged in same-sex love, generally for a limited period, as preparation for romantic and sexual relations with their future husbands, especially as youths at school. Same-sex love was a precarious and, for many, distasteful affection that had increased with the spread of secondary and postsecondary education. Consequentially, China—along with Japan, the United Kingdom, Germany, Italy, and other nations that figured in the profusion of sexuality-related psychological, sexological, and educational literature by Edward Carpenter, Havelock Ellis, Pan Guangdan, and others—faced a potential crisis of modern affect: alarmists worried that women's same-sex love, if it grew unchecked, could undermine human reproduction and scuttle attempts to improve the "race-culture" of the nation via eugenics.

In their diaries and other writings, Tao and Liu recounted the emotional and carnal nature of their bond forthrightly, sometimes poetically. The explicit erotic nature of their prose was ruled obscene, causing the courtroom to be cleared whenever diary evidence was discussed—although newspaper and magazine publishers rushed their words into print. Their transgression against gender and sexual norms was therefore not in question. This testimony and the savagery of Tao's evisceration of Liu led many to presume that her mental state was immature or was otherwise abnormal, leaving her unable to repress the momentary urge to commit murder. Nonetheless, her deportment in prison, especially in light of her demonstrated Buddhist piety and initiation as a nun, convinced some Buddhists and others that she had recovered her right mind. Her behavior was thus understood to have been due to transitory confusion and neurasthenia. If she had developed incorrigible same-sex love, the physiological damage to her brain and other organs would have been permanent, and she would have been unable to recover. Tao had practiced "same-sex love" and had been physically and mentally harmed by it; she had seemingly been vulnerable as a result of temperament, neurasthenia, the school environment, and other factors. Same-sex love had proven so noxious to her body and mind that she, a talented artist and highly educated young woman, had inexplicably gutted her classmate and same-sex lover. Her story thus exemplified the potential risk of same-sex school friendships. Nonetheless, the "typical Salomé" was redeemed: Restored to physical and mental health, she no longer practiced same-sex love. Rather, she was reintegrated into society, ending up the wife of a county government official.

     PETER J. CARROLL

1   See "Liang nusheng zhi yimu canju"; Ren, "Tongxing'aizhi buliang jieguo"; and "Nüxuesheng tongxing'aizhi eguo."

2   See Zhenlan, "Tongxing'ai shi shenshengdema?"; "Ciduo huixiede riji"; "Gao-fayuan jinchen kaishen"; "Mingriqi benbao zhuri pilou Tao Sijin yuzhong riji"; "Dai Tao nüshi dugengzheng"; Zhou, *Salomé* in China," 295, 300–311; and "Sharende xiaojie."

3   Ren, "The Writer's Art," 1–17 and passim.

4   "Tao Sijin jinmian yisi."

5   "Xu Qinwen fangwenji."

6   "LiuTao'an panjue quanshu."

7   "Liang nüsheng zhi yimu canju."

8   See Zhang, "Tao'an taolunhui"; Cao, "Sanjiaolian'ai jiejuefa"; Cao, "Taolun (weiwan)"; and Cao, "Taolun (xu)."

9   See "Du. Dangrande jieguo"; Qian, "'Du' shi nanzimen de zhuanlipinma?"; Chen, "Nüxing jidude jiepou"; and You, "Xingyu yu duji."

10 Xu, "'Tongxinglian'ai yu sanjiaolian'ai."

11 See Haiyan Lee's perceptive analysis, *The Revolution of the Heart*, 152–55. Eugenia Lean's *Public Passions*, 49–179, contrasts the general approval shown to murderous revenge motivated by filial piety vs. the opprobrium and concern provoked by violence stemming from romantic jealousy.

12 This archive brings to mind Jennifer Robertson's notable article "Dying to Tell: Sexuality and Suicide in Imperial Japan," which examined the lethal nature of social codes: Women in same-sex relations in Taishō Japan essentially had to die (or, to apply the same logic to Tao and Liu, die or murder) to have their story publicly told in such detail. See also Sang, *The Emerging Lesbian*, 127–60; and Kang, *Obsession*, 90–96.

13 "'Ai' de ziwei."

14 Jiyun, "Tao'an taolunhui."

15 Sang, *The Emerging Lesbian*, 106–09.

16 Gregory M. Pflugfelder, "'S' Is for Sister," 133–90.

17 Shanzai, "Funü tongxingzhi aiqing."

18 Some progressive voices agreed with Carpenter to argue that same-sex love signified society's progress, and even contemplated an erotics of pedagogy between teachers and students of the same sex as central to education. Liu Mengying's murder and the fact that her suspicions regarding Tao's entanglement with Liu Wenru may have precipitated it likely undercut the legitimacy of such theories. See Furuya, "Tongxing'ai zai nüzi jiaoyushangde xinyiyi," 1,064–69; and Ellis, *Studies in the Psychology of Sex*, 215, 373.

19 Shen, "Tongxing'ai yu jiaoyu." Regarding Ellis, see Hsu, "The 'Ellis Effect.'"

20 Ren, "Tongxing'aizhi buliang jieguo."

21 Jin and Huang, "Funü yu jiatinglan."

22 "Shisheng lian'aizhi mimi"; "Ziyoulianai'de mimi"; "Nüxueshengde damimi"; "Nannüxuesheng lian'aide mimi"; "Nüxuesheng jisude damimi"; Zhentan, "Nan maiyinde mimi"; and Jiying, "Tongxinglian'aide mimi."

23 Guai, "Sanjiao tongxinglian'aizhi zha."

24 "Zhao Mengnan wei tongxinlian'ai er si"; "Zhao Mengnande sishi"; and "Zhao Mengnan cansi Xihu."

25 *Shenbao* and the English-language press were more circumspect, although one can read between the lines. See Wuchen, "Guanyu tongxinglian'ai"; "Two Young Americans in Murder and Suicide Tragedy"; "Young American Ex-Banker Sought in Fatal Shooting of Fellow Countryman Here"; and "Sharenzhe zisha."

26 Wuchen, "Guanyu tongxinglian'ai."

27 China, *The Criminal Code*, 7, 21, 77.

28 "Lüshi dabianlun jingshenbing nanduanding."

29 Wu, "A Disorder of Qi," 324–26.

30 Zhang, *Nannü shengzhiqi xing shenjingshuairuozhi yufang ji zhiliao*, 12; "Lian'ai fasheng."

31 Sensheng, "Qingnian nannü yu xingde shenjingshuairuo," 12–13; Bi, "Sheping," 12–16; and Wu, "A Disorder of Qi."

32 Shapiro, "The Puzzle of Spermatorrhea in Republican China," 551–96.

33 Zhang, *Nannü shengzhiqi xing shenjingshuairuozhi yufang ji zhiliao*, 1–2.

34 See Sensheng, "Qingnian nannü yu xingde shenjingshuairuo"; and Gu, "Nüzide shouyuin."

35 Zhenlan, "Tongxing'ai shi shenshengdema?"

36 Yan, "Pingtan."

37 Pan, "TaoLiu dusha'ande shehui zeren," 25–26.

38 Gu, "Cong TaoLiu dusha shuodao nüzi tongxing'ai he nüxing fanzui yu xingjineng (zhong)"; and Gu, "Cong Taoliu dusha shuodao nüzi tongxing'ai he nüxing fanzui yu xingjineng (xia)."

39 "Yuejing yu chunü mo."

40 Song Meiling and Zheng Yuxiu were also female legislators, but they had not taken their seats. Zhang served as a supplementary legislator in their stead. Pan, "Wudu yououde tongxing jiansha'an"; "Yaoshi Zhang Mojun lai shenli LiuTao'an Tao Sijin jue wushengwang"; and Pan, "Zaiti TaoLiu dusha'an."

41 Pan, "TaoLiu dusha'ande shehui zeren."

42 "Tao Sijin yuzhong songjing"; Zhang, "Tao nüshi chanhuiji"; Shuiguo, "Tao Sijin chaodu qingchou"; "Renwu: Tao Sijin nüshi."

43 "Xiuzhen xinwen."

44 Duggan, "The Trials of Alice Mitchell," esp. 308–311; Duggan, *Sapphic Slashers*, passim; and Lindquist, "Images of Alice," 31, 61.

     PETER J. CARROLL

CHAPTER 6

CHANGING SEX IN THE URBAN PRESS

Scientific Modernity and the Shaping of Transsexual Subjects in Twentieth-Century China

HOWARD CHIANG

IN THE HISTORIOGRAPHY OF SEXUALITY, ESPECIALLY AFTER MICHEL Foucault's seminal work, scholars have tended to privilege science and medicine as the epistemic leverage for the formation of modern gender and sexual identities.[1] This method has influenced the writing of the history of transsexuality in twentieth-century China. Two widely publicized examples of this involving human sex change are the case of female-to-male Yao Jinping in mid-1930s Shanghai and the case of male-to-female Xie Jianshun in early 1950s Taiwan. These examples shed light on the significance of the urban press in influencing popular categorizations of gender and sexuality through its interaction with medical and scientific knowledge. Major urban newspapers and tabloid print media constituted a space that enabled writers with sufficient cultural capital to comment on these rare yet fascinating stories of bodily transformation. These published and circulated writings provided intrigued readers with an unusually wide range of perspectives. The press also became a central vehicle for the agents of elite medico-scientific discourse to engage with the wider public, filtering novel and complicated ideas about sex and its plasticity for lay readers. In this chapter, I argue that this social milieu provides a promising ground for the historian to capture a process whereby common understandings of sexuality were shaped not only by dominant secular discourses of medical science, but also by the participants of this quotidian venue for voicing competing visions for themselves and the nation.

Around the turn of the twentieth century, the scientific concept of sex slowly entered the Chinese lexicon.[2] Since the late Qing period, biologists and medical doctors had introduced Western anatomical concepts of the human body.[3] Promoting a vision of sexual dimorphism, they construed the physical morphology and function of the two sexes as opposite, complementary, and fundamentally different.[4] In the May Fourth era, iconoclastic intellectuals such as Zhang Jingsheng and Pan Guangdan emulated the work of European sexologists by collecting "data" on the sexual lives of Chinese people and by translating foreign sexological classics on the psychology of sexual variations. Sex, in their formulations, was no longer something to be observed in nature, but something to be desired.[5]

In the second quarter of the twentieth century, the urban intelligentsia began to envision a more fluid definition of humanity. They no longer drew on the limited language of anatomy to talk about two different but equal sexes; rather, they started to think of men and women as two versions of a universal human body. Over time, Chinese sexologists came to embrace the plausibility of sex transformation based on the vocabulary of sex endocrinology, famous sex-reversal experiments on animals, and a new scientific theory of universal bisexuality. They turned to indigenous Chinese frameworks for understanding reproductive anomalies, such as eunuchs and hermaphrodites, and relied on them as a conceptual anchor for grasping new and foreign ideas about sex. Throughout the Nanjing decade (1928–37), Chinese scientists entertained the possibility of human sex change and even offered scientific explanations for it, but they oftentimes retreated to biologically anomalous cases such as castration and intersexed subjects. They had yet to articulate a vision of individuals as agents capable of seeking surgical and hormonal sex transformations for themselves.

The idea that nonintersexed individuals could change their sex began to reach a wider public in the mid-1930s when the press reported on a woman from Tianjin named Yao Jinping, who had become a man and taken the name Yao Zhen in 1934. On March 17, 1935, news of Yao's sex transformation appeared in major papers, including *Shenbao* (Shanghai news) and *Xinwenbao* (The news), and soon became the spotlight of urban public discourses in China. By April, Yao's name had formed such a major part of ordinary parlance that new stories of sexual metamorphosis almost always began by referencing it.[6] According to Yao's grandfather, the family had lost contact with Yao's father, Yao Yotang, after his army was defeated by the Japanese troops and retreated to Xinjiang. Yao cried day and night and would rarely

          HOWARD CHIANG

get out of bed until one night in the late summer of 1934, when a lightning strike hit the roof of the family's house. Yao suddenly felt something physically different. On the next morning, Yao reported a possible sex change to her grandmother, who felt Yao's covered genital area and was confident that Yao had turned into a man. Yao's bodily metamorphosis earned the uniform label *nühuanan* (woman-to-man) in the media.[7]

Although surprised by the transition at first, Yao's grandfather eventually decided to bring Yao to Yao Yotang's senior officer, General Li Du, who played an important role in defending Northeast China from Japan in the 1930s. They explained the situation to him in Shanghai. On the day before Yao's news appeared in print, reporters met Yao in person but mainly spoke to Yao's grandfather, who assumed the responsibility of communicating the details of Yao's bodily change to the press. Yao's grandfather presented several pieces of "evidence" to prove Yao's former biological femininity, including a diploma indicating Yao's graduation from a female unisex elementary school in 1930. The most striking evidence that Yao's grandfather showed the reporters were two photographs of Yao, taken before and after the sex change. These photos were printed and distributed in most, if not all, of the newspapers that featured Yao's story.[8] Apart from this crucial proof, journalists drew attention to other fragmented hints of femininity, including Yao's pierced ears and slightly bound feet. Given these indications, Yao's account in *Shenbao* stated, "Evidence points to the factual status [of Yao's sex change] and awaits examination by experienced physiologists."[9] *Xinwenbao* described the Yao story as "something similar to a fairy tale" and the evidence brought forth by Yao's grandfather as "nothing like the *biji* [notebook] genre . . . but hard facts."[10]

On the second day of publicity, Yao finally opened up and spoke to the reporters, in part because the reporters soon considered the details provided by Yao's grandfather "inconsistent." Upon hearing Yao's own recollection, enthusiastic reporters jumped to ask about psychological changes. They were eager to find out whether Yao had begun to experience "sexual feelings toward women," especially in light of Yao's decision to cancel an arranged marriage. Yao expressed unease upon hearing this question and refused to respond directly. Instead, Yao wrote on a piece of paper: "I am currently no different from a normal man. One hundred days after my physical sex change, I started to experience an admiration of some sorts toward other women." At this point, Yao's grandfather stepped in and told the journalists that although Yao's genital area had masculinized, it remained underdeveloped. The reporters recommended that Yao undergo a physical examination. But Yao's grandfather insisted that Yao still needed to rest and recuperate, only after which the family might consider a full medical exam. Meanwhile, General Li Du, Yao's father's senior official, promised to schedule a full physical checkup for Yao. He also expressed a strong willingness to support Yao financially so that Yao could eventually go back to school.[11]

On the same day, reporters asked a handful of medical experts to deliver professional opinions on Yao's case. The most important input came from the president of the National Shanghai Medical College, Yan Fuqing. (Yan had received his medical degree at Yale University in 1909; following the fate of many intellectuals in China, he would later suffer and in fact die in Shanghai during the Cultural Revolution.) Yan suggested that Yao's bodily changes were likely symptoms of a *cifuxiong* condition, or pseudohermaphroditic female-to-male sex transformation. Nonetheless, he insisted, the truth behind Yao's case could only be confirmed with a thorough physical examination following strict scientific standards. Xu Naili, the acting chair of the Chinese Medical Association, concurred that although a case like Yao's was indeed rare, the facts remained to be fully uncovered. A definitive diagnosis of Yao's condition must not be formulated based on unfounded speculations.[12]

On the following day, other interlocutors from the medical profession chimed in. A gynecologist, Mao Wenjie, paid Yao a visit on the morning of March 18 and asked to inspect Yao's body. Yao refused to disrobe, so Mao proceeded with an assessment of Yao's genital region in a fully dressed situation, which was identical to the way Yao's grandmother had verified Yao's transformation previously. Based on this indirect observation, Mao conjectured that Yao's condition was congruent with what doctors normally called "female pseudohermaphroditism," or what was more commonly known in Chinese as "*ci* becoming *xiong*." Mao testified that Yao's male organ remained underdeveloped, because although Mao could sense a penis that was immediately erected upon physical contact, he could not detect the presence of testicles. He also called attention to specific residual female traits, such as a large right breast (but a small left one) and a significant amount of vaginal secretion that left a strong odor in Yao's lower body.[13]

While most experts who spoke up were enthusiastic about the potential breakthroughs Yao's case might bring to the medical field, all of them remained careful not to arrive at a conclusive diagnosis too hastily prior to a physical exam. On the day Yao was transported to the National Shanghai Medical College, Yan Fuqing met with General Li Du and was surprised to learn that Yao's sex change had occurred abruptly. According to Yan, the female-to-male transformations resulting from female pseudohermaphroditism were typically gradual. In order to figure out what was really going on

     HOWARD CHIANG

behind Yao's self-proclaimed sex change, Yan promised to assign the best practitioners in the hospital to this case, including the chair of the gynecology department, Dr. Wang Yihui, and the chair of the urology department, Dr. Gao Rimei.[14]

Word that Yao's story was merely a hoax soon shocked the public. On March 21, the *Shenbao* coverage of Yao's clinical examination was introduced with the headline "Yao Jinping Is Completely Female." The *Shenbao* journalists had confirmed this startling finding with General Li over the telephone in the evening of March 20. According to Li, because Yan Fuqing highly valued the groundbreaking prospect of Yao's case, he had assigned six of his best doctors (two Western and four Chinese) to conduct a thorough examination. At nine o'clock in the morning (of March 20), they tried to persuade Yao to disrobe so that the medical team could examine Yao's body closely, but Yao persistently refused to cooperate. Eventually, the team had to rely on anesthesia to bring Yao to sleep, and, upon close investigation, the doctors realized that Yao's body was genuinely female, without the slightest hint of genital transformation. This disappointing discovery was confirmed by eleven o'clock in the morning. Pressed by Li immediately afterward, Yao explained that in self-presenting as a man, Yao's sole intent was to join the army in Xinjiang and reconnect with Yao's father. This was not feasible for a woman. Li quickly forgave Yao and promised the family annual support of three hundred yuan plus the cost required to send Yao back to school in Tianjin.[15] According to *Xinwenbao*, the deceiving erected male organ detected (indirectly) by Yao's grandmother and Dr. Mao Wenjie was nothing more than a bundle of cloth wrapped in a rodlike fashion.[16]

The press coverage of Yao Jinping generated a "public passion" on an unprecedented scale toward the issue of sex change.[17] In light of the level of publicity that it received, the Yao story provoked interest in nearly every corner of urban Chinese culture in the spring of 1935. In contrast to Yao's bogus transformation, some magazines claimed, stories of genuine sex change prevailed in foreign countries such as Japan, Egypt, and the United States.[18] Some commentators stressed the importance of gathering sufficient scientific evidence before jumping to any hasty conclusions about Yao's bodily change; others, following the leading voice of doctors, assumed that Yao's sex change was already real and argued the other way around: Yao's experience was valuable for unlocking the secret of nature and thus advancing scientific progress.

For the most part, the general public viewed Yao Jinping neither as a freak nor as someone embodying the negative connotations conventionally attached to the *renyao* (human prodigy or fairy) figure.[19] Instead, when confronted with this highly sensationalized case of sex transformation, Chinese readers of the press reacted in a surprisingly sympathetic manner. The case was often perceived with a growing sentimentalism that framed Yao's behavior and motivations in extraordinarily positive (usually filial) terms.

On March 18, the day after Yao Jinping's name first made headlines in China, a commentary had appeared in *Xinwenbao* that attempted to offset the sudden peak of public interest and anxiety surrounding Yao's story. The writer, Du He, began by pointing out the prevalence of both female-to-male and male-to-female transformations in the Chinese historical record. The popular tendency to dismiss these cases as outright impossible, according to Du He, should be corrected. In fact, around this time another case of female-to-male transformation was being widely reported outside China. The message was clear: this coincidence of "Sino-Western reflection," in the author's words, suggested that Yao's experience was not exceptional. Locating the cause of Yao's transformation in congenital physiological defects, Du He argued against viewing it as an irregular or surprising event. Here, the view articulated by Chinese sexologists (such as Liu Piji) in the 1920s had filtered down to the popular level: Modern science could throw light on puzzles of life previously less well understood.[20]

Interestingly, Du He insisted that Yao was already a man regardless of his physiology. Du consistently referred to Yao with the masculine pronoun "he" instead of "she," and the article's entire discussion proceeded on the assumption that Yao had undoubtedly turned into a man. To the author, Yao embodied a masculine gender worth praising rather than being disparaged:

> Yao Jinping missed his father deeply when he was a girl. He cried
> day and night. Now that he has become a man, he promised him-
> self to find and reconnect with his father. It is evident that he is
> not only filial but also masculine-hearted by nature. People like
> him and those who are associated with him should be applauded
> and granted extra love and care. With positive support, he can
> turn into a "good man" [*haonan'er*]. His physiological changes
> should not be the focus of discussion, which would render him
> as a biological oddity.

By placing an equal, if not greater, emphasis on gender embodiment, the author differed from the sexological elites who upheld science as the only answer to all aspects of sexual life. Notwithstanding his reinforcement of gender stereotypes, Du He wanted to convey a larger point regarding the societal treatment of people who changed their sex: that their social status should not be stigmatized by scientific standards and narratives of abnormality.[21]

Others perceived the relationship between science and Yao's unconventional metamorphosis in a less antagonistic way. According to a March 21 article that appeared in the Shanghai tabloid newspaper *Crystal* (Jingbao), "Research on Female-to-Male Transformation," the significance of Yao's experience and the value of scientific research should be more adequately understood in reciprocal terms. The author—a woman named Fang Fei— also opened with the observation that there had been plenty of historical documentations of sex change in China—"but, without reliable evidence, they are not trustworthy." Fang claimed that Yao Jinping's transformation, on the other hand, provided a rare and important opportunity for the scientific assessment of similar phenomena. Even "the pierced ears and the bound feet" in Yao's case "do not constitute solid evidence, because they are the result of human alteration"; in contrast, such natural changes in Yao's physiology as genital transformation, the flattening of breasts, the development of an Adam's apple, and, according to Fang, "the most surprising observation that all of these were induced by a strike of lightning" needed "to be investigated further by researchers."

By and large, Fang's discussion endorsed the spirit of scientism bolstered by May Fourth sexologists. In her view, Yao's case presented researchers and medical doctors a golden opportunity to study the nature of sex transformation based on hard evidence and, by extension, to advance the status of the Chinese scientific community. Because actual human sex change was "such a rare event in life," Fang encouraged experts in medicine and biology to not let this opportunity slip. Similar to Du He, Fang's assumption here, before knowing the eventual outcome of Yao's story, was that Yao had already become male. But unlike Du He, Fang did not take science as a powerful force of cultural authority that necessarily pathologized and marginalized the social status of people like Yao Jinping. Fang instead argued that precisely due to its rarity, Yao's unique experience should actually make Yao proud after "abandoning any feeling of shame and offering [herself] as a candidate for scientific research."[22]

At the peak of Yao's publicity, some tabloid writers followed the leads of earlier sexologists and brought to public discourse similar bodily conditions, such as hermaphroditism and eunuchism. In a *Crystal* article titled "Reminded of A'nidu because of Yao Jinping," the author Xiao Ying recalled a woman named A'nidu—a foster parent of the famous Shanghainese courtesan

Wendi Laoba—who had passed away a few decades before the Yao incident. According to Xiao Ying, A'nidu's body was masculinized in ways similar to Yao's: A'nidu "had a *yang* presence but a *yin* face," and "she wore women's clothes to emulate a *ci* [female] appearance, yet her large physique resembled a man's." When A'nidu was still alive, many assumed that she was an "underdeveloped man" (*fayu weiquan zhi nanzi*). Xiao Ying regretted that A'nidu's body was not subjected to postmortem examination. For Xiao Ying, the difference between a man and a woman (*nannü zhibie*) could not be determined on the basis of genital appearance alone: the internal structures of the reproductive system mattered too. Writing in a language similar to Chai Fuyuan's notorious *ABC of Sexology* (especially his discussion of "incomplete male growth"), Xiao Ying applied some of Chai's sexological ideas about natural reproductive anomalies to the case of A'nidu.

With respect to Yao, Xiao Ying's main point was that any claims put forth about Yao's sex change could only be inconclusive before a thorough medical examination of Yao's body. "Although Yao Jinping is publically known to have transformed from *yin* to *yang*," Xiao Ying carefully asserted, "her lower body parts have not been properly investigated. The claims that her grandfather, Yao Qingpu, made about her penile development have not been verified. Most doctors judge the case to be the *cifuxiong* type, but it seems to be too early to draw this conclusion." Unlike Du He and Fang Fei, Xiao Ying did not assume that Yao Jinping had already undergone a sex transformation. Xiao Ying brought up A'nidu precisely to underscore the importance of a careful physical checkup, especially in order to achieve a reliable assessment of Yao's anatomical status. "It would be most welcome," Xiao Ying added, if "the determination of Yao Jinping as either *ci* or *xiong* by doctors" could "be reported in various newspapers and print venues." In arguing that the result of Yao's sex determination should be publicized, rather than emphasizing Yao's marginal and stigmatized status, Xiao's intention, similar to the previous two writers, was to promote the value of science in an age of social and political uncertainties.[23] Another article embraced this scientific faith by criticizing the media's emphasis on a "lightning strike" and a "strange dream" as ungrounded explanations for Yao's transformation.[24] This echoed some of the criticisms leveled by medical experts about superstitious claims.

Four days after the article on A'nidu appeared, Xiao Ying contributed another piece to *Crystal*, titled "Reminded of Eunuchs because of Yao Jinping's Female Body." News of Yao's unchanged female sex had been widely reported by this point, reflected in the article's opening sentence: "The female

      HOWARD CHIANG

status of the self-proclaimed female-to-male Yao Jinping was confirmed after being medically examined by a group of seven doctors—Chinese and Western—at the National Shanghai Medical College." But Xiao Ying did not offer a straightforward rendition of what happened:

> The doctors discovered that her fake male genital appearance was made possible by a phallic-like bundle of cloth and not the result of an actual transformation of the reproductive organ. This bears striking similarities to the castration surgeries operated on eunuchs for the immediate effect of dismemberment. [Upon uncovering the truth behind Yao's sex change,] Professor Yan Fuqing and his medical team must have enjoyed a good laugh.[25]

Yao Jinping reminded Xiao Ying of castration in both realistic and metaphoric ways. Yao's female body was literally laid bare in front of medical experts, like a eunuch's body lacking a penis. In Xiao Ying's metaphoric formulation, the doctors' discovery of Yao's true sex became a performative restaging of castration itself—the public enactment of a medical procedure that "removed" Yao's highly publicized male identity. Whether Yao Jinping was reminiscent of the hermaphroditic body (via A'nidu) or the allegorical experience of castration (via eunuchs), Yao's intention to pass as male was never abhorrent to Xiao Ying. Xiao Ying merely approached Yao's sex change from the angle of rendering medical science as the cradle of truth.

In these tabloid accounts, not a single author passed moral judgment on human sex change. None of the commentators cast Yao Jinping in a negative light; before she was medically examined at the National Shanghai Medical College, some observers even described Yao's bodily state as a rare, unique biological condition that could potentially provide scientific researchers and medical doctors a multitude of research possibilities. All of them invoked medical knowledge to *naturalize* birth defects and human anomalies. But more importantly, Yao Jinping's story played a pivotal role in turning the mass circulation press into a platform for expressing a normative ethos of scientism. This gradually transformed "sex change" into a more general category of human experience not confined to congenital bodily defects. Despite its shocking outcome, Yao's story invited a wide range of reactions that looked beyond the single medical explanation of pseudohermaphroditism. As the commitment to the power of science deepened, the idea that even nonintersex individuals could change sex gradually took shape in Chinese popular culture by the 1940s.

On August 14, 1953, the *United Daily News* (Lianhebao) announced the striking discovery of an intersex soldier, Xie Jianshun, in Tainan, Taiwan. The headline read "A Hermaphrodite Discovered in Tainan: Sex to Be Determined after Surgery."[26] By August 21, the publication had adopted a radically different rhetoric, trumpeting, "Christine Will Not Be America's Exclusive: Soldier Destined to Become a Lady."[27]

Considered by many to be the "first" Chinese transsexual, Xie was frequently dubbed the "Chinese Christine" (Zhongguo Kelisiding). This was an allusion to the famous American transsexual star Christine Jorgensen, a former GI who had received her sex reassignment surgery in Denmark two years prior and become a worldwide household name immediately afterward due to her personality and glamorous looks. The analogy reflected the growing influence of American culture on the Republic of China at the peak of the Cold War.[28] Within a week, the Taiwanese press transformed Xie from an average citizen whose ambiguous sex provoked uncertainty and national anxiety to a transsexual icon whose fate helped globally stage Taiwan on a par with the United States.

Dripping with national and trans-Pacific significance, Xie's experience made *bianxingren* (transsexual) a household term in the 1950s.[29] She served as a focal point for numerous new stories that broached the topics of changing sex, human intersexuality, and other atypical conditions of the body.[30] People who wrote about her debated whether she qualified as a woman, whether medical technology could transform sex, and whether the two Christines were more similar or different.

But Xie never presented herself as a duplicate of Jorgensen. As Xie knew, her story highlighted issues that pervaded post–World War II Sinophone society: the censorship of public culture by the state, the unique social status of men serving in the armed forces, the limit of individualism, the promise and pitfalls of science, the relationship between military virility and national sovereignty, the normative behaviors of men and women, and the boundaries of acceptable sexual expression. Her story attracted the press, but the public's avid interest in sex and its plasticity prompted reporters to dig deep. As the press coverage escalated, new names and medical conditions grabbed the attention of journalists and their readers.[31] The kind of public musings about sex change that had saturated Chinese culture earlier in the century now took center stage in Republican Taiwan.[32]

When the story of Xie first came to public spotlight, the *United Daily News* appended a direct reference to Jorgensen: "After the international frenzy surrounding the news of Miss Christine, the American ex-GI who turned into a lady after surgery, a *yin-yang* person [hermaphrodite] has been discovered at the 518 Hospital in Tainan." This opening statement reflects a transitional moment whereby sex change surgery developed from a common clinical management of intersexuality into a new basis of sexual subjectivity. The *United Daily News* article suggested that Xie had been fully aware of having feminine traits since childhood, but had kept those traits a secret until their recent "revelation" under the close attention of doctors in Tainan. A native of Chaozhou, the thirty-six-year-old Xie had joined the army at sixteen, lost his father at seventeen, and lost his mother at eighteen. He came to Taiwan with the Nationalist army in 1949. "At the age of twenty," the article explained, "his breasts developed like a girl, but he had hidden this secret as a member of the military force rather success-fully. It was finally discovered on August 6, upon his visit to the Tainan 518 Hospital for a physical examination due to recurrent abdominal pains and cramps, by the chair of external medicine, Dr. Lin. He has been staying at the hospital since August 7."[33]

The first turning point in the framing of the Xie Jianshun story in both medical and popular discourses came with Xie's first operation. The press collaborated with Xie's physicians closely and kept the public informed about their progress. On August 20, the day of the first operation, the *United Daily News* published a detailed description of the surgical protocols sched-uled for three o'clock that afternoon.[34] By bringing the reader's eyes "inward" toward Xie's internal anatomical configurations, the communique repeated the epistemological claims of the medical operation intended for sex deter-mination. Step by step, the newspaper article, presumably relying on the information provided by Dr. Lin's team, told its reader the surgical proce-dures and criteria for the establishment of Xie's female sex. Yet no symmet-rical explanation was given for establishing a male identity for Xie. The narrative only concluded with the brief remark, "Otherwise, Xie will be turned into a pure male." One wonders what would have happened if Xie's interior anatomy had been found to be drastically different from a normal woman's. What were the doctors planning to do, then, with Xie's "sealed vaginal opening"? If Xie could be transformed into a "pure female" by simply cutting off a "symbolic male genital organ," what would a transformation into a "pure male" entail? Would that also involve the removal of something? Or would that require the adding on of something else? Even if female gonads were found inside Xie's reproductive system and the second opera-tion followed, what would happen next if Xie's vaginal interior showed signs of anatomical abnormality? On what grounds would the doctors evaluate the resemblance of Xie's vagina to an average woman's, at this stage? To what degree could Xie's vagina deviate from the internal structure of a "normal" vagina before it was considered too "abnormal"?

The journalism picked up momentum, but answered none of these questions. Under the pretense of keeping its readers informed, the press actually imposed more assumptions (and raised more questions) about Xie's "real" sex. *Taiwan New Life Daily News* (Taiwan xinshengbao) asserted that it was "easier to turn Xie into a woman than into a man," and *China Daily News* (Zhonghua ribao) learned that Xie had been anxious enough to cry numerous times about the potential makeover.[35] By the day of the first operation, the medical and popular discourses had congruently prepared the lay public for a sensational outcome—an unprecedented sex change episode in Chinese culture. Xie's sex was arguably already "determined" and "transformed" before the actual surgery itself. This reciprocated the ambiguity surrounding the purpose of the first operation: was its goal the determination or transformation of Xie's sex?

On the following day, August 21, the Taiwanese public confronted a lengthy summary of Xie's surgery in the abovementioned *United Daily News* piece. Its subtitle, "Soldier Destined to Become a Lady," echoed the headline of the New York *Daily News* front-page article that had announced Jorgenson's sex reassignment in December 1952: "Ex-GI Becomes Blonde Beauty." The *United Daily News* piece included a more telling subtitle: "The *Yin-Yang* Person's Interior Parts Revealed Yesterday after Surgery: The Presence of Uterus and Ovaries Confirmed."

From this point on, Xie was frequently referred to as the "Chinese Christine." Whereas reporters had always used either the masculine pronoun "he" or both the masculine and the feminine pronouns in the first week of publicity, they changed to the feminine pronoun entirely in referring to Xie in all subsequent writings. In publicly sharing his views of Xie's operation, Dr. Lin asserted that "Xie Jianshun should be converted into a woman in light of his physiological condition," stating that this procedure would have "a 90 percent success rate." The August 21 *United Daily News* report described Xie's first surgery with remarkable detail. It thus familiarized the reader with the clinical proceedings of Xie's surgery, reinforcing Xie's status as an object of the medical gaze even after the surgery itself. Ultimately, this careful textual restaging of Xie's medical operation translated its *clinical* standing into a glamorized *cultural* phenomenon in postwar Taiwan.[36]

When Republican government officials took a more serious interest in her case, Xie resisted their top-down decisions. Xie's second operation was initially scheduled to take place within two weeks of the first, but the only

   HOWARD CHIANG

news that had reached 518 Hospital four weeks after her exploratory lapa-rotomy was a state-issued order to transport her to Taipei. Xie refused the order, however. She immediately wrote to bureaucrats to express a firm preference for staying in Tainan and being operated upon there again.[37] To her dismay, Xie paid a price for challenging the authorities. They neglected her and delayed her operation for at least three weeks following her request. The press reappeared as a viable venue for voicing her dissent. On October 17, Xie disclosed her deep frustration with her last menstrual experience, which had occurred roughly a month before. "Given her vaginal blockage, wastes could only be discharged from a small [genital] opening, leading to extreme abdominal pains during her period," a *United Daily News* article with the title "The Pain of Miss Xie Jianshun" explained. Since another menstrual cycle was just right around the corner, she urged Dr. Lin, again, to perform a second operation as promptly as possible. But Dr. Lin despairingly conceded that he had to receive a formal response from the central government before he could initiate a second surgery. All he could do at this point, as one might have expected, was to reforward Xie's request to the higher officials and wait.[38] By late November, the prolonged waiting and the accumulated unanswered requests had forced Xie to agree bitterly to relocate to a hospital in Taipei.

The media had heretofore functioned as a key buffer among the medical professionals, Xie Jianshun, and the Taiwanese public. The national dailies, in particular, had served as the primary means through which readers could learn Xie's thoughts and gauge her opinions. Those who followed her story relied chiefly on the press for the ins and outs of her treatment. Doc-tors had even allowed news reporters to witness the first exploratory lapa-rotomy operation and, afterward, disclosed their decision to turn Xie into a woman, before telling Xie herself. Similarly, Xie considered the press the most immediate (and perhaps reliable) way to publicize her desire to remain biologically male before the operation and her unwillingness to leave Tainan afterward. Almost without the slightest degree of hesitation, both Xie and her physicians readily collaborated with journalists to escalate the initial scoop of media reporting into a nationwide frenzy.

Although the reporters continued to clamor, Xie's coverage took a dip near the end of 1953. In 1954, only three articles in the *United Daily News*, one article in *Min Sheng Daily*, and one article in the *Central Daily News* (Zhongyang ribao) followed up on Xie's situation. After her relocation to Taipei, an update on Xie's health condition came in mid-February 1954. The months of silence in the press coverage had less to do with the public's declining interest than with a mutual agreement between Xie and her attending physicians to refrain from speaking to media representatives. This constituted the second turning point in the evolving relationship between the medical profession and the coverage of Xie in the mass media. The popular press no longer played the role of a friendly intermediary between the public, the doctors, and Xie herself. To both Xie and her medical staff, the publicity showered on them after the first operation seemed to impede rather than help their plans. Xie, in particular, might have considered the authorities' indifference toward her request to stay in Tainan to be a consequence of nationwide media coverage, thereby holding her prolonged waiting against the reporters.

The mysterious aura surrounding Xie Jianshun's fate did not last long. The public's avid interest finally pushed medical experts to step up and come clean about Xie's situation. On October 28, 1955, the No. 1 Army Hospital finally released a full-length official report on Xie, claiming "the completion and success of Xie Jianshun's sex change operation."[39] The official report, published in the *United Daily News*, revealed numerous aspects of the Xie story that overthrew earlier speculations. Of these revelations, the most surprising was probably the fact that Xie's most recent operation was actually her fourth, and not her third, operation. (Recall that Xie's second operation had received little publicity in the previous year.) By June 1954, from reading the scattered newspaper accounts, interested readers could gain a vague impression that doctors in Taipei had performed a second surgery on her, but its date, nature, and purpose were unclear. According to this official 1955 report, however, Xie's second operation—an exploratory laparotomy, with the additional step of removing parts of her male gonadal tissues—had taken place on April 10, 1954.

Based on the samples extracted from her body during this operation, the doctors had confirmed Xie's status to be that of a true hermaphrodite, meaning that she had both ovarian and testicular tissues in her gonads. The doctors also clarified that at that point, her "testicular tissues were already deteriorating and unable to produce sperm," but her "ovarian tissues were still functional and able to produce eggs." In light of a stronger presence of female sexual characteristics, the medical team performed a third operation on August 26, 1954. After the surgery, Xie's penis was replaced by an artificial vaginal opening. A year later, on August 30, 1955, Xie's most recent and fourth genital surgery was simply a vaginoplasty. With her "normal woman's vaginal interior," Xie Jianshun's "transformation from a soldier into a lady is now indisputable."[40] Brought to light by the mainstream press, Xie's personal triumph encapsulated postwar fears and hopes about the possibilities of medical science.[41]

   HOWARD CHIANG

The final media blitz surrounding the Xie story peaked in the late 1950s. The press announced that Soon Mei-ling, Chiang Kai-shek's wife, and a number of celebrities had visited Xie in Taipei, and that she had begun working at the Ta Tung Relief Institute for Women and Children under the new name Xie Shun—after *nine*, not four, surgeries.[42] Ever since the birth of "the Chinese Christine," the comparison of Xie to Jorgensen had intrigued, satisfied, and resonated with observers time and again, but never without its limits.

The widespread coverage of sex transformation in the urban press reveals pertinent aspects of the relationship between medical science and the formation of sexual subjectivities. Although the two case studies examined here stem from radically different sociopolitical contexts—1930s treaty-port Shanghai and 1950s Cold War Taiwan—together they illustrate distinct methods of writing the history of sexuality. Although some critics have challenged the Foucauldian approach of social constructionism by highlighting the limited role of the medical paradigm in the historical shaping of queer subcultures,[43] these cases suggest that in the context of early- to mid-twentieth-century China, medical science did not merely generate a pathologizing language about gender and sexual deviance, which marginal subjects subsequently appropriated in a "reverse discourse."[44] In fact, many writers—queer or not—who contributed to the mass media often drew on the enlightening nature and cultural authority of modern science to promulgate public discussions of sex change. The popular media and the mainstream and tabloid presses thus offered a rich, vibrant space for the social negotiations and contestations of queer identification.[45] For historians, such sources expand the parameters of pivotal categories such as "science" and "sexuality" beyond the hegemonic standards of the modern West and offer exciting new perspectives on methods and approaches.[46]

NOTES

For a more extensive treatment of the materials in this chapter, see Chiang, *After Eunuchs*.

1   Foucault, *The History of Sexuality, Vol. 1*; Faderman, "The Morbidification of Love between Women"; Laqueur, *Making Sex*; Hausman, *Changing Sex*; Terry, *An American Obsession*; Oosterhuis, *Stepchildren of Nature*; Davidson, *The Emergence of Sexuality*; and Minton, *Departing from Deviance*.
2   Jia, "Zongguoren xing guan chutan"; and Rocha, "*Xing*."
3   Rogaski, *Hygienic Modernity*; Elman, *On Their Own Terms*; and Heinrich, *The Afterlife of Images*.

4   Chiang, "The Conceptual Contours of Sex in the Chinese Life Sciences."

5   Sang, *The Emerging Lesbian*; Kang, *Obsession*; Chiang, "Epistemic Modernity and the Emergence of Homosexuality in China."

6   See, for example, the April 1935 article "Hongchuan Hui'an quanxian Luo Rongzong nanhua weinü."

7   "Nühua nanshen zhi Yao Jinping yeyi di Hu."

8   See, for example, "Nühua nanshen zhi Yao Jinping yeyi di Hu"; and Dan, "Nühuanan."

9   "Nühua nanshen zhi Yao Jinping yeyi di Hu."

10   "Yao Jinping yeyi di Hu."

11   "Yao Jinping huanan fangwen ji."

12   Ibid.

13   "Yao Jinping xi fushen huananti"; and "Yao Jinping nühua nanshen."

14   "Yao Jinping zuoru yiyuan jianyan"; and "Zuo song Shanghai yiyuan jianyan."

15   "Yao Jinping wanquan nüershen."

16   "Yao Jinping yanxi wanquan nüshen."

17   The term "public passions" is adopted from Lean, *Public Passions*.

18   See, for example, "Nübiannan"; "Nübian nanshen"; and Xu, "Nübiannan qiwen."

19   On the concept of *renyao* in Chinese history, see Huang, *Queer Politics and Sexual Modernity in Taiwan*, 53–81; and Chiang, "Archiving Peripheral Taiwan."

20   Liu, *Renjian wujie de shengwu*.

21   Du, "Nühua nanshen."

22   Fang, "Nüzhuan nanshen de yanjiu."

23   Xiao, "Yin Yao Jinping huixiang A'nidu."

24   Bai, "Nühua nanshen."

25   Xiao, "Yin Yao Jinping nüshen xiangqi taijian."

26   "Nanshi faxian yinyangren jiangdong shoushu bian nannü."

27   "Burang Kelisiding zhuanmei yuqian dabing jiang bianchen xiaojie."

28   On Christine Jorgensen, see Meyerowitz, *How Sex Changed*.

29   The word *transexual* was first coined by the American sexologist David Cauldwell in 1949. Cauldwell wrote: "When an individual who is unfavorably affected psychologically determines to live and appear as a member of the sex to which he or she does not belong, such an individual is what may be called a *psychopathic transexual*. This means, simply, that one is mentally unhealthy and because of this the person desires to live as a member of the opposite sex." See Cauldwell, "Psychopathia Transexualis," 275. In 1966, endocrinologist Harry Benjamin used the word *transsexual* in his magnum opus, *The Transsexual Phenomenon*. This book was the first large-scale work describing and explaining the kind of affirmative treatment for transsexuality that he had pioneered throughout his career. On the intellectual and

social history of transsexuality in the United States, see Hausman, *Changing Sex*; and Meyerowitz, *How Sex Changed*.

30 In this chapter, I adopt the feminine pronoun when referring to Xie both generally and in the specific contexts after her first operation. I only use the masculine pronoun to refer to Xie in discussing her early media publicity, because she expressively refused sex reassignment before the first operation.

31 See Chiang, "Gender Transformations in Sinophone Taiwan."

32 On the vibrant discourse of sex change in Republican China, in addition to my book *After Eunuchs*, see Dikötter, *Imperfect Concepts*, 74–81; Chiang, "The Conceptual Contours of Sex in the Chinese Life Sciences"; and Wong, "Transgenderism as a Heuristic Device."

33 "Nanshi faxian yinyangren jiangdong shoushu bian nannü."

34 "Yinyangren Xie Jianshun jinkaidao biancixiong."

35 "Yinyangren jingshenti"; and "Yinyangren shinan shinü jintian fenxiao."

36 "Burang Kelisiding zhuanmei yuqian dabing jiang bianchen xiaojie."

37 "Xie Jianshun gaizao shoushu huo jianglai Taibei kaidao."

38 "Xie Jianshun xiaojie de yintong."

39 "Lujun diyi zongyiyuan xuanbu Xie Jianshun shoushu chenggong."

40 "Sici shoushu yibianerchai Xie Jianshun bianxing jingguo."

41 For voices that challenged the propriety and authority of the official report, pointing out that its explicit content was too invasive of Xie's privacy and that its "scientific" tone did not pay sufficient attention to Xie's postoperative psychology, see, respectively, "Fabiao Xie Jianshun mimi weifan yishifa buwu shidangchu"; and "Heyiwei Xie Jianshun."

42 See "Xiri dabing tongzhi jianglai fulian huiyuan"; "Yishi chuangzao nüren wunian duding qiankun"; "Xiri shachang zhanshi jinze jingru chuzi"; "Xiaoyangnü Fu Xiuxia zhu Tatong Jiaoyangyuan"; and "Xie Jianshun guanxiongfu."

43 See Chauncey, *Gay New York*, 125; and Wang, "Shame, Survival, Satisfaction."

44 Foucault, *The History of Sexuality, Vol. 1*, 101.

45 On the role of the popular press in the shaping of sexual subjectivities, see also the seminal work of Duggan, *Sapphic Slashers*; and Meyerowitz, *How Sex Changed*.

46 For recent attempts to rethink the boundaries of sexual science in the framework of global translation and circulation, see the essays in Bauer, *Sexology and Translation*; and Fuechtner et al., *A Global History of Sexual Science, 1880–1960*.

CHAPTER 7

A REPARATIVE RETURN TO "QUEER SOCIALISM"

Male Same-Sex Desire in the Cultural Revolution

SHANA YE

IN A 1993 REPORT ON BEING GAY IN CHINA IN THE TORONTO *GLOBE and Mail*, the awakening of subject Yang Tao's gay identity unfolds amid the 1989 Tiananmen upheaval, a political event that marked the climax of intensified social conflicts resulting from China's economic reform since the late 1970s.

> The night of the bloody crackdown at Tiananmen Square was the moment Yang Tao began to face up to his homosexuality. He had gone to the square to demonstrate on that evening in June, 1989, when soldiers suddenly started shooting. He leaped over a fence and ran to safety. . . .
>
> "It was a narrow escape. I could have been killed," said Mr. Yang. . . . "I thought: Why should I live with a mask? This is the way I am."[1]

As the narrative suggests, the precarious queerness of Yang Tao, who was both gay and a political dissident, was threatened by socialist totalitarianism. But it was precisely at his moment of confronting state violence that his queer self was able to fledge.

The figures of the "wounded queer" and the "oppressive socialist state" have been central in narrating the emergence of Chinese queer subjectivity and LGBT activism. We often hear stories of communist prosecution of sodomites, police harassment of homosexuals, and governmental crackdowns on LGBT organizations. These stories frame queer subjects as victims *par excellence* of state socialism, positing a strong link between queer liberation and Western-style political and economic modernity. The *Globe and Mail* article is one such narrative. As the story continues, we learn that Yang Tao "was enrolled in an elite language school where he learned to speak English fluently." In the "darkness" of "confusion," "despair," and "hard struggle" with himself, Yang Tao "came across the words 'gay' and 'homosexual'" in foreign books. In 1986, he spent a year in the United States, where he discovered a gay subculture, "bought gay magazines, watched gay videos and went to gay bars." Yet it was the 1989 killing that made Yang Tao realize that "the situation was hopeless in China" for both gays and liberal-minded political dissidents. Thus, he decided to break free by escaping to the United States.[2]

This type of "traumatic-dramatic historiography" utilizes historical injuries to justify postsocialist queer liberalism and normalization, a process commonly used to produce knowledge of Chinese queer sexuality. The construction and maintenance of the socialist-oppression/postsocialist-liberation dichotomy has created an epistemological blind spot and methodological dead end that not only "closet" socialist queerness, but also foreclose our ability to imagine radical queer alternatives.

The *tanbai jiaodai*, or "honest confessions," narrated by men who engaged in same-sex behavior during the Cultural Revolution (1966–1976), are an important source type that instead reveals the dynamic interplay between power and pleasure, in which state socialism relies on queer subjects' expression of their sexual selves. The "evidence" of queerness these narratives provide adds new material to the understanding of queer existence in the Maoist era; it also enables an epistemological shift from the question of whether socialism hinders sexuality to the question of whether historical, cultural, and affective processes have sustained knowledge producers' attachment to oppression and injury.

QUEERING THE SOCIALIST "CLOSET"

Prevailing accounts of Chinese queer history have understood China's pre-reform years (1949–1978), marked by centralized state socialism and Maoism, as a dark time, wherein shadowy figures of homosexuals, reframing Lord Alfred Douglas's words, "dared not speak their names." Homosexual, gender-variant, and sexually variant individuals have commonly been perceived as living in a "socialist closet," fearful of social stigmatization and political persecution.

The absence of current scholarship on queers in socialism fueled my desire to retrieve and preserve lost histories when I began fieldwork in 2014.

On my way to the National Library in Beijing for my first day of archival digging, I overheard a conversation about selling antiques between two men at the bus station; I asked the dealer whether he by chance had material from the Cultural Revolution. When he replied "Yes," I inquired about material on homosexuality, which led to my first piece of male same-sex material—and later, to some five hundred pages of documents, including sodomy indictments, court judgments, legal records, personal confessions, and victim testimonies. In contrast to the presumption that homosexuals were hidden, the salacious language and explicit descriptions of male same-sex behavior in these pages reveal pronounced sexual energy and sexual culture in Maoist society and the socialist state system.

The abundance of sexual expression in the Cultural Revolution period has been supported by several recent historical studies. Citing cultural historian Harriet Evans's work on public education about love, sexual hygiene, and marriage, researchers Elaine Jeffreys and Haiqing Yu argue that despite prevailing conservative attitudes, "public discussions of sex and sexuality were not exactly 'taboo' in the Maoist period."[3] Historian Emily Honig points out that there were no official declarations prohibiting sexual relationships, and that the state never overtly promoted sexual repression in Maoism.[4] In fact, novels and personal memoirs released after the Cultural Revolution indicate that the Cultural Revolution provided previously inconceivable opportunities for youth to explore sex, love, and romance.[5]

Although this evidence has provided a new look at the sexual history of China's state socialist era, simply recuperating lost history and supplementing it with examples of homosexuality is insufficient. Digging out the amphora of same-sex practices in socialism is nothing queer—on the contrary, the existence of queer sexuality is, for lack of better words, the most ordinary thing throughout history. What is interesting, instead, are two questions: Regardless of the plenitude of sex, what has sustained the repeatedly told story of sexual suppression and loss? And what would Chinese queer theorization of history gain if we let go of our attachments to loss, and instead embraced an epistemological turn to "radical abundance"?[6]

Moving away from the question of whether socialism suppresses sexuality, "queer socialism" asks how our desires and intentions to recover the suppressed queer past—from the standpoint of the postsocialist, neoliberal present—could have "closeted" queer subjects, concealed the ordinary everyday queer practices in socialism, and weakened queer connections across time and space.

The "closeting" practice hinges on the abovementioned practice of "traumatic-dramatic historiography"—a method that characterizes much

　　　　SHANA YE

of the scholarship on historical sexuality in China, in which historical writings utilize injury to fulfill future-oriented narratives of liberation. This dialectic construction has been well captured by many queer historians. As scholar Heather Love sees it, the desire to overcome historical injury and the commitment to "progress" are "at the heart of the collective project of queer studies and integral to the history of gay and lesbian identity" across the twentieth century.[7] Within this narrative, gays and lesbians are marked as heroic norm-resisters who occupied a position to overthrow the tyranny of repressive regimes, respectability, decency, and domesticity. Insofar as this narrative is appealing, it is—as gender and queer theorist Jack Halberstam writes—a "self-congratulatory, feel-good narrative of liberal humanism that celebrates homo-heroism."[8]

Opposing the liberatory understanding of gay and lesbian identity fostered by progressive enlightenment, Michel Foucault leads us to see the effects of a "reverse discourse":[9] On one hand, modern homosexual identity is continually seen as a form of damaged or compromised subjectivity; on the other hand, gay freedom is produced in response to the history and discourse of damage. The contradiction of Euro-American queerness as "both abject and exalted,"[10] as Love sees it, explains this impulse to turn the dark side of queer representation to "good use" in both the realm of subject formation and politics. This oxymoronic construction is rooted in the project of Western modernity: "The idea of modernity—with its suggestions of progress, rationality, and technological advance—is intimately bound up with backwardness. The association of progress and regress is a function not only of a failure of so many of modernity's key projects but also of the reliance of the concept of modernity on excluded, denigrated, or superseded others. . . . If modernization in the late nineteenth and early twentieth century aimed to move humanity forward, it did so in part by perfecting techniques for mapping and disciplining subjects considered to be lagging."[11]

If the abject, "lagging" queers in the past serve as the domestic "others" of Western modernity, the technology to create and discipline backward cultural "others" through racializing "deviant" queer figures facilitates modernity's imperialist global project. Queer theorist Jasbir Puar uses the term "homonationalism" to describe how—in a post-9/11 and post–*Lawrence v. Texas* context—the advancement of neoliberal politics and the technologies of biopolitics have created an image of the United States as queer-friendly, through selectively including white homosexual subjects and excluding Muslims as sexual-racial "others" (or even terrorists). This ideology installs an opposition between queers and Muslims, which fortifies US exceptionalism—a political rhetoric that frames the United States as epitomizing a "higher" level of civilization, whereas the Middle East is understood as backward and uncivilized and therefore a national enemy upon whom to wage war.[12]

In the context of Chinese socialism, the abject queer repressed by the socialist regime serves as both the temporal and spatial "other" of "proper" modernity. As anthropologist Lisa Rofel shrewdly points out, the post-socialist collective project of neoliberal globalization relies on a revisionist historical account—one that views Maoist socialism as hindering China's capacity to embrace proper modernity because of its repression of sexuality.[13] This sly construction of a socialist sexual past allows a postsocialist allegory—presenting the desire to free one's gendered and sexual self from the socialist totalitarian state—to emerge. Writing in response to Rofel's theorization of "desiring China," the scholar and author David Eng states, "The social stakes of homosexuality's expressive desire unfold upon a political horizon of *becoming*, a political horizon of great significance for Chinese modernity and for Chinese citizen-subjects alike"; thus, "the appearance of expressive queer desire promises to mark China's proper, though belated, place within a 'cosmopolitan globalized world.'"[14]

The postsocialist queer is discursively and materially produced by queers themselves—activists and scholars—as a cosmopolitan consumer-resister, through the discourse of global capital. The trope of desire has given post-socialist queers the power to refashion the stereotype of socialist blue ants dehumanized by class consciousness and state-controlled economy, fulfilling the national allegory of China's inevitable transition. In this narrative, queers in the past not only suffer, but suffer for us—if we knew state socialism was hellish, we would feel at ease with the decision we'd made to pursue a neoliberal future, even though neoliberalization also comes with its own violence and erasure. The drama of the inevitable postsocialist transition is made possible by sustaining the trauma narrative of the past.

However, as sociologist Jeffrey C. Alexander reminds us, not all injury, pain, and suffering become social and collective trauma. What trauma narrative wins out is "a matter of performative power."[15] The successful circulation of this trauma-drama, based on a national catastrophe (in this case, violence against homosexuals in an oppressive socialism), relies on the discursive and affective suppression of a less visible trauma (China being "othered" as socialist). To understand this process, a brief overview of Chinese contemporary history is helpful.

Since China's defeat by Western powers in the First Opium War (1840–1842), nationalist discourse has attributed China's weakness to its seclusion from the outside world, and sought to strengthen and revive the nation by

SHANA YE

appropriating Western technology. During the May Fourth Movement in the early twentieth century, nationalist intellectuals and reformers advocated for Western democracy and science to solve pressing crises of the semifeudal, semicolonial society. It is worth noting that China's condition of not being officially and completely colonized led to its ambivalent relation with colonialism and its later forms in the era of globalization; while it allowed China to seek an alternative path to modernity through communism and socialism, the country's lack of colonial history cultivated a national feeling of exclusion from the global world marked by capitalism. This sense of seclusion and exclusion was also galvanized by Cold War–era Orientalism, which invariably constructed China as a politically and culturally abnormal "other" in contrast to Western normality. On one hand, desire for becoming "normal" and equivalent to the liberal, modern West has driven China's economic reform and shifts toward globalization; on the other hand, Orientalized Chinese difference and internalized imperialism have sustained an affective inferiority in the Chinese psyche, strengthening China's determination to transition from a despotic, planned, and dark past to a democratic, free, and bright future.[16]

Would the attachment to queer consumer-subjectivity have looked the same if queers in the socialist past refused to be redeemed by the global neoliberal present? Would the liberatory agendas of rights and marriage have achieved their dominant status in LGBT movements if we could learn more creative methods of resistance from our socialist queer forebears who managed to succeed in survival and accretion? Would the allegory of inevitable transition still have taken hold if we could decipher how its power relies on an erasure of queer experience and a perpetuation of different forms of violence? A return to "queer socialism" involves casting a turning-back gaze upon queer knowledge production, and fearlessly posing challenging questions—even when those questions might lead to more tensions, ruptures, enmities, and alienations—lest queer intellectual and activist practices become a closet of themselves in their own right.

THE CULTURAL REVOLUTION ARCHIVE OF AFFECT

The disastrous movements of the Great Leap Forward (1958–1962) and the commune program, the withdrawal of Soviet support, and severe food shortages in the 1950s incited intellectual dissidence against Mao Zedong among the top leaders of the Communist Party. Acting on fears of denunciation of his leadership, Mao launched a socialist education campaign in 1962, in the name of rooting out revisionism and capitalism and purging political dissidents. The Communist Party's internal political conflicts quickly spread to the larger society as Mao called on Chinese citizens to identify and fight class enemies, in order to strengthen class struggles and the proletarian revolution.

In the literary and cultural field, Mao launched a campaign in 1963 to eliminate harmful bourgeois influences and prevent dissident intellectuals from using literature to promote anti-party thoughts and activities.[17] During the Cultural Revolution (1966–1976), ideologically unsound literary works were severely criticized and prohibited. In the 1960s, literature and art that depicted the old ruling class, their values and ideologies, and some foreign literary works from capitalist countries were considered "poisonous" and "counterrevolutionary."[18] Works concerned with love and romance were strongly opposed because they were regarded as "bourgeois and revisionist."[19] Sexual immorality—which included premarital and extramarital sex, male same-sex relationships, and sex with children—was framed as political impurity that required severe punishment. Yet as a result, previously unspeakable sexual behaviors became highly pronounced and recorded for the purpose of guarding socialism. Cases of "immoral sex" were disclosed and denounced in public, in struggle sessions or on big-character posters (*dazi bao*), as bad examples that would educate the masses and transform convicts. (This public denouncement of sex, ironically, frequently aroused the masses; one informant I spoke with in 2014 recalled that he got an erection when reading the words "male-male implicit relationship"—*nannan guanxi*—on a *dazi bao* in 1973.)

The Cultural Revolution archive discussed herein consists of documents of men who committed the crime of sodomy (*jijian zui*) or the crime of hooliganism (*liumang zui*);[20] the collection includes individual dossiers, police indictments, records of crimes and misdeeds (*fanzui shishi*), court judgments, confessions, and victim testimonies.[21] The men in these archival materials range from peasants and workers to communist cadres whose male same-sex behaviors were disclosed and reported to their local Communist Party committees. Some of them participated in struggle sessions or reported to the police station for arrest, while others were arrested, sentenced, and persecuted. Although China had no laws that criminalized homosexuality, and the attitude of the Supreme Court toward consensual male sexual relationship was ambiguous—even tolerant[22]—prior to the Cultural Revolution, individuals who committed such behaviors were still referred to as criminals and convicts.[23] The penalty for these crimes varied, given the fact that the new socialist law system was not formalized until 1979;[24] also, the power of the Party and the Red Guard during the Cultural

     SHANA YE

Revolution overrode the juridical authority and law. In the archival dossiers, some people were given warnings within the Communist Party, or expelled from the party. Others were sentenced for three to eight years of jail time, without trails. In the worst case, a convict who was involved in sex with minors was sentenced to death with reprieve.

The Cultural Revolution archive is an archive of affect. It contains narratives about intimate life, and the desire and affective labor embedded within its constitution and reception deserve critical analysis. Unlike US lesbian and gay archives[25] that characterize grassroots queer scholars' efforts to preserve erased histories,[26] the Cultural Revolution archive comprises texts from institutionalized documentation and official state records. In documenting and revealing sexuality in the form of crimes, the state and its representatives encountered the sexual and affective lives of queer individuals, allowing the state to be queered and sexualized. Thus, the Cultural Revolution archive is simultaneously an archive of the state's desire to govern and an archive of unexpected erotic interactions of bodies—of the queer individual, the state official, the historian, and the future reader—that take place in the collaborative process of making sexuality in state socialism. This dynamic relation requires new methods of archival work, heeding how subjects are produced in the efforts to document and interpret, as well as noting the process "through which the bodies and desires of others [and of ourselves] . . . enter historicity"[27]—an intimate unraveling and tracing that the following sections explore further.

QUEER SUBJECTIVITY IN *TANBAI JIAODAI*

This chapter focuses on *tanbai jiaodai* from Cultural Revolution archival sources. *Tanbai jiaodai* share many characteristics with the Mao era's diary writings. As with Mao-era diaries, the subjects in *tanbai jiaodai* have wholeheartedly devoted themselves to the Communist Party, Chairman Mao, and the revolution. They actively engage in self-criticism for the revolution, and show strong commitment to transform themselves under the leadership of the party and through Marxist-Leninist and Maoist thoughts. Distinct from subjects in Maoist diaries who frame themselves as disciplined, ideal revolutionary men and women,[28] the subjects of *tanbai jiaodai* manuscripts often describe themselves as lacking political consciousness and indulging in a bourgeois lifestyle. As examples of failure, they must confess how bourgeois thoughts corrupted them in detail, in order to conquer the evil forces of the bourgeois class and transform themselves to serve the proletarian revolution.

It is precisely through the state's coercive compulsion to confess these evil deeds that the subject finds a space to speak about an intimate sphere of personal life that is otherwise discouraged, if not completely prohibited. Contrary to the postulation that "private writing that deviates from public discourse is . . . dangerous and impossible,"[29] the confessor in *tanbai jiaodai* is not only encouraged but *required* to write about how they deviated from the official discourse and ideology. According the Maoist principle of self-criticism, the more details that a confessor writes about their deviances, the more sincere they become in committing to transforming themselves. As a result, the subject is allowed queer space to construct a sexual self while conforming to a socialist ideology. Apart from historian Yue Meng's understanding of Maoist private and public space as an "absolute hierarchy,"[30] these "place-making practices" enabled queer subjects to engage "the new understandings of space" and to produce queer counterpublics.[31] In this sense, *tanbai jiaodai* confessions are rare autobiographic sources that allow readers to understand the intricate interplay between socialist disciplinary power and a subject's self-making.

It is also important to keep in mind that we ought not to conflate *tanbai jiaodai*, a specific form of Maoist confession, with Foucault's historicization of confession in Victorian society, despite the similarity that—insofar as the officials who repressed sex ironically became the producer of sexual subjects—seems to confirm Foucault's famous assertion that resistance is internal to power relations, and the exertion of power generates multiple sites of unpredictable subversion. In *The History of Sexuality, Vol. 1*, Foucault stresses that techniques for regulating sexuality "were formed and, more particularly, applied first, with the greatest intensity, in the economically privileged and politically dominant classes" as "the bourgeoisie began by considering that its own sex was something important, a fragile treasure, a secret that had to be discovered at all costs."[32] For Foucault, sexuality was deployed not to limit the pleasure of others by the "ruling class," but to elaborate and establish the privileged classes through self-affirmation.

The socialist and Maoist tradition of criticism and self-criticism (*piping yu ziwo piping*) that informed *tanbai jiaodai* originated as a major mechanism of inner-party decision-making and discipline among Chinese political elites. It emerged as a form of mass mobilization and education during the Cultural Revolution, resulting from a series of structural changes in the Chinese system of communications.[33] Different from Foucauldian confession, which relied on religion and subjugated the subject to medical authority in order to distinguish a bourgeois ruling class, Chinese confession had a clear political purpose: to educate and transform wrongdoers, rather than

    SHANA YE

punish them. This mechanism of confession was supposed to serve a socialist ideology that advocated for eradicating class differences and homogenizing society under the rule of a single proletarian class.

If Foucauldian confession emphasizes constructing class differences and privileges through making distinct sexual subjects, Chinese confession is more ambiguous in terms of class difference and privilege. In China, socialist power operated in a complicated fashion in everyday life—here, the making of sexuality and sexual subject through confession was predicated on interactions of multilayered factors and desiring subjects. This understanding goes beyond the rigid analytic categories so often embedded in the study of Chinese socialism, such as "state" and "society," "party" and "people," and the "ruling class" and the "oppressed."

The protagonist of the *tanbai jiaodai* analyzed below is Zhang S. P., a thirty-four-year-old inventory worker in the province of Henan. Zhang's writings are from two distinct time periods: from October 12 to 25, 1973, and from July 31 to August 8, 1975, as he was called on to respectively confess and reconfess after his same-sex practices were disclosed.

In the first confession, dated October 12, 1973, Zhang begins with three lines of revolutionary doggerel that were common in Mao-era writings. He spends most of the pages describing how the proletarian revolution has triumphed across the world and how the Communist Party under the leadership of Chairman Mao has led the Chinese people to great victories. In this four-page confession, he only spends six lines in the middle of the second page vaguely describing his same-sex behaviors. He writes,

> Because my bourgeois worldview has not been completely transformed, and additionally I did not spend enough effort to study Mao Zedong's thoughts, and I was not well aware of the party's goals and class struggle, I committed such a mistake. One night I came back from the city and I did not go back to my dorm directly. Instead I went to a workmate's dorm. It was late, so I shared a bed with him. Then I started to touch his penis to see whose was longer. At the time, I thought it was just fooling around. I didn't think it was such a severe problem.[34]

A day later, on October 13, Zhang wrote another, supplementary confession. Differing from the first, the majority of the content Zhang details here involves sexual contact with a workmate, Little Wang. In this three-page additional document, Zhang reveals when he went to Little Wang's dorm, what their conversation was like, and how they went to bed together.

The twin-size bed in the dorm was very small, so we were very
close to each other. My hand was beside his penis and I felt he
had an erection. So I held his penis to see if his was longer than
mine. He moved a little and I thought I woke him up. So I stopped
and went to sleep.[35]

Although we do not know what happened between these two initial
confessions, the title of the second confession, *"Buchong cailiao"* (Supplementary material), suggests that the party committee was not satisfied with
Zhang's first confession—it included too much doggerel and too little information about the "crime." For the party committee, the sparse detail in the
first confession would have showed Zhang's lack of consciousness about his
crime's severity and his limited commitment to redeem his mistake.

Under the name of "completely transforming the bourgeois worldview"
and "return[ing] to the correct revolutionary road," seven days later, on
October 20, Zhang turned in another writing, revealing different details
about his "crime." In this version, he does not use the small bed as an excuse
for his sexual contact with Little Wang, and he discards the part about
comparing penis size. Instead, Zhang writes the following:

At first we slept on opposite sides of the bed. . . . Around 3:00
or 4:00 a.m., I woke up and saw Little Wang was still sleeping
soundly. I thought that he must be sleeping heavily because he
had drunk so much that day. I sat up and turned to his side of the
bed. . . . I put my hand into his underwear and started stroking
his penis. I got closer to him and started to put his penis into my
anus. I wanted to make him ejaculate.[36]

In his fourth confession, dated October 25, Zhang revises his story
again. This time, Zhang clarifies that the sexual incident was not spontane-
ous but planned:

Little Wang told me that [Little Wang and five other guys] had
drunk about four *jin* [two kilograms] of liquor today . . . so I
thought Little Wang must sleep very heavily tonight. I could
share the bed with him and play with his penis after he fell
asleep. . . . Around 11:00 p.m., Little Wang asked me if I had a
place to stay. I responded immediately, "No, my place is taken
by some guests."[37]

Reading these four confessions side by side, we see that Zhang's narrative of his sexual contact with Little Wang shifts from accidentally "fooling around" to actively planning and pursuing sex. Zhang's framing changes: from presenting himself as a passive actor who has made a mistake, he shifts toward portraying himself as an agentic subject who has actively carried out his own desires. His narrative's transition from "fooling around" to searching for the reasons behind his behavior indicates the emergence of agency in forming identity, self-understanding, and subjectivity.

Interestingly, in his fourth confession, Zhang also overtly admits to nonconsensual sex, which could be framed by the party committee as a more severe crime than illicit sex between men. It remains unknown if this change was due to Little Wang testifying and depicting Zhang as a rapist in order to sideline his own involvement in the sexual practice and avoid punishments during Zhang's confession. The change could also represent Zhang's attempt to protect Little Wang by portraying himself as the sexual initiator. But Little Wang's question of whether Zhang had a place to stay also offers the possibility that the sexual behavior in this case was consensual—Little Wang may have been alluding to having sex with Zhang as well. In all three readings, Zhang and Little Wang are active sexual subjects.

What is also interesting is that the transformation of Zhang's sexual self and the possibility for him to articulate that self were both made possible by the mechanism of socialist confession, which was intended to create and patrol proper class subjects at the cost of sexuality and gender. Originally, Zhang did not think it was "a big deal,"[38] but it seems likely that the party committee kept pushing, with or without violence, in order to shepherd Zhang back to the "correct revolutionary road." In his third confession, Zhang caters to such a need, admitting,

> When the party first asked me to confess and reflect on my mistake, I did not realize the severity of it. With the help of the party and other comrades, I realized that the occurrence of my mistake was by no means fortuitous. In the winter of two years ago, I played with another workmate's penis and made him ejaculate. But till today, I have not reported this mistake to the party. It led me to continue making mistakes.[39]

Regardless of whether he forgot or intentionally withheld the fact of his previous sexual encounter, Zhang's confession indicates that he had never clearly or thoughtfully reflected on his sexuality—or, at least, he had never had an opportunity to speak about it. The confession process guided him to remember his past and make a connection with the present. "The act of remembering one's past necessarily calls for interpreting one's old self," theorist Wenying Xu notes, and "illuminates the person's new identity."[40] Zhang had to see his past and present behaviors as consistent—a basis for a sense of coherent identity. His formation of identity took place through the process of forced confessions, fostered by both the state's desire to regulate citizen-subjects and the individual desires of representatives of the state— namely, the Communist Party officials, police, and legal functionaries.

Through multiple confessions, Zhang reconstructs an old, unconscious self and narrates the transition to an awareness of a new identity. Although the identity has no proper name at that time, it has potential for collective actions and community-building.

In a project that sets out to disrupt queer liberalism, the discussion of identity—a concept rooted in a specific Euro-American Enlightenment tradition—might be risky. Yet identity has held an important role in Chinese queer study since the late 1980s. In the early study of queer sexuality in China, a central debate featured the conflict between a unique premodern, pre-Western-imperialist sexual culture and a hybridized, globalization-influenced sexual culture. In his influential work on Chinese homosexuality, historian Chou Wah-shan makes a distinction between traditional Chinese homoeroticism and the translation of "homosexuality," emphasizing that "the notion of the homogenous, universal and gender-inclusive *gay* identity' did not exist in China." Chou explains, "Even when sexual activities are categorized, they never refer to a specific minority of people, but to specific behavioral practices that can involve everyone in certain social relations." As Chou suggests, unlike Foucault's homosexuals as a "species," nonnormative sexual subjects were never a "generic personality possessing a unique psycho-sexual essence."[41]

The question of whether Chinese nonnormative sexual subjects are a "species" with self-identification has been important to the history of queer emergence and politics. In the scholarship on nonnormative sexuality in China from the 1990s onward—either defined by sociological, medical, or psychological approaches,[42] or occurring within the transnational study of sexuality emphasizing the globalization of LGBT status through capitalism, intellectual institutions, or international NGO networks—the process of "naming" homosexual, LGBT, *tongzhi* ("comrade"), queer, and other categories of identity is crucial. It seems that only through naming is the queer subject able to become tangible, and therefore a political subject entitled to protection and rights.

     SHANA YE

This process of naming and identity politics is believed to be the basis for collective resistance. At the same time, the process raises a number of questions and problems—foremost among them, the problem of identity and colonialism. Historian Petrus Liu points out that "Chinese *tongzhi* studies often results in what Johannes Fabien has described as the 'allochronism' of racial time"; Liu notices that "a good way to denaturalize heterosexuality is to historicize the invention of the homosexual/heterosexual distinction, but the historicizing effort inevitably provokes debates about whether some human cultures are prehomosexual, prequeer and altogether different from the West."[43] In this light, if a distinct sense of gay identity came to shape in the late 1980s and early 1990s in China as the country started to integrate itself into the global economy, we could conclude that Chinese gayness is belated, therefore trapping ourselves in the colonialist logic of progressive lineal time. If an identity of sexually variant and gender-variant people existed before China's reform, on the other hand, we would argue for a unique and independent gay culture in China. This would then counter the import-export model of global gayness. Both ends of the spectrum are highly charged with the affects of either desire for global queering or Chinese exceptionalism.

Looking at how Cultural Revolution–era queers, such as our protagonist Zhang S. P., come to understand their sexual and political identity sheds new light on the dilemma of historicizing homosexuality. Zhang's construction of identity complicates the binary stance between Western imported identity and exceptionalist understanding of Chinese same-sex practices as solely behavioral. Cultural theorist Stuart Hall points out that identity is a linchpin for understanding the interplay of agency and structure in the social world; Hall conceptualizes identity and identification as a contextual, conditional process that responds to the changing material situations and discourses nonnormative subjects face. "I use 'identity to refer to the meeting point, the point of suture, between on the one hand the discourse and practices which attempt to 'interpellate,' speak to us or hail us into places as the social subjects of particular discourses, and on the other hand, the processes which produce subjectivities, which construct us as subjects which can be 'spoken,'" he writes. "Identities are thus points of temporary attachment to the subject positions which discursive practices construct for us."[44] As Zhang's confessions suggest, his sense of identity was constructed through the affective experience of being "interpellated" as a sodomite; but this discursive construction also formed a sense of a recognizable individual and collective subject position, resisting the reductionist, discursive naming of the "sodomy criminal."

Perhaps more intriguing is Hall's stress on "a radical historicization" in theorizing identity in order to capture the constantly transforming process of identity. He pushes queer historians and critics to think about questions of how to use "the resources of history, language and culture in the process of becoming rather than being." What holds more currency is "not 'who we are' or 'where we came from,'" but "what we might become, how we have been represented and how that bears on how we might represent ourselves."[45] Hall connects the subject of history and the viewer of that history; he asks for a historically specific understanding of changing processes of identity, while also asking for what purpose, and to whom, the question of identity matters. This is a valuable vantage point for postsocialist queer scholars, critics, and activists to attain when producing knowledge of queer history.

REPARATIVE READING OF SOCIALIST BODIES AND DESIRES

In one of his 1973 confessions, Zhang details how he attempted to convince another workmate, Little Li, to have sex with him. Zhang tells Little Li that "anal penetration is better than the New Year celebration" and "ejaculation feels better than all other things." He writes,

> I asked him, "Have you ejaculated before?" He said, "No." Then I asked, "Are you able to ejaculate?" He said, "I don't know." . . . I then stroked his penis for a while, and he said he was too tired because of work and he [was unable to] ejaculate.[46]

That Zhang frames his question as "Are you able to ejaculate?" (*Ni huibuhui liujing*?) may seem odd to present readers, as we generally assume that the ability to ejaculate is a natural bodily function of a potent adult man. Scholar Everett Zhang tells us, however, that since male bodily function was highly politicized and moralized during the Maoist period (and particularly in the Cultural Revolution), nonlaboring functions such as ejaculation, with the exception of involuntary nocturnal emission, were considered indulgent, immoral, and shameful.[47] Admitting the ability to ejaculate could put Little Li at risk of contravening Communist Party ideology.

At first glance, Zhang S. P.'s odd question and Li's response about losing sexual function because of work could indicate that bodies and sexualities disappeared within the Cultural Revolution[48]—that the official ideology sublimated all desires into desire to work for the revolution, desexualizing the actual body as a mere implement of socialist labor. However, this

SHANA YE

reading might risk reinforcing what Eve Kosofsky Sedgwick calls "paranoid reading"—a practice that aims to expose the already-known systemic oppression but does not necessarily follow what needs to be done about those hegemonic relations. Sedgwick further tells us that other forms of reading—for example, one involving a reparative motive and positionality—while rendered "invisible and illegible under a paranoid optic," are "not only important but also *possible*," and already well evident in queer experience.[49] To practice other-than-paranoid forms of knowing is to nurture an affective culture around the texts, histories, and subjects we engage that could facilitate plentitude, accretion, interruptive richness, and surprise. Such an affective culture would allow us to enjoy the pleasure and erotic fulfillment of such labor. The following pages experiment with such reparative methods through a rereading of Zhang's confessions.

As the confession unfolds, we learn that before Zhang entered Li's dorm, he peeked inside Li's window and caught Li playing with his own penis. Instead of exhaustion from work, the real explanation for Li's inability to ejaculate might lie in his having just masturbated. Both Zhang and Li are well aware of each other's indulgence in sexual pleasure—but instead of directly talking about sex, they engage in a conversational and sexual exchange made possible (and also conditioned by) the socialist ideology of work. By appropriating the official ideology, Zhang and Li insist on reinserting bodies and sexualities into the socialist discourse, resexualizing the desexualized socialist male body.

Historians Horacio Ramirez and Nan Boyd argue that "the sexuality of the body (or bodily desires) is an important, indeed material, aspect of the practice of doing oral history work," since "the body, and how and what it remembers . . . are particularly significant for narrators drawn to discussions of sexual consciousness, erotic desire, and gender expression."[50] The inseparable link between the body and oral history sheds light on how the subject in archival texts narrates, as well as how the historical subject and its readers interact. Zhang's first encounter with another queer body, when he spots his workmate's masturbation, can be seen as a site for potential productive knowledge about sex and communities; in fact, such knowledge production did happen, through a dance between a coding of unspeakable sexuality and the highly pronounced ideology of class. It is not sex that subjugates itself to class; instead, the language of class becomes a medium for the articulation of sex.

In late 1975, two years after Zhang's initial confession and at the final stage of the Cultural Revolution, he was caught again committing sodomy and called on to write *tanbai jiaodai*. Compared to his confessions in 1973,

in 1975 Zhang's writing style changes significantly: he is able to exercise
the skill of self-writing, and has become increasingly blatant about his sexuality. In all of his seven confessions from July 31 to August 8, 1975, Zhang
barely talks about the Communist Party, his bourgeois thoughts, or the
revolutionary road. He begins with a brief quote from Mao Zedong and
ends his confessions with two lines at most thanking the party's education and other comrades' support. In the content, Zhang enumerates basic
information about his sexual encounters with other workers, with minimal
narrative. Words such as "penis," "anus," "erection," and "ejaculation" appear
repeatedly in these pages. This change—his willingness only to provide
abstract words, rather than details—may signal Zhang's indifference toward
his crime and his resistance toward authority.

Yet a more dynamic reading is also possible: Zhang caters to the libidinal curiosity of the party committee members by teasing them with arousing words, but not fully fulfilling their desire to know, therefore leaving
imaginary space for fantasy. In Zhang's 1973 writings, the "root cause" of his
mistake was "bourgeois pornographic material and texts."[51] From this clue,
we can guess that Zhang was well aware that the unpublished stories that
he claimed had corrupted him had originated in past sexual criminal confessions.[52] He could also be aware that his own confessions might become
the source of unpublished copies that would be circulated to arouse other
individuals.

If we understand Zhang anticipating that his confession would be read
by his work unit's cadres, officials, and other potential audiences, we could
view Zhang's changing style as his intention to produce pornographic texts,
thus allowing him to be a pleasure producer rather than a denigrated criminal and repressed victim. We could also read Zhang's confession as opening
up space, in scholar Françoise Lionnet's words, for "the subject of history
and the agent of discourse" to "engage in dialogue with each other"[53] about
sexuality, violence, and power across past and future. This silent but potent
call for connection, a complex interplay of agency and conformity, is not
something current vocabularies of visibility and empowerment would capture. Refusal or inability to see the "opacity"[54] of Zhang's invitation to com-
municate about sex, desire, and pleasure with others through his *tanbai
jiaodai* embodies the unfortunate myopia of theorizing socialist queerness
from the perspective of global neoliberal desire.

As we can see from the above sections, beneath the surface of an individual who was supposed to sublimate himself to the party and the revolution—
as well as to a coercive culture that forced the private into the public—there

SHANA YE

was also a mixture of fear, deviation, desire, and pleasure. The oppressive apparatus and space where self-making was carried out led to unexpected outcomes, rendering the sexuality of state socialism queer. Marked by passion and tensions, the Chinese queer self was at odds not only with the official discourse of the revolution at the time, but also with the present representation of the past. Such an oddity, or queerness, leads back to political questions: How do we do queer history without simplifying historical injury? What are ethical relations that we, as queer historians, researchers, activists, and policymakers, could develop? And how do we imagine a radical queer politics that simultaneously attends to violence, damage, and homophobia as well as epistemological, affective, and methodological limitations of our own that closet ways of conceptualizing and being "queer"?

POWER AND PLEASURE IN "QUEER SOCIALISM"

I was surprised to learn recently that Zhang S. P. was still alive. I wanted to know what exactly had happened to him, how he felt when forced to confess, and how his life had turned out. Knowing that the pain, suffering, and pleasure of queer historical forebears mirror the pain, suffering, and pleasure of queers in the present could strengthen our queer community across time and place, and the touch of historical figures could reaffirm that no matter how difficult life was or is, "We're here. We're queer. Get (fucking) used to it!"[55]

But I also feared what Zhang might tell me. His *tanbai jiaodai* could have been read many ways by his coevals, historians, and future readers— he could be seen as a failed socialist man who seduced and corrupted his workmates, a desiring subject who pursued his sexual self and aroused others, a queer antihero whose coyness sexualized the party and the state, et cetera. The juiciness of these texts and the richness of their constitution and interpretations resist a prescriptive method that diminishes queer life to agendas organized around neoliberal values of consumer citizenship and homonationalist liberatory rhetoric. But what if the "real" Zhang was nothing like the one depicted in my readings and projections? Would the impulse to know resurrect the paranoid reading that these texts resist? Would "facts" from his own mouth obfuscate the imaginative close readings? Would my resistance to know in order to fertilize agentic reading of the past undermine the subject's own agency and desire in the present?

When I shared these concerns with a queer friend, he commented, "I've been wondering how come we haven't seen much BDSM-playing based on socialist plots, if socialism has impacted our culture and behaviors so deeply. When you were talking about Zhang and Little Li's conversation about being unable to ejaculate, I thought it could be a good source for an orgasm-denial play." As Zhang had surprised me by his writings, this remark surprised me by showing how historiography can be erotic, as bodies in historical encounters clash and become tools to "effect, figure, or perform that encounter."[56] There is never a set boundary between felt history and understood history. Cognitive and rational modes of apprehending history are often intertwined with the sensory and the emotional, opening space for inserting desires, pleasures, and surprises. The dichotomous construction of socialist oppression and postsocialist liberation has left us only one version of socialist sensory disposition: exalted abjection. If this disposition has disabled our erotic imagination and ability to feel pleasure in learning about the past, a reparative return to "queer socialism" then allows us to revive our bodily and epistemological ability to be surprised, to explore pleasure and eroticism in imaginative reading of historical encounters. For this very reason, I decided not to meet Zhang, so that other readers could be surprised and be encouraged to retell socialist history, presenting it in varied and surprisingly queerer ways.

NOTES

1   Wong, "'I Lived in Darkness.'"
2   Ibid.
3   Jeffreys and Yu, *Sex in China*, 5.
4   Honig, "Socialist Sex," 145.
5   See also Honig and Zhao, "Sent-down Youth and Rural Economic Development in Maoist China"; and Min, *Red Azalea*.
6   Arondekar, "In the Absence of Reliable Ghosts," 99.
7   Love, *Feeling Backward*, 3.
8   Halberstam, *In a Queer Time and Place*, 143.
9   Foucault, *The History of Sexuality, Vol. 1*, 101.
10 Love, *Feeling Backward*, 3.
11 Ibid., 5.
12 Puar, *Terrorist Assemblages*.
13 Rofel, *Desiring China*, 12.
14 Eng, "The Queer Space of China," 465.
15 Alexander, *Trauma*, 2.
16 Wang, *China's New Order*, 4–5.
17 Du, "From Taboo to Open Discussion," 134.
18 Ibid.
19 Ibid.

          SHANA YE

20 Historically speaking, China has no law against homosexuality, since homo-
    sexuality was not officially recognized by the state authority until 2004 (Guo,
    Zhongguo fashiyexiade tongxinglian, 61; Zhou, *Aiyue yu guixun*, 209; and
    Kang, "The Decriminalization and Depathologization of Homosexuality in
    China," 232). *Jijian* (sodomy) was criminalized under Qing dynasty laws as an
    illicit behavior (Sommer, *Sex, Law, and Society in Late Imperial China*, 119–
    30), a designation that continued in the state socialist era. "Hooliganism" is
    a broad category of illicit, punishable behaviors that include loitering, public
    indecency, and gang fights (Guo, *Zhongguo fashiyexiade tongxinglian*, 61; and
    Kang, "The Decriminalization and Depathologization of Homosexuality in
    China," 233). Male same-sex behavior was criminalized under the provisions
    of "disruption of social order," rather than as a sex crime (Kang, "The Decrim-
    inalization and Depathologization of Homosexuality in China," 233). During
    the Cultural Revolution, individuals who engaged in male same-sex practices
    were classified as *huai fenzi* (bad elements) in the revolutionary lexicon.

21 Alongside the archival sources discussed here, which I collected in the
    course of my fieldwork, a small number of similar archival sources have also
    been previously found and analyzed by legal scholars such as Xiaofei Guo
    and Dan Zhou as evidence for studying socialist laws. See Guo, *Zhongguo
    fashiyexiade tongxinglian*; and Zhou, *Aiyue yu guixun*.

22 See the 1957 Heilongjiang province Supreme Court case in Kang, "The
    Decriminalization and Depathologization of Homosexuality in China,"
    235–36.

23 In original material I collected.

24 Kang, "The Decriminalization and Depathologization of Homosexuality."

25 For example, the Lesbian Herstory Archives in Brooklyn, New York, and the
    GLBT Historical Society archives in San Francisco.

26 Cvetkovich, *An Archive of Feelings*, 8.

27 Marshall et al., "Queering Archives," 2.

28 Windscript, "Hopes and Collisions."

29 Ye, "Keeping a Diary in China."

30 Meng, "Female Image and National Myth," 124.

31 Halberstam, *In a Queer Time and Place*, 6.

32 Foucault, *The History of Sexuality, Vol. 1*, 120–21.

33 Dittmer, "The Structural Evolution of 'Criticism and Self-Criticism,'" 709.

34 Zhang S. P., October 12, 1973.

35 Zhang S. P., October 13, 1973.

36 Zhang S. P., October 20, 1973.

37 Zhang S. P., October 25, 1973.

38 Zhang S. P., October 12, 1973.

39 Zhang S. P., October 20, 1973.

40 Xu, "Agency via Guilt in Anchee Min's *Red Azalea*," 208.

41 Chou, *Tongzhi*, 22–23.

42   Li and Wang, *Tamende Shijie*; Zhang, Beichuan, *Tongzinglian*; Fang, *Tong-xinglian zai Zhongguo*; and Pan, *Zhongguo Xinggemming Zonglun*.

43   Liu, *Queer Marxism in Two Chinas*, 47.

44   Hall and du Gay, *Questions of Cultural Identity*, 5–6.

45   Ibid., 4.

46   Zhang S. P., October 20, 1973.

47   Zhang, "The Birth of *Nanke* (Men's Medicine) in China," 498.

48   See Meng, "Female Image and National Myth," 124.

49   Sedgwick, *Touching Feeling*, 127, 147, 150 (emphasis in original).

50   Ramirez and Boyd, *Bodies of Evidence*, 1, 7.

51   Zhang S. P., October 25, 1973.

52   In my fieldwork, many men who engaged in same-sex behaviors revealed that they had learned about sexuality from "hand-copied books" (*shouchao ben*). Some of these books were created by policemen or people who had interrogated former confessions. In Zhang's 1973 confessions, he wrote that he had written many pornographic texts; these texts were hand-copies. It is my speculation that Zhang might know these texts were from former confessions.

53   Lionnet, *Autobiographical Voices*, 193.

54   De Villiers, *Opacity and the Closet*, 2–7.

55   A rallying slogan popularized by AIDS activist organization Queer Nation in the 1990s.

56   Freeman, *Time Binds*, 95.

CHAPTER 8

THE IRONY OF SIZE

Male Smallness and the Rise of China

EVERETT YUEHONG ZHANG

IN OUTPATIENT CLINICS IN BOTH BEIJING AND CHENGDU, WHERE I was conducting fieldwork on the "epidemic of impotence," I often heard men worry about the small size of their penises.[1] The intensity of this worry extended far beyond the clinic. One evening in the early 2000s, I attended the live broadcast of *Whispering* (Qiaoqiao hua), a well-known sex-education radio call-in show in Tianjin that featured a male doctor of Chinese medicine. Such call-in shows had become popular since the 1990s.[2] I was unexpectedly asked by Ms. Liu, the host of the show, to join the doctor in taking listeners' questions. One of the questions was about penis size. An eighteen-year-old man thought, on the basis of his observations in the public shower room, that his penis was abnormally small compared to those of other men. As a result, he no longer dared to go to the shower room, as he could not bear to have others see his genitals. Without thinking too carefully, I said:

> This is a rather common anxiety. In my current fieldwork, I've
> been in contact with many patients who were worried about
> their small penises. In general, the worry was unnecessary. Many
> men became aware of the length of their penises by comparing
> them with other people's penises. But the way they made these
> comparisons was not accurate.
>
> First, what matters about the penis is its length in erection.
> If a penis can become long enough to penetrate after erection, its
> length is fine. Science has emphasized time and time again that

the length of the penis is not the most important factor in helping a female partner to reach orgasm.

Second, in Chinese history, there have been cases of *suoyangzheng* [the syndrome of penis-shrinking]. This syndrome is actually anxiety that leads one to believe that his penis is not only becoming smaller and smaller, but also shrinking into the body.

Another characteristic of Chinese society in the past that worsened this anxiety was that there was not much private space for taking a shower or bath, so most people had to go to a public shower room. Those who were worried about their small penises often discovered that everyone else in the shower room had a bigger penis. Once, I told a man who was worried about his penis: "Look, since everyone who thinks he has a small penis feels it is too shameful to go to the public shower room and so always stays away from it, all you can see in the public shower rooms are the bigger ones." This is another place where people make erroneous comparisons.

I know there have been a good number of studies about the size of the penis in China. Doctors like Shi Chengli in Gansu, Cao Jian in Beijing, and someone in Shanghai all did surveys about this. The studies showed a wide range of variation in size.

Even though I had tried to touch on Chinese aspects of this anxiety, I had framed the issue scientifically and treated it not too differently from the way psychologists in Western countries deal with "size anxiety."[3] And missing from my discussion was any mention of race or ethnicity, both of which figure prominently in people's perceptions about their bodies. What were difficult to address in my limited time on the air were the questions of whether worry about small penis size reflected a collective anxiety shared by many Chinese and, if so, why this would be the case at a time when the Chinese nation was moving to a level of prosperity and strength not seen before.

The sense of inadequacy in Chinese masculinity and its connection with the nation have been examined in Chinese studies.[4] Yuejin (Eugene) Wang analyzes a "femininity complex" in Chinese masculinity in which "feminine wits" outdo overblown masculine figures—a scenario facing a new fascination with "tough guys" in foreign movies.[5] The anthropological fieldwork discussed here explores a sentiment about Chinese male sexual inadequacy and its unique conditions—how the experience of the individual body has

     EVERETT YUEHONG ZHANG

informed and been reinforced by the developmental status of the Chinese nation. The "small male sexual organ" stands as a legitimate articulation of the desire to become "big." Ironically, the desire to strive solely for "bigness" could reveal an unenlightened "smallness" in the psyche, even amidst the rise of China.

TWO TYPES OF "SMALLNESS"

In some cases, doctors consider a small penis to be a real problem of physical underdevelopment. In other cases, doctors call men's concern about small penis size "unnecessary anxiety." Mr. Sima, a twenty-year-old migrant worker from Hebei, came to the clinic where I was doing fieldwork to complain about his small penis. He'd had sex with his girlfriend three or four times, and he'd had no problems achieving erection or penetrating her. But because he had heard people say that his penis was small, he tried to hide it from his girlfriend, particularly when it was flaccid. He told his examining doctor, "When I took a shower in the public shower room, I felt that other people's were bigger. So I don't go to public shower rooms anymore. Now I only take a bath in the company's bathroom, or I simply wash my body at home."

The doctor asked Mr. Sima, "Since you have no problem having sex, what's wrong with the penis, even if it looks small when flaccid?" Mr. Sima responded, "I feel I am not normal." The doctor, a bit impatiently, asked, "Then tell me: How 'abnormal' are you?"

Mr. Sima replied, "Its function is normal, but its size isn't. It's over ten centimeters long when erect, but only four centimeters long when flaccid."

The doctor asked Mr. Sima to drop his pants and show him his penis. After taking a look at it, the doctor raised his little finger, saying, "If your penis is like this, it's small." Then, he raised his thumb, saying, "If your penis is like this, it's not small at all." The doctor was trying to convince Mr. Sima that length was not the only indicator of penis size; diameter and other measures also had to be taken into account.

Mr. Nie, a twenty-six-year-old salesman for an Internet company, and Mr. An, a thirty-nine-year-old civil servant, also complained about their small penises; both men had originally come to see doctors about premature ejaculation, but their concern with penis size came up in their consultations. Unlike Mr. Sima, Mr. Nie and Mr. An were Beijingers; both had college educations, and both were professionals. It seems that the preoccupation with smallness was not limited to one stratum of society.

The large number of cases involving size anxiety in *nanke* (men's medicine) prompted me to conduct a survey about men's (and in a separate set of questions, women's) perceptions of the penis. I carried out the survey among two groups: *nanke* patients and college students (the latter group containing both men and women).[6] I asked, "Is it the case that the bigger the penis, the better?" Those who responded "yes" made up a small percentage of respondents.

Then I asked the male survey respondents, "What do you think of your penis in terms of size?" The majority considered their penises to be average-sized, but those who considered theirs smaller than average outnumbered those who considered theirs bigger than average—by a two to one margin in Chengdu, and by a seven to one margin in Beijing.

The answers to the last question in my survey were most revealing. I asked male respondents to choose between the following two hypothetical situations: "Would you rather have a twelve-centimeter (nearly five-inch) penis and be 165 centimeters (about five feet five inches) tall, or would you rather be 180 centimeters (about five feet eleven inches) tall and have an eight-centimeter (about three-inch) penis?" Among the *nanke* patients of both Beijing and Chengdu, the majority (71.4 percent and 73.8 percent, respectively) went with the first choice: a longer penis but a shorter body. They did so even though only a small percentage had responded that a bigger penis is better (19.5 percent in Beijing and 13.1 percent in Chengdu). A clear majority preferred a longer penis over greater body height, even though a Chinese folk saying has called men shorter than 170 centimeters (five feet seven inches) *ban canfei* ("half crippled"). Responding to the same question, 52 percent of the male college students preferred greater penis size to greater height; 48 percent preferred the reverse. This result showed that, among the two groups of men, the impotence patients were more inclined to worry about small penis size. (When asked, though, about penis size comparison between Chinese men and white Westerners, patients' and male students' responses were quite consistent.)

Despite men's reluctance to endorse the extreme position ("the bigger, the better"), their general preference for a longer penis rather than a taller body demonstrated that an "average-sized" (eight-centimeter-long) penis was not the ideal for many men. The survey results suggest a desire for optimal male potency, represented by the size of the sexual organ. This desire does not come out of a neutral place; instead, it emerges from a historical context wherein nothing is neutral or natural, and the average can sink into abnormality. Being "average" here indicates a body size short of normality, a masculinity not up to the standard, and a deficiency that seems primordial and perpetual.

ESSENTIALIZED ANXIETY

Under what conditions did the average size of the Chinese male become "abnormal"? Where does normality lie? It is tempting to infer that penis envy is an essential male Chinese worry, passed down from premodern times to modern times. But it's perhaps more interesting to ask, Has the practice of modernity in China exacerbated men's worries about penis size?

The small penis has long been a medical concern in Chinese history. Pre-Qin Mawangdui scripture records prescriptions of *nanxing meiyao* (masculinity-enhancing medicine) for penile enlargement.[7] Prescriptions to cure *yujingxiao* (small jade stem—that is, a small penis) were recorded in medical literature of the Song period (960–1279) that was based on literature from previous periods.[8]

Some literary representations in ancient China suggest that women enjoy large penises—particularly women characterized as especially luscious.[9] Other texts focused on bedchamber arts, meanwhile, downplay the importance of size.[10] But even the need to downplay size's importance implies that men had an exaggerated concern about the matter. In Li Yu's pornographic novel *The Carnal Prayer Mat* (Rouputuan), written in the Ming period, Weiyang Sheng, the hero, feels humiliated by his small penis after another man comments on it, even though his wife seems satisfied. In desperation, he gets help from a *shushi* (adept) who teaches the bedchamber arts. The adept implants a dog's erect penis in Weiyang's penis. Weiyang gains sexual power through this huge, half-human, half-beast penis; it enables him to realize his ambition of sleeping with all the beautiful women in the world.

Leaving aside the plot point of extreme genital transformation, what is noteworthy about this novel is that Weiyang Sheng's unease about his small penis size results from another man's comments and Weiyang's own subsequent constant self-comparison with other men. Driven by this unease, Weiyang singlemindedly pursues enlargement in defiance of common sense; he ignores warnings that the large size he aspires to would hurt virgins and young women, and he also flouts social norms by ignoring the damage the transplanted dog penis could do to his reproductive ability. Weiyang eventually suffers consequences for his extreme sexual lust; his wife becomes a prostitute and encounters him, without his being aware of her identity, in a brothel, where she commits suicide. After being beaten up by other clients, he recognizes his wife. In desperation and agony, he castrates himself, mutilating the source of his pleasure as well as his anguish. The critical overtone of the caricatured pursuit of a large penis and the anxiety about smallness was obvious.[11]

Based on his study of erotic fictions, particularly those of the Ming period, scholar Keith McMahon makes an argument for the historical discontinuity of penis envy in China: "Although I am all for looking for continuity between 'premodern' and 'modern,'" he states, "I think that contemporary complexes of impotence, while often retrieving premodern material or auras, are very different. . . . The contemporary scene is heavily mediated by intrusions between it and the premodern formation."[12] Men certainly experienced inadequacy in premodern times—but it can be argued that this feeling of inadequacy was transformed into a complex of the Chinese by encounters with the West in modern and contemporary times. If Weiyang Sheng aims to have a bigger penis in order to "outdo women" in his time, then, as McMahon argues, under modernity, many men want to have a bigger penis in order to win the male competition by "outdoing other men." This argument might imply that as male dominance over women's bodies tended to weaken, the anxiety to outdo other males grew.

Among both male clinic patients and male college students, more of my survey respondents believed that white Western men had a bigger penis than Chinese men than believed African American men had a bigger penis. In two separate questions (comparing white Western males with Chinese males, and comparing black males with Chinese males), among clinic patients, 62 percent in Beijing and 64 percent in Chengdu believed white Westerners had a bigger penis in response to the former question, whereas only 45 percent in Beijing and 59 percent in Chengdu gave the size advantage to black men in response to the latter question. Among college students, 62 percent in Beijing and 65 percent in Chengdu assigned the larger size to white Westerners in response to the former question, whereas about 50 percent in Beijing and 53 percent in Chengdu gave it to black men in response to the latter question. These results might contradict some racial stereotypes in the US analyzed by identity politics critiques. "African American men are overmasculinized studs" (akin to "the mindless body" in anthropologists Paulla Ebron and Anna Tsing's formulation), "while Chinese American men are feminized nerds" (akin to "the bodyless mind"), because the white man stands in between as the norm.[13] This norm was perceived by the Chinese respondents in my surveys as even more unilinear and absolute.

  EVERETT YUEHONG ZHANG

I once asked a doctor whether studies existed documenting the "normal size" of the "Chinese penis" or, more specifically, the "Han Chinese penis." I was told that there had been quite a few; I eventually collected sixteen such studies, a collection that's likely far from complete. Table 8.1 gives a sense of what the studies were about.

Several characteristics of these studies deserve to be noted. First, fifteen of the sixteen studies were conducted over the last two decades of the twentieth century, suggesting an increasing concern about penis size occurring exactly in the midst of the post-Mao reform (from the late 1970s to the present). The timing does not seem coincidental.

Second, even though Beijing and Shanghai were the two major sites for these studies, provinces such as Gansu in the northwest, Jilin in the northeast, Shandong in the east, Sichuan in the southwest, and Guangxi in the south were also covered. The research populations of the sixteen surveys varied; some were defined on the basis of province-wide systematic random sampling, whereas others were special populations (military personnel, schoolchildren, college students, men about to get married, and clinic patients). Researchers ranged from nationally known urologists to county clinic practitioners; research interest in the issue seems to have spread rhizomically and extensively.

The primary motivation behind the studies, according to several researchers—including Dr. Shi Chengli, who pioneered penis size research in China in the 1950s and 1960s—was to collect data for use in the manufacture of condoms. But, in the 1980s and 1990s, this motivation gave way, gradually but steadily, to others, until ultimately the major research goal was to generate data about what was "normal." In answering the question "What is the normal size of a Chinese penis?" an individual organ could be designated "abnormal" by falling outside the normal range at either end, large or small. Interestingly, though, most of the research gravitated toward addressing the ultimate question "How small is too small?"

THE SLIPPERY TRUTH AND THE REAL ANXIETY

From a statistical perspective, an *average* penis size might be considered *normal*. But people's concern about normality entails more than establishing what is average. In his famous midcentury work *The Normal and the Pathological*, the French physician and philosopher Georges Canguilhem

	Name of study	Principal investigator	Date of publication and research location	Number of men measured	Ages
1	A report measuring penis size and the size of condoms made in China	Shi Chengli	1963 Lanzhou, Gansu	1,412	20–30
2	The criteria for normal external reproductive organ size of Chinese adult males	Liu Guozheng	1981 Beijing	1,000	18–30
3	An investigation of sexual development of 470 young and adolescent males	Jiang Yu	1985 Shanghai	470	7–18
4	An analysis of the result of measuring 464 normal children's scrotums and penises	Liu Yibin	1986 Changsha	464	0–14
5	The normal size of the penises of adult males in Zibo city	Wang Cunzhang	1987 Zibo	846	18–57
6	An investigation of 2,029 adult males' reproductive organs	Zhang Sixiao	1988 Sichuan	2,029	Over 18
7	A comparison in penis size between ethnic Han and Korean young and middle-aged males	Jin Changtao	1988 Yanji	884	Over 18
8	An analysis of the measurement of the penises and scrotums of 990 men in Shanghai as premarital checkup	Zhu Huibin	1990 Shanghai	990	Over 20
9	A report on the results of measuring the penises of 1,149 married men	Xing Guowu	1990 Chifeng	1,149	20–40
10	An exploration of the method of measuring the penis and its normality	Wu Weicheng	1992 Beijing	2,547	Average 19.4
11	An analysis of the results of measuring 2,906 adult males' scrotums and penises	Xie Yuhua	1992 The Navy	2,906	17–40
12	A discussion of the relationship between scrotum and penis size and marital or reproductive life	Zhu Huibin	1993 Shanghai	868	Average 28.9
13	A report on the flaccid and erect penis sizes of 300 men	Feng Yuming	1994 Jinshan, Shanghai	300	Average 23.6
14	An investigation of infertile males' penis size	Huang Yufeng	1999 Shanghai	500	Over 18
15	A report of 220 normal males' penis lengths in erection	Zhang Puzhong	1999 Tianjin	220	20–40
16	An analysis of the result of measuring 500 men's penis size	Qin Zhengxing	1999 Nanning	500	22–33

Sources: Shi et al., "Yinjing tiji"; Liu and Cao, "Zhongguo chengren"; Jiang et al, "470 li"; Liu, "Zhengcheng ertong"; Wang et al., "Ziboshi chengren"; Zhang et al., "2,029"; Jin et al., "Chaoxianzu"; Xing and Tian, "1,149"; Zhu et al, "Shanghaishi"; Wu and Lu, "Yinjing celiang"; Xie et al., "2,906 li"; Zhu and Chen, "Gaowan yinjing"; Feng and Zhu, "300 li"; Huang and Xu, *Nanke zhenduanxue*; Zhang et al., "220 li"; and Qin et al., "500 ming."

disputed the idea that normality is based on statistical truth; he placed concern about health at the center of the discourse concerning normality. In Canguilhem's formulation, it's not statistical truth—the average—but the ability of the body to adapt to its surroundings that is important.[14] Canguilhem argued against absolutism in understanding the body and health, putting resilience first in judging the normal against the pathological. From this point of view, the penis size surveys listed above were overshadowed by the sense that an absolute standard existed by which to judge penis size in the specific social world of Chinese modernity.

Dr. Shi and his fellow researchers made comparisons with the limited data they had managed to obtain about average size in foreign countries— primarily, the United States. This use of foreign data forced comparisons between the Han Chinese and white Westerners. Shi et al. conducted their work in the early 1950s, from 1950 to 1956; the non-Chinese data they used for comparison were from two works in English (a 1949 work on human sexual anatomy by Robert Latou Dickinson, and the 1952 work *Urological Pathology* by Dr. Peter A. Herbut) and one work in Chinese published in 1950.[15] Because of the implicit comparison of the Chinese norm with the "international" norm (primarily the Western norm), the results of most of the studies since the 1980s produced a dilemma. Those studies found that most Chinese men's worries about small penis size were groundless, and that they did not deviate significantly from the average size. However, most of the studies done in the 1980s and 1990s determined a smaller average size than Shi's early study had[16]—perhaps in part because methods for measuring penis length were more clearly defined.

EXPERIENCING "SMALLNESS"

My survey asked male respondents about their beliefs regarding the relative penis sizes of white Western men, Chinese men, and African American men. Of the *nanke* patients I surveyed, over 60 percent (62.4 percent in Beijing and 63.9 percent in Chengdu) believed that Chinese men had smaller penises than did Western white men. Among male college students, 61.5 percent held the same view.

How did they develop this perception or belief? The penis-size surveys discussed above were published mostly in medical journals; most men were not likely to have been familiar with them. The perception more likely came from comparisons the men made in their everyday lives.

One opportunity for men to compare their bodies with other men's occurred in the process of relocating from rural areas to urban ones. Mr. Guo, a twenty-one-year-old security guard at a state-owned company in Beijing, was originally from a rural area in Shandong. He had first had sex at fourteen, when a girl of twelve came to play in his home. He said the sex was consensual. "She didn't even have pubic hair or breasts. I entered her; she said she felt pain, so I withdrew. Later, I had sex with her many times," he recalled. Something had changed, though, in Guo's perception of his own body since he'd moved to Beijing. He continued:

> When I was growing up in the rural area, I saw other people's penises, but didn't pay much attention to them. Last year, I came to Beijing. I often took a shower in the public shower room, finding that my penis was smaller than others'. I now live with seven men in the employee dormitory room of the company. I started to regret that I had sex so early with the girl. I also regret that I masturbated almost every day for quite a while when I was going to high school. I think [those experiences] had a bad impact on the development of my penis.

Guo "discovered" his small penis after coming to the city at the age of twenty. The public shower room was where he built his perception of the smallness of his penis. (Most patients in my survey—76.7 percent in Beijing and 68.9 percent in Chengdu—became aware of their penis size in public shower rooms, as did 69.4 percent of male college students.) After his discovery, Mr. Guo started to subscribe to the ideal of a large penis.

Over the past several decades in China, massive migration of peasants has involved an extensive restructuring of the relationship between rural residents and city dwellers. From the 1980s onward, the flow of migrant workers disrupted the order of the socialist past with its centralized control of the border between the city and the countryside, intensifying to reach the level of over 200 million persons a year. The number was over 262 million in 2012; among them, 163 million worked beyond local townships.[17] While physically surviving the new challenge of city life, migrant workers faced a restructuring of their self-perception in the new world of urban consumption. Their perception of their own bodies also shifted as they were made naked in their new surroundings.

Mr. Guo's experience was not universal. Some migrant workers I interviewed mentioned radically different experiences. One man from a village in Hubei recalled how he had been slightly terrified upon seeing the naked

        EVERETT YUEHONG ZHANG

body and big penis of a military man bathing in the river in his village. An artist from Shaanxi recalled a game his peers had played in the countryside, where his family had been sent for political reasons: young boys went into a hillside cave, took off their pants, and masturbated together while shouting out the name of a girl in the village, singling out a different girl each time. They even competed to see who had the biggest and hardest penis, which was determined by hanging a sickle on each boy's erect member. This kind of masculine competition could be seen in many places. But the particular implication of such competition for men like Mr. Guo—members of the "floating population," a term describing a growing population that consisted primarily of migrant workers (*nongmingong*), who started to move around and have worked regularly in cities as wage laborers since the 1990s—was the deficiency it revealed in their lives. That sense of deficiency ignited a desire for self-transformation—a desire to replace poverty with affluence, to be modern. Moreover, the migrant-worker experience in China signified the existence of a hegemonic definition of modernity, in terms of a standard, normal, and, in the end, ideal mode for the body and life. In psychoanalytic terms, those men's self-identification coalesced around not just a penis, but a large penis. As the physicist and postcolonial critic Homi Bhabha writes, "Identity is never a priori, nor a finished product; it is only ever the problematic process of access to an image of totality."[18] For men like Mr. Guo, subscribing to the ideal of bigness constituted a primary psychodynamic striving for masculine totality that could also fuel an unfulfilled, unrealizable desire in the symbolic world at a distance.

Comparisons of penis size were not confined to the shower room, but were explicit or implicit aspects of many activities. They surfaced, for instance, when men watched pornographic videos, which had become a widespread practice by the late 1990s. Pornographic videos, VCDs (video compact diskettes), and DVDs (digital discs) were produced in Hong Kong, Taiwan, Japan, Korea, and mainland China. Most porn products featured Asians, and not unusually featured Westerners, such as Americans. In the clinic, few who watched such videos reported deriving satisfaction from it; doing so, for many, led to the discovery or reinforcement of a feeling of "smallness."

Mr. Cui, a thirty-three-year-old civil servant, showed me an advertisement for penile enlargement surgery. The ad boasted that one month after surgery, the penis would grow by five centimeters. Even though Cui's clinical problem was premature ejaculation, his worry about "smallness" was obvious. "I started to watch pornography as soon as I could buy it in the street," he recalled. "After a while, I became bored with it, because the scenes of intercourse were all basically repetitive thrusting. *Yangren* [Westerners'] penises were indeed very big—compared to theirs, my own is only about ten centimeters when erect, and very small when flaccid."

Mr. Yan, a thirty-nine-year-old engineer, also came to see the doctor about premature ejaculation. He, too, had size concerns. He had started to watch pornography in his twenties (in the 1980s). After watching, he felt that his penis was too small.

Mr. Qiu, a twenty-five-year-old worker, suffered from erectile difficulty. He recalled watching pornography (that featured Westerners) for the first time in 1995 at a coworker's home. He concluded from this experience that Westerners were physically strong and that their *xingqiguan* (sexual organs) were big—larger, he said, than the average Chinese man's.

Pornography that contained images of Westerners and other sources of erotic imagination contributed to what might be called a worship of bigness. One migrant worker from Anhui said, with a naïve, awestruck look on his face, "I heard that the penises of the Soviets were big—when erect, they could strike the ground." He didn't mention ever having watched pornography. His "knowledge" about the phallic superiority of the Soviets had a Cold War–era flavor, from before the Soviet Union fell apart in the early 1990s. The legendary size of the *yangren* penis (here, the Soviets were racially equated with Westerners) predated the era of "voyeurism gone national"—a time in the 1990s in which watching pornography became increasingly common across society and was not confined to one section or layer of society, but was less permissible than it would be later.[19] It seemed that increasing access to images of Western bodies had reinforced an established sense of the inferiority of Chinese men's bodies, sexual organs, and potency.

ZHANG JINGSHENG'S APPEAL

In 1927, Zhang Jingsheng, a professor of philosophy at Peking University, published an article entitled "The Aesthetics of Sex" in the journal *New Culture.* Zhang Jingsheng was known for his liberal philosophy; he advocated building a new society by changing the Chinese outlook on issues of love, sex, physical and ethical education, and so on. He promoted a utopian society, organized around the aesthetics and ethics of love and beauty.

Zhang's liberal philosophy concerning sexuality—and his controversial experiment in soliciting and publishing autobiographies of people's sex lives in the summer of 1925—won him the nickname "Dr. Sex." He launched an attack on Chinese culture by denouncing the Chinese body, which he considered unsexy and even ugly; Zhang criticized Chinese men for having an underdeveloped *yangbu* ("*yang* part," or penis). He claimed, "Sexual beauty doesn't exist in either the Chinese male or female. The ugliness lies at the reversal of male and female. The male is feminized, the spirit of virility being turned into a pale-faced scholar. . . . Because of the weak *xingbu* [sexual part, or penis] of the Chinese male, he has feeble limbs, and is low-spirited."[20]

Zhang argued that the way Chinese people made love was responsible for men's feminization. Because Chinese men and women were not fully engaged in a state of abandon and pleasure when having sex, he believed, the male and female embryonic elements could not completely separate: "It's no wonder that after the male grows up, he doesn't have a beard, nor does he have a developed *yangju* ["*yang* instrument"—an alternative term for penis]. . . . He looks inert, like a woman."[21] He concluded, "Most of the men in our country suffer from impotence, and ejaculate as soon as they barely have an erection."[22]

To be sure, Zhang Jingsheng was an unconventional scholar, even compared to the pioneers of the May Fourth movement. His works on sexuality had been unavailable to Chinese readers in the People's Republic of China from 1949 until the late 1990s, but his portrayal of the Chinese body—particularly, the "weakness" of Chinese male sexuality—was echoed in self-critiques of Chinese culture in the 1980s, when China was opened to the outside world.

OPEN TO NEW COMPARISONS

Comparisons between the Chinese body and the Western body took different forms in Maoist China than they did during the Republican period. Direct quantitative comparisons were greatly limited during the Cold War because of China's isolation during that period. Still, some comparative studies were done. Shi, Liu and Zhang's Mao-era penis-size survey, referred to above, measured the penis size of about 1,400 men and compared the results to the available foreign data.[23]

The later Chinese studies of penis size I collected (from the 1980s and 1990s), as noted, reported smaller average sizes than the Mao-era study did. This discrepancy may stem from the shock effect of the encounter with the outside world in the post-Mao era. In the Maoist period, particularly during the Cultural Revolution, direct contact with Westerners was a rarity, particularly in places beyond Beijing and Shanghai. I remember walking one evening in 1973 in downtown Chongqing when, suddenly, someone shouted with excitement, "Look! Foreigners! Foreigners!" Everyone walking along the street stopped to look at a procession of vans passing by, whose passengers were looking back at them no less curiously. The vans were carrying members of one of the earliest US delegations to China after Richard Nixon's historic visit in 1972; they were traveling through the city on their way to the Three Gorges on the Yangtze River. To the pedestrians on the street, the Westerners looked like Martians. (Around the same time, I heard that a curious crowd had followed foreigners walking in downtown Chongqing and had caused traffic jams.)

It is no wonder that, after the isolation of the Maoist era ended, many ordinary Chinese, who had been told that two-thirds of the world's population were *shenghuo zai shuishen huore zhi zhong* ("living under deep water and scorching heat"—that is, living miserable lives), were fascinated by the mere sight of foreigners. During the high tide of the Cultural Revolution, historian Joseph Levenson at Berkeley famously predicted, "China will join the world again on the cosmopolitan tide."[24] But joining the world was not as smooth as it might look. Its psychological impact disturbed the sediments of historical memory. I heard people express eye-opening experiences while watching a television report showing the house of an ordinary working family in Detroit around the time of Vice Premier Deng Xiaoping's visit to the United States in 1979: "Look, they're workers—they have everything we don't have!" This was also the time when the masculine images of "real men" represented by Sylvester Stallone and Takakura Ken made inroads with Chinese audiences. It was in this larger context that studies found the average size of the Chinese penis to be smaller than earlier studies had.

PENIS WORSHIP AND *SHANGHAI BABY*

As the Chinese penis shrank in scientific studies, the Western penis grew in some popular discourse. Since the mid-1980s, many literary works in China have dealt with the topic of impotence. The most graphic portrayal of the contrast between the potent Western man and the impotent Chinese man is found in Wei Hui's 1999 novel *Shanghai Baby* (Shanghai baobei). Coco, the heroine, who is in her twenties, has sexual relationships with two men: her Chinese boyfriend, Tiantian, and her German lover, Mark. The two men are depicted in direct contrast to each other in terms of masculinity. Tiantian, a helpless drug addict and parasite who relies on his mother to survive, suffers from impotence. He is unable to give Coco, the woman insatiably searching for her identity through sexual fulfillment, what she wants. In contrast, Mark, a businessman in Shanghai, aggressively pursues Coco and satisfies her with his sexual prowess (and, significantly, with his large penis). The portrayal of Mark's sexual organ focuses on its threatening size and the ostensible jouissance Coco discovers in the mixture of pain and pleasure that it provides:

> Then he enters me; his gigantic penis scares me and makes me feel pain in the swelling. . . .
>
> I see long-legged Mark at the intersection of Yongfu Road and Fuxing Road. He dresses up neat and fragrant, standing under the streetlamp as though he'd just walked out of a movie and floated over the Pacific Ocean. My foreign lover has a pair of beautiful, mesmerizing blue eyes, unmatchable protruding buttocks, and that big stuff that scares me to death. . . .
>
> His stuff, which looks like it is made of rubber, is forever in erection, never admitting any defeat, never showing any look of fatigue.[25]

Even though, in the end, Mark returns to Germany to be with his wife and family, leaving Coco dissatisfied by their lustful yet empty relationship and confused about who she is, worship of the Western phallus builds throughout the story. Tiantian, meanwhile, eventually dies of his drug addiction; his masculinity withers away.

The worship of the Western phallus portrayed in *Shanghai Baby* may be extreme. But my conversations with many people—men and women, professionals and migrant workers, rich entrepreneurs and laid-off workers, cadres and college students—revealed agreement, often taken for granted, that the Western male sexual body was superior to that of the Chinese male. Even the sexual jokes I encountered in the late 1990s, in Beijing and Chengdu, were illuminating in this regard. Consider these two examples:

> Jiang Zemin, president of China, is having dinner with Bill Clinton, president of the United States, in a Western restaurant. They order the same food, but are served differently. Clinton is served a sausage with two boiled eggs; Jiang is served a toothpick with two grapes.

> Deng Xiaoping wants to improve his potency, so he goes to the United States and has surgery to replace his penis with somebody else's. After the surgery, he's more potent than ever. Seeing the miracle in Deng, Yang Shangkun, the former president of China, follows in Deng's footsteps and has the same kind of surgery in the United States. Unfortunately, his potency doesn't

improve. Disappointed, he consults with Deng. Deng offers to take a look at Yang's new stuff. As soon as he sees Yang's new penis, Deng says, "No wonder yours isn't working. The one you have now was originally mine!"

These jokes deploy the technique of separation—separating ordinary people from their leaders and making the leaders the butts of ridicule. These jokes also draw a distinction between the better-off (Deng, in his successful "grafting" of the West) and the worse-off (Yang, in his awkward imitation of Deng) and make the latter look stupid. The implications of such political irony aside, a collective sentiment about the contrast between the "big" (the Western white male) and the "small" (the Han Chinese male) is clearly manifest. Just as, according to Freudian psychoanalytical theory, jokes, slips of the tongue, and dreams are often the best clues to and outlets for what is repressed in the unconscious, the jokes cited here may be clues to and outlets for repressed ideas in the Jungian collective unconscious.

THE DOUBLE STANDARD

In discussing potency, men and women often gave me unexpected answers, sometimes betraying interesting contradictions in their logic. Ms. Cai, a thirty-year-old civil servant, told me, "Several girlfriends of mine in my unit like to chat about men. We've discovered that men who look *dakuaier* [tall and strong] often *bu zhongyong* ["are not very useful"—i.e., are not very good at sexually satisfying women]. It's the skinny, short men who turn out to be very good at sex."

I asked, "What do you think of Westerners? Are they good or bad in terms of *xingnengli* [potency], since they normally look stronger and taller than the Chinese?"

She thought for a while, then answered, "Westerners are good at sex, probably because they're of a different race."

On another occasion, Mr. Wu, a thirty-five-year-old worker, said, "Are you asking me who's more potent—the tall man, or the short man? Let me tell you something. Have you heard the saying 'Those who eat a lot [i.e., who look fat and tall] turn out to be bad at sex'?"

After I asked him to apply this saying to Westerners, he hesitated before saying, "They're of a different race. We can't match them."

For many, race appeared to be the ultimate explanation for differences in sexual potency. Yet many who emphasized race often also cited Westerners' dietary regimens as crucial to the development of their taller, stronger bodies, and therefore their better potency. Mr. Tang, a fifty-five-year-old cadre, said, "I've sometimes watched pornographic videos. I think those scenes of strong potency are made up for the sake of making movies. But I do think Westerners have stronger potency than the Chinese. It's because they eat more beef and lamb. Beef and lamb strengthen *yang*. The Chinese are not good, because we primarily eat carbohydrates. In terms of meat, I only eat chicken, duck, fish, and pork."

Mr. Zi, a thirty-four-year-old street vendor, said, "The Chinese can't match Westerners, because Westerners eat more beef and lamb. I can't eat beef, because as soon as I eat beef, I *shanghuo* ["have fire that goes up"—that is, have excessive internal heat that unbalances *yin* and *yang*]."

The perception that Westerners' consumption of beef made a huge difference in their potency seemed common. Once, joining a group of professionals for hot pot—a meal featuring all kinds of meat, including beef, as well as vegetables and delicacies—I asked the question, "Are Westerners stronger?" A journalist responded, "Of course, Westerners are stronger, because they like to eat be—" He stopped in the middle of his answer, suddenly aware of how much beef he himself consumed in general, and was eating at that moment. Over the preceding two decades, Chinese consumption of meat, including beef, had increased significantly; the journalist's unthinking repetition of a common belief was interrupted when he became aware of his own behavior. He continued, "Probably the whole potency thing has to do with one's confidence."

Assigning such a significant role to beef-eating as a Western determinant of potency offers another example of a double standard—just as Ms. Cai and Mr. Wu, above, delinked potency from physique in relation to their fellow countrymen, yet made a positive association between the two factors in relation to Westerners. Here, in accordance with the double standard, a high-protein diet could lead to potency in Westerners, but not in Chinese. The logic in these double standards reveals the social and psychological processes that heightened the Chinese sense of male inadequacy.

IDENTIFICATION IN MISRECOGNITION

One afternoon in October 1999, I was riding a trolley car on Ping An Boulevard, reading the *Beijing Evening News* after finishing my field observations at a Beijing hospital. Glancing up from the paper, I became aware of someone staring at me from a seat across the aisle—a beautiful young woman in her mid-twenties, wearing a green dress and a blue scarf. I finished reading another news item, then raised my head again; her eyes were still focused on me, apparently conveying interest in communicating. Out of curiosity, I turned to her and asked, "How are you?" She smiled and continued to stare at me. After a moment of silence, she asked, "Where are you from?"

I immediately understood the woman to mean "What country were you born in?" I was often asked this question by people in China. Perhaps I looked slightly different from other Han Chinese, and perhaps my body language had changed after many years in the United States. On another day, I'd surprised a Chengdu taxi driver by speaking in Sichuan dialect after looking up from the newspaper I was reading and discovering he was taking me on a detour to overcharge me. He'd assumed I was a foreigner.

I often took the question about my birthplace as an opportunity to start a conversation. That afternoon on the trolley, I asked, "Can you guess?" I expected the woman to guess as others had: that I was from Xinjiang, in Western China. She surprised me: "Are you German?"

These days in Beijing, reading a Chinese newspaper and speaking Chinese do not necessarily guarantee that one will be ascribed a Chinese identity. A taxi driver once said to me, "Nowadays, *yangguizi* ["foreign devils"—i.e., foreigners] can speak Mandarin so wonderfully!" On numerous occasions, I had been taken for a foreigner: Indian, Filipino, Mexican, Iranian, Pakistani. But this was the first time someone had thought I was German. The woman seemed interested in continuing our conversation as the trolley rolled along the newly reconstructed boulevard.

Past experiences of having been misrecognized as a foreigner flashed through my mind. Curious how she would react, I said, "No, I'm Chinese." I could tell immediately that she was disappointed and turned off by my confessed identity, even though nothing had changed in me. Had she not harbored a negative feeling toward Chinese men, she probably would not have expressed so blatant a change of attitude.

WOMEN'S DESIRE

The woman on the trolley resembled the cosmopolitan Japanese women in Karen Kelsky's ethnography (*Women on the Verge*) who demonstrate "the fetish of the white man" through their "romantic or sexual rejection of Japanese men" and pursuit of white Westerners. In Kelsky's account, this pursuit is more about the women's disgust with Japanese gender relations and their curiosity about "respectful" white men than it is about bodily, sexual experience. The desire manifests itself as a social and cultural critique of a dominant Japanese masculinity they are reluctant to live with. This cultural critique is also expressed in bodily terms: one Western white man observes that Japanese men "have small dicks" and are "hung like hamsters," and a female Japanese writer states that "Japanese men have no dicks."[26]

The convergence of the "emasculating impulses of Western Orientalism and the oppositional agendas of internationally bound Japanese women" poses a challenge to the study of women's desire under globalization:[27] How can we separate cosmopolitan desire as an oppositional agenda and social critique of one's own society from colonial desire informed by Western hegemonic understanding of the body? In the context of my study, the question becomes, How is one to read the fetish of the white phallus as a social critique of a kind of Chinese masculinity that Chinese women, including perhaps the woman on the trolley, were reluctant to live with?

The fetishization of penis size and the worship of the Western phallus reached extreme expression in *Shanghai Baby*. In contrast, medical discourse in China has downplayed the importance of penis size in women's ability to achieve sexual pleasure. Yet this discourse has not seemed to affect men who suffer from small-penis anxiety, particularly those who have little sexual experience. An eighteen-year-old vocational school student, seeking advice about his small penis, wrote to a urologist who showed me the letter: "I've read many books. None of them offered a solution to this problem. They all said that the problem of size won't constitute an obstacle to sexual life in the future. What is the use of this kind of shit?! It may give some comfort to people, and lure people away from reality. If we want to face reality, we will not listen to this shit."

The doctor had received a great many letters that were no less desperate. Deep suspicion of medical discourse's sincerity paralleled the tendency to associate potency with Western white men, and to attribute the gap between Chinese men and white men to essential racial differences. A doctor once explained to me: "A comparison *within huangzhong ren* [the yellow race] is different from a comparison *between* the yellow race and the white race in terms of penis size. The latter comparison has to do with racial differences. Comparatively, the Chinese are indeed not up to the level of *yangren* [Western whites] in sports such as track and field and soccer. This is a problem of *tizhi* [the quality of the body], and therefore a problem of racial differences."

On the one hand, this doctor attributed the obsession with penis size to men's lack of skill in sex. On the other hand, he made it clear that he did not mean that size was unimportant, although he downplayed its importance to ease his patients' worry. To be fair, his view on racial differences seemed more flexible than many other doctors' views, leaving room for other indicators to offset the supposed inadequacy of size. He put more emphasis on skill and technique than on penis size for sexually satisfying women, even though, in the final analysis, he accepted that white men enjoyed an essential physical advantage over Chinese men.

To what degree did Chinese women agree with this doctor? The doctor said that he had not yet encountered a female patient who, after having sex with white men, complained about Chinese men's small size. I talked to several women about the importance of size; Ms. Yao, a thirty-two-year-old employee of a joint venture in Beijing, said that she had had sexual relations with white men. I had a conversation with her one afternoon in the early 2000s in the coffee shop of an elite club in Beijing. Ms. Yao began by speaking English, to circumvent eavesdroppers, and our conversation continued in that language. To my question "Do you think white men are more sexually potent than Chinese men?" her answer was "Absolutely." She thought Chinese men were inferior to white Western men. However, she added, feelings took priority over penis size in giving her pleasure: she enjoyed cuddling and tenderness more than sheer potency. She even said, "Big dicks hurt me."

Her words reminded me of our first conversation, a year and a half earlier. In criticizing Chinese men, she'd listed what she perceived as their many problems: "They don't wash their hair. They don't cut their *bimao* [nostril hairs]. They lie in a chair rather than sitting in a chair. They dress clumsily—for instance, wearing white casual socks with leather dress shoes." She added, "*China Can Say No* didn't portray a real picture of the relationship between white employers and their Chinese female employees. In joint ventures, those foreign bosses are very respectful of female employees."[28]

From our two conversations, I concluded that her perception of white men's virility focused less on sex than on feelings of being respected and loved, and on the white man's better social demeanor. Size was not an issue for her at all. Coco (from *Shanghai Baby*) and Ms. Yao represented two contrasting poles in terms of women's attitudes toward the sense of smallness. The former refers to her German lover Mark's "big penis," and the latter refers to the "respectful demeanors" of Western men. A simple morality does not work here, but women's desire has become increasingly relevant and crucial in this discussion—a topic that needs to be addressed in a different study.

A FANONIAN QUESTION

The beginning of China's reform and opening to the outside world in the late 1970s was a unique historical moment—one in which the self-confidence of the Chinese, based on ignorance of the outside world, gave way to a

     EVERETT YUEHONG ZHANG

heightened sense of inferiority concerning the status of the country's economic development. China has transformed itself from a nation that instituted food rationing in the Maoist period to one of incipient prosperity in the twenty-first century; how have changes in the social context affected the complex of inferiority?

In 1999, I had a conversation in Beijing with the executive editor of a men's magazine—a high-style publication targeting professionals and running advertisements of solely foreign fashion brands. Noticing that the masculine figures on the covers were all Western, I asked this editor, a confident woman in her early thirties, to explain. She said, "Well, as soon as we ran cover photos of Chinese men, circulation went down." She said this only half a year after anti-NATO demonstrations had broken out and soared through Beijing's streets. However unrelated the readers of this magazine and the demonstrators might be to each other, I took the polarized feelings toward Westerners as possibly symbolizing two faces of a shared sentiment of inadequacy.[29]

In *The Wretched of the Earth*, written during the Algerian struggle for independence from French rule, philosopher and psychiatrist Frantz Fanon discussed how devastating colonization is to the psyche of the colonized. Among the cases he described was one of impotence. A twenty-six-year-old Algerian man Fanon interviewed had joined the resistance; the man's wife was questioned about his whereabouts and was repeatedly raped by French soldiers. With other soldiers present, one of her rapists said to her, "If ever you see your filthy husband again, don't forget to tell him what we did to you."[30] Later, she told her husband about the rape; her "dishonor" angered him. Not long afterward, he found himself impotent on several occasions. He told Fanon: "If they'd tortured her or knocked out all her teeth or broken an arm I wouldn't have minded. But that thing—how can you forget a thing like that? And why did she have to tell me about it all?"[31]

Fanon pointed out, "The hitherto unemphasized characteristics of certain psychiatric descriptions here given confirm, if confirmation were necessary, that this colonial war is singular even in the pathology that it gives rise to."[32]

This "pathology," a direct impact of colonial rule on the psyche of the colonized, had a lasting impact: It generated conflicting and contradictory feelings in the postcolonial body. It produced ambivalent identity embroiled in a constant struggle between polarized feelings, leading to the emergence of what Bhabha calls a "third space,"[33] beyond the binary of traditional outland provincialism versus postenlightenment nationalism.

Despite the fact that China was never a colony, its forced encounter with the industrial West particularly since the nineteenth century had a unique social and historical impact on Maoist socialism. In the Maoist period, the sense of inferiority about the male body might not have been as acute as it became in post-Mao times, simply because of the lack of opportunity for comparisons. More importantly, the state effectively fostered a sense of Chinese superiority under isolation, portraying Western powers as reactionary and evil. There was little room for the ambivalence Bhabha describes.

The underdeveloped economy and low standard of living in the Maoist period contributed to self-questioning and self-doubt when the post-Mao reform began. This complex is largely an unintended effect of the post-Mao transformation, in its interaction with the rejuvenation of the past. As Marxist teleology was abandoned in the post-Mao period, a teleology of modernity—the desire for modernity disrupted by the political campaigns in the Maoist period—started to occupy the national center stage. Entering the twenty-first century, numerous numbers in China's development can be cited to prove China's "bigness" under globalization. Now the question is, Will an inferiority complex continue to define, however implicitly, Chinese nationalism and even Chinese modernity?

Evidence conflicts regarding where this complex stands. A more nuanced understanding of development has begun to be articulated since the early 2000s. In the late 2000s and the 2010s, people I talked to, including cadres, were less likely to gloat over the nation's economic achievements than they had been. Instead, they often directed my attention to problems facing China's development.

Tellingly, perceptions of Western masculinity have also changed. In 2009, the popular TV drama *Woju* (Dwelling narrowness) portrayed Mark, a Westerner living in the city of Jiangzhou (reminiscent of Shanghai), as a caring, considerate, and, most importantly, sexually disciplined and spirited gentleman in his relations with Chinese women, particularly with his Chinese-language teacher, Haiping. This character stands in stark contrast to the Mark of *Shanghai Baby* a decade before.[34]

Two possibilities exist. This inferiority complex may be so intransigent that the country's changing materiality will not affect its deeply rooted feeling of inadequacy, because the self-perception of smallness—a result of identification with bigness—has taken on a life of its own. Absent enlightened choice, many magnificent moments for the Chinese nation may well continue to reproduce the inferiority complex.

Alternatively, the complex may fade away. If the inferiority complex is an unenlightened state of feelings and reasoning, then Chinese society must make enlightened choices and adopt the good norms while discarding the

          EVERETT YUEHONG ZHANG

bad norms of Western modernities. Enlightened choices will allow confidence to develop, and when that happens the inferiority complex will no longer have a place.

Perceived male smallness embodies the national sentiment that has rearticulated the desire to become big in the reform era—an ironic experience in the midst of China's rise. It demonstrates more the failure of Maoist socialist utopia and the problematic logic of teleological modernity than the retrieved memory of humiliations.

As far back as 1996, the news that China had finally become the number-one producer of iron and steel in the world went somewhat unnoticed. This was because, worldwide, production had shifted—long before the 1990s—away from developed countries and into less developed countries, for reasons that do not bode well for those countries, such as the high pollution and high energy consumption associated with such production. Thinking back to the disastrous Great Leap Forward campaign of 1958, which set the whole nation to producing iron and steel with the goal of overtaking Western industrial countries, one cannot help but reflect on how Chinese society might make different choices to avoid similar disastrous mistakes. The difference may lie in building enlightened confidence with which the rise of "bigness" does not, ironically, convey "smallness."

NOTES

For the fieldwork and particularly the survey I conducted for this chapter, I received support from people in Beijing and Chengdu. For their kindness, I want to thank Li Lianxiang, Ma Xiaonian, Sun Chuan, Wan Jingbo, Wang Jiuyuan, Wu Jian, Xu Yin, Yan Jianjun, Yang Yusheng, Zeng Tong, Zhang Lan, Zhang Shuwu, and Zhao Xudong. This chapter has been revised quite a number of times, in different contexts. I want to thank Lawrence Cohen, Aihwa Ong, Arthur Kleinman, Nancy Chen, Susan Greenhalgh, Wilt Idema, Keith McMahon, Louisa Schein, Giovanni Vitiello, Robert Weller, and Mayfair Yang for comments and suggestions on its previous versions. I want to thank two reviewers for suggestions. I thank the editor Howard Chiang for having worked diligently to put the volume together and to improve this chapter. I want also to thank copyeditor Anne Mathews for her fine editing.

1   Zhang, *The Impotence Epidemic.* This chapter shares anthropological fieldwork sites with this book.
2   Zhang, "Flows between the Media and the Clinic," 139–71.
3   Zilbergeld, *The New Male Sexuality,* 266–67.
4   Shih, *The Lure of the Modern,* 110–27; and Brownell, *Training the Body for China,* 213–37.

5   Wang, *Red Sorghum.* Kam Louie's analyses of how Chinese masculinity privileges "cultural attainment" over "martial valor" resonates with the revelation of such a femininity complex (Louie, *Theorizing Chinese Masculinity,* 1–57). See also Zhong, *Masculinity Beseiged.*

6   This survey was administered to 240 patients and about 600 college students. The latter population, though not chosen based on random sampling, was based on a sampling with a relatively even distribution of gender (male vs. female), major (science vs. nonscience), and location (five universities).

7   See Li, *Zhongguo fangshu zhengkao,* 363.

8   See Tamba, *Yixinfang* [*Ishinpo*], 597–98. At the same time, there were recipes for curing the problem of *yumenda* (too large a jade gate—that is, an oversized vagina).

9   See, for example, Liu, "Hejian zhuan," 794–95, and Xu, "Ruyijun zhuan," 1–49.

10   See, for instance, Anonymous, *Sunü miaolun,* section 6. This Ming period text incorporates parts of bedchamber-art texts from previous periods; the section in question discusses the issue of penis size.

11   See Li, *Rouputuan.*

12   McMahon, personal communication, 2003.

13   Ebron and Tsing, "From Allegories of Identity to Sites of Dialogue," 132–33.

14   See Canguilhem, *The Normal and the Pathological,* 151–79.

15   Yin, *Xing de shengli he bingli.*

16   Shi's study found that the average penis size of the Chinese participants in the study was 8.4 cm in 1963 (Shi et al., "Yinjing tiji celiang baogao"). Later studies found averages of 6.55 cm in 1981 (Liu and Cao, "Zhongguo chengren nanzi wai shengzhiqi zhengchang biaozhun"), 9.05 cm in 1985 (Jiang et al., "470 li nanxing qingshaonian xingfayu qingkuang diaocha"), 7.7 cm in 1987 (Wang et al., "Ziboshi chengren yinjing zhengchang biaozhun"), 7.21 cm in 1988 (Zhang et al., "2029 li chengnian nanxing shengzhiqiguan diaocha baogao"), 7.15 cm in 1988 (Jin et al., "Chaoxianzu yu hanzu qingzhuangnian yinjing daxiao de bijiao"), 8.02 cm in 1992 (Wu and Lu, "Yinjing celiang fangfa de tantao ji zhengchang biaozhun"), 7.1 cm in 1999 (Huang and Xu, *Nake zhenduanxue*), 8.75 cm in 1999 (Zhang et al., "220 li zhengchang nanxing yinjing boqi changdu de celiang baogao"), and 7.2 cm in 1999 (Qin et al., "500 ming nanxing yinjing celiang jieguo fenxi").

17   Statistic Bureau of the People's Republic of China.

18   Bhabha, *The Location of Culture,* 51.

19   Zhang, "China's Sexual Revolution," 112–15.

20   Zhang, *Zhang Jingsheng wenji,* 279.

21   Ibid., 280.

22   Ibid., 281.

23   Shi, Liu and Zhang, "Yinjing tiji."

24   Levenson, *Revolution and Cosmopolitanism,* 55.

25   Wei Hui, *Shanghai Baobei,* 61, 207, 239 (my translation).

26 Kelsky, *Women on the Verge*, 152, 184–85.

27 Ibid., 184.

28 She was referring to Song, Zhang, and Qiao, *China Can Say No*, a book with
    a fiercely anti-Western tone.

29 I do not mean to make a judgment on whether or not the demonstration,
    as an outburst of nationalism, was justified. I suggest that such an uproar
    of collective anger reflected more than one type of psychological makeup.
    I point out one of them.

30 Fanon, *The Wretched of the Earth*, 255.

31 Ibid., 258.

32 Ibid., 252.

33 Bhabha, *The Location of Culture*, 53–56.

34 *Woju*, July 2009.

CHAPTER 9

SEX AND WORK

HIV/AIDS and Elite Masculinity in Contemporary China

ELANAH URETSKY

KONG CHUIZHU, THE VICE-GOVERNOR OF YUNNAN FROM 2003 THROUGH 2013, committed suicide on July 12, 2014. He was likely a victim of President Xi Jinping's severe anticorruption measures, which had aimed to rid the government of "tigers and flies" (senior officials and low-ranking cadres).[1] Kong had been linked to Shen Peipeng, another former vice-governor of Yunnan, who had been placed under investigation for graft the preceding March. Kong may have seen the writing on the wall after Shen Peipeng revealed some of Kong Chuizhu's corrupt practices during an investigation.[2]

The spate of official suicides that began after Xi initiated his anticorruption campaign is tragic, yet not completely surprising. Officials who foresaw their fate chose to end their lives rather than endure the torture and humiliation that could befall them. The more surprising aspect of Kong's death was that he had learned before he died that he was HIV positive; also, his death had occurred after his third attempt at suicide. He made his first attempt in Beijing during the 2014 National People's Congress: he returned to his hotel room one night and cut his wrist, arms, and neck with a broken wine glass. Doctors who treated him performed a routine HIV test that diagnosed his positive status.

News of an elite HIV-positive member of society or government is surprising from the perspective of the public-health-focused discourse that dominates research and programming on HIV/AIDS. Global paradigms have long painted a picture of HIV/AIDS as a disease of vulnerable and marginalized populations. Even within that paradigm, we expect HIV-positive people to carry identities of commercial sex workers, injection drug users, or men who have sex with men.[3] Notice of a heterosexual HIV-positive man automatically brands him as a "client of a sex worker"—an epidemiologic appellation that places him within the standard public health paradigms that govern global HIV/AIDS discourse. But few, if any, such men would respond to this type of constructed identity.

More than a decade of experience conducting research on the relationship between elite male sexual practices and HIV in China has taught me to not be surprised at the news of an HIV-positive government official. News of such officials is rarely made public and is extremely protected, for fear of marring party legitimacy, but my research has revealed that these powerful men are extremely vulnerable to HIV infection because of the role commercial sex plays in the work that promotes their economic and career advancement. Despite this experience, though, I was surprised to hear of Kong Chuizhu's positive HIV status. I had met Kong several times, ten years before his untimely death, each time on a tennis court in Kunming. I had always held him up in my mind as a pioneer who was accomplishing his career advancement on the tennis court, rather than in the brothel. I had obviously only seen one side of Kong Chuizhu. The other side of him shared a tight sexual network with Shen Peipeng that at once promoted their careers and exposed them to HIV. This network extends throughout the province and results in HIV infections among other government officials.

Politically and economically, powerful Chinese men are, ironically, placed within the same field of vulnerability to HIV as those who are marginalized in society and more readily identified with a disease like HIV/AIDS. This is related to the role that sex has played in determining the economic and political success of elite Chinese men in post-Mao China. Sex, for these men, is not necessarily about expressing sexuality, but about expressing a desire to amass economic and political power. Within this context, sex has quite simply become an aspect of work, rather than the simple individual behavior it is treated as within public health discourse. Such realization has implications for the prevention of sexually transmitted infections (STIs) and HIV among this class of men and their sexual partners. Realistically, "sex work" should not be a term reserved solely for marginalized women; it should also be used for the men who engage in commercial sex for the purposes of work, and who gain a use-value (i.e., the value or usefulness a commodity offers in its consumption) out of commercial sex equivalent to that which Marx associated with work.[4] This argument also has implications for the way we employ global discourses of sex work.

Sexuality has historically been an integral aspect of Chinese society, celebrated for the essential value it offered in maintaining health and social structure. Taoist tradition viewed the bodily fluids emitted and exchanged during sex as a crucial part of the natural universe, necessary for maintaining the balance of *yin* and *yang* energy within the body—a fundamental measure of primordial mortality.[5] This perspective was reflected in imperial Taoist manuals on social conduct, which included proper sexual technique among their guidance for practicing and maintaining proper health and hygiene.[6] China's resultant culture of sexuality focused more on building and maintaining social order, which was also seen as an integral part of stable political order. Elite men, responsible for governing China through their mastery of the literary arts, were partially socialized through their interaction with courtesan women, who primarily served in entertainment roles but could also provide sexual services.[7] None of this was socially prohibited; it was seen as necessary for maintaining political stability.

Sex involved eroticism, which, according to Confucian doctrine, was seen as chaotic and potentially disturbing to the home and family. Because Confucian code viewed the family as a microcosm of the state, any chaos in the home was believed to pose a threat to political stability. Confucius thus relegated the conduct of extraneous erotic behavior to spaces outside the home, as a means for maintaining cosmic, and hence state, order.[8] A government official would accordingly choose a wife who was worthy of joining his kinship network, mothering heirs, and gaining access to the economic resources of his lineage; she was also chosen for her ability to support her husband's political and social status, without concern for love. She was not, however, associated with the provision of erotic pleasure, which a man could seek elsewhere.

China's newly emergent market economy has engendered a new class of elite men who are defined by money, rather than scholarship. Many of these men have lived through a period of tight political controls and suppressed sexuality. The new spaces for personal expression opened up by the post-Mao recession of the government from the social sphere have encouraged many men to reclaim the sexual privileges historically reserved for them. This has led to the rise of a contemporary class of Chinese men who often identify as "Confucianists" (*rujia*) and feel entitled to relations with women who play various social and sexual roles in their lives.

Contemporary discourse around sexual culture in post-Mao China is often framed in terms of a "sexual revolution" that allegedly occurred when

   ELANAH URETSKY

imported Western values incited a shift away from sexual austerity, following implementation of Deng Xiaoping's economic reform measures.[9] Such a sudden surge in foreign cultural behavior is unlikely, though; endorsing this theory would be, as Zygmunt Bauman has argued, "like accepting the alchemist's authorship of the gold found in the test tube." Bauman suggests that "it takes more than greed for profit, free competition, and the refinement of the advertising media to accomplish a cultural revolution of a scale and depth equal to that of the emancipation of eroticism from sexual reproduction and love. To be redeployed as an economic factor, eroticism must have been first culturally processed and given a form fit for a would-be commodity."[10] It is true that we are witnessing a more palpable surge of sexual expression in post-Mao China, but it is more attributable to a sudden emerging space that has allowed men to once again realize the entitlements available within their own sexual culture, rather than a revolution in favor of a foreign sexual culture.

This essay's discussion of sexuality focuses on men and their masculine practices—a topic that often conjures up visions of men showing off their sexual prowess. This macho notion of masculinity and male sexuality, which has limited use even in the Latin American context where it was developed, is further limited in the Chinese context, where masculinity is socially and not sexually constructed.[11] Masculine identity, in China, occurs at the center of important relationships, both inside the home and outside in the broader social, economic, and political sphere, rather than acting as a representation of gender status.

This masculine taxonomy sets the stage necessary to understand what sex means to the many businessmen and government officials who engage in risky sexual practices that expose them to various sexually transmitted infections, including HIV. The exchange of sex in this context is frequently conducted for the construction and generation of social relations, rather than as an individual behavior. These social relations, used to define and maintain "social fields" in China, have become an integral part of the work that defines success for urban businessmen and government officials.[12] Addressing sexually transmitted HIV in this context thus requires a reconceptualization of both "work" and "sex work." This connection between men, work, and sex may not apply globally, but it is a useful framework for revisiting the way we conceptualize sex work in Asia; it also reminds us that we must ultimately look at sex work as a functional category, rather than a behavioral category, in our work to prevent sexually transmitted infections.

This chapter draws from a larger ethnographic project examining how trends of masculinity and male sexual culture in contemporary urban China can expose men to STIs and HIV.[13] That study focuses on the social, cultural, politico-economic, and historic structures that prompt urban Chinese men to seek sexual experiences outside of marriage, exploring how they negotiate, use, and experience sex with various partners. Research was primarily conducted in Ruili, a border region in southwest China that is home to the country's first concentrated HIV epidemic. The significant role Ruili plays in the history of China's HIV epidemic, as well as its active cross-border trade with Burma, make it an ideal location for studying the interaction between male sexual culture and HIV in China. Men who engage in trade in this region rely on entertainment, including sex work, as a way of fostering communication with the officials who have the power to govern their success.

Observation of, and in-depth interviews with, men and women occupying varying roles in restaurants, hotels, massage parlors, hair salons, karaoke clubs, saunas, and brothels provided the foundation for a comprehensive characterization of the daily lives of urban Chinese men engaged in professional networking activities. These interviews and observations also facilitated a detailed understanding of the relationship between the activities occurring in these venues and the work required for political and economic success in contemporary China. The following section describes a typical day for many of the successful businessmen and government officials encountered in the course of this project's research; it depicts scenarios that are typical in the way post-Mao China is governed.[14]

A "TYPICAL" WORKDAY

The official workday in China begins at 8:00 a.m. and ends at 6:00 p.m., with a three-hour break from 11:30 a.m. to 2:30 p.m. for lunch and siesta (*xiuxi*). Government employees are required to work five days a week, from Monday to Friday. Many men seeking political or economic success, however, frequently engage in work-related duties that do not allow them to return home until 2:00 a.m. In addition, while offices are closed on the weekend, many men are still unofficially required to attend to late-night work-related duties outside the office.

Government officials and businessmen in Ruili frequently begin their workday at 8:00 a.m., hosting a guest at a breakfast spot serving food typical

　　　　　　ELANAH URETSKY

of one of the local ethnic minority communities. Guests are other government officials or businessmen who have come from elsewhere to evaluate local officials' work or prospect new business opportunities. Breakfast at one of these popular local establishments consists of local delicacies—rice noodles with spicy beef, pork, or a hot pudding made from yellow peas (*doufen*). Coffee served with sweet condensed milk is also on the breakfast menu. Breakfast provides a good introduction to the area, and a perfect way to begin a relationship with a government official who can provide access to necessary elements of success for a local official or businessman.

Breakfast is usually followed by a trip to the field, to view and inspect a local site of either business or government operations. This provides evidence of the host's capacity to carry out either his official duties or his intended business venture. True success, however, depends upon establishing a trusting relationship with one's guest. This involves continued demonstration of respect, through a series of shared ritual networking practices collectively referred to as *yingchou*. These practices that have been central to the demonstration of trust and loyalty between elite men in China since the Song dynasty (960–1279) include ritualized forms of smoking, banqueting, drinking, and female-centered entertainment that can culminate in sex.[15] Any discussion of yingchou must thus consider these practices as one fluid ritual, not as individual customs; the sexual behaviors that often act as a coda to *yingchou* are understood in the same way as the feasting and drinking central to the ritual.

The central role of food and drink in building bonds of trust among the Chinese male elite was first recorded in the *Liji* (Book of rites), a Confucian text that described the proper order for such rituals.[16] Today these same rituals dominate the time of many government officials and businessmen, helping them cement relationships among peers.[17] Networking practices in China, as stated earlier, also include an entertainment component that often involves the provision of sex from a sex worker.[18] This part of the *yingchou* ritual—reminiscent of the tradition of courtesans serving elite men during China's later imperial era—serves to distinguish these men as elite.[19] This type of entertainment has become central to the *yingchou* process because it underscores a man's power and authority in post-Mao society, but the ritual is still primarily grounded in the core practices of drinking and feasting.

Most men understand that the ritual gesturing does not end after their first meeting. As with the loyalty a party member demonstrates to the party, loyalty and respect must similarly be repeatedly demonstrated between men throughout the duration of their relationship. Consequently, a morning of breakfast and surveying is typically followed by a luncheon banquet at 11:30 a.m., wherein local delicacies and strong alcohol are used to demonstrate mutual respect through a ritual hierarchical exchange of formal toasts.

During the brief siesta that follows lunch, a woman who sells sex may visit the guests. Official work-related duties resume from 2:30 p.m. until 5:30 p.m. The host always invites his guests to an evening dinner banquet that consists of more local delicacies and strong alcohol. After dinner, hosts typically invite their guests out for entertainment, which can include massage, foot reflexology, hair washing, or a trip to a local disco and karaoke club. This is often followed by a midnight meal. This entertainment can be coupled with sexual services, provided by a woman who works at the establishment. Alternatively, a guest can be offered services from a brothel-based sex worker who is discreetly solicited to his hotel room. Cigarettes are constantly exchanged between host and guest throughout the day, again as a means of initiating and maintaining communication and respect. This typical day of hosting and entertaining can define six or even seven days of the workweek for officials and entrepreneurs in Ruili.

DEFINING WORK IN CHINA

The outside observer may view this schedule as a day filled with leisure activities. Indeed, Western government officials, businesspeople, and public health workers encountered during this project often viewed these behaviors as merely sophomoric activities, influenced by Western cultural values entering China alongside increased access to wealth. To the Chinese men engaged in these activities, though, these unofficial business practices, stemming from the tradition of *yingchou,* are integral to their work and necessary for success in China's post-Mao era. This use of the term *work* may seem inappropriate from a Western institutional perspective, structured by activities directly related to the operation of government, the economy, and society. But in China, where work is defined both functionally and institutionally, sex (in addition to banqueting, drinking, and smoking) has become an official part of labor in official sectors of society. Observations from this and other similar projects demonstrate that successful men in China conduct their work inside entertainment establishments as often as they do inside the four walls of an office compound.[20] A successful man is one who rarely goes home; a man who occasionally goes home is considered mildly successful, and a man who regularly goes home at the end of the official workday is surely unsuccessful. This has become true, in part,

  ELANAH URETSKY

because of the measures men must pursue to position themselves within certain social fields in contemporary China.

Chinese society was traditionally organized around a rigid hierarchical structure imposed to maintain social and political order. During China's mid-late imperial era the literati (aka the scholar-gentry), who were responsible for the proper governance of imperial China, occupied the top of this hierarchical structure, followed by peasant laborers, artisans, and then merchants and traders. A strict social division continues to establish and maintain order in contemporary China, but modern order is dictated by the current Leninist political system, which distinguishes between party and nonparty members rather than along traditional cleavages of social hierarchy. The party rules and lay members of society (*laobaixing*) are expected to follow as loyal subjects. This same structure affects the concept of work in China, which is divided between effort performed for the party and effort performed for individual profit (i.e., effort not performed for the party). Preserving these boundaries, which define China's modern social fields, has become essential for maintaining party legitimacy.[21] These boundaries are also useful for maximizing the material and nonmaterial profit and authority of those at the top of the hierarchy, by creating a structure that sees them as the legitimate holders of "economic capital, cultural capital (legitimate knowledge of various sorts), social capital (various kinds of relations with significant social others), and symbolic capital (prestige and social honor)."[22]

To "have work" or "have a job" (*you gongzuo*) in China implies employment in a state-owned enterprise or work unit (*danwei*).[23] Work in nongovernment contexts is categorized according to its particular function, which is also closely associated with identity. For instance, a businessman (or businesswoman) is said to "*zuo shengyi*" (do business); a peasant is said to "*laodong*" (labor); and a migrant worker is said to "*dagong*" (do manual or menial work). The party maintains control over the resources of production, which, under Leninist code, are distributed to other members in exchange for their loyalty and hard work. This creates a stark divide between the party and *laobaixing* that also serves to protect party members' legitimacy as state authority. This distinct divide between party and nonparty, however, presents great challenges to the development of China's market-oriented economy, because it depends on communication between government officials inside the party and entrepreneurs (who may lie outside the party). The process of *yingchou*, a mechanism that has historically aided the establishment and maintenance of loyal relationships among Chinese men, enables officials and entrepreneurs to work around the requirements of a Leninist system that reserves resources for loyal party members.

Under China's Leninist system, government officials are primarily responsible for properly allocating distribution of state-owned resources. What they do in their work to carry out this function, however, is ambiguous. Leninist doctrine instructs that they distribute resources as a reward to those who are indoctrinated with party values, which includes party members and employees in government work units.[24] In an environment where a Leninist bureaucracy must support the development of a market-oriented economy, government officials have had to reinvent the requirements for distributing state-controlled resources that determine market and entrepreneurial success. The market mechanism promotes private resource ownership and exchange facilitated through money, which is not allowable under the guise of a Leninist state. As a way of negotiating this challenge to the free flow of resources necessary for operating a market economy, government officials have turned to the traditional institution of *guanxi* (dyadic personalistic relations). *Guanxi* allows officials to capitalize on a cultural institution grounded in personal loyalties characteristic of traditional Chinese authority and patrimonialism. Relationships akin to these personal loyalties are also crucial to operation of China's market economy but go beyond the personal relationships typically characteristic of *guanxi* ties. In these cases, people are able to build loyalty through an impersonal *guanxi* relationship to gain access to the state-controlled resources that are reserved for those who can demonstrate personal loyalty to the party.[25]

Guanxi is inherent to kin or even quasi-kin relationships in China. The needs of the market economy, however, give cause for businessmen and government officials to develop *guanxi* relationships beyond the natural boundaries of kinship. This artificial construction of *guanxi* is daily accomplished through the shared networking practices of *yingchou*. Today, these practices are used as a way of informally governing the distribution of resources. As a result, drinking, smoking, banqueting, entertainment, and casual sex—all considered leisure in the West—have become an unofficial but expected aspect of work for men seeking political or economic success in post-Mao China. So, while visits to commercial sex workers and informal sexual relations in exchange for access to positions and resources have almost become normalized for businesspeople and government officials in China, they often occur within the guise of their official capacity or position, without official endorsement or acknowledgement. If viewed from a Marxian perspective, these work-related functions, though not officially related to men's jobs, do nevertheless produce the same type of use-value necessary for achieving the compensation Marx associates with work.[26] Many of these men, in fact, view these duties as required.

 ELANAH URETSKY

THE COMPELLING NATURE OF SEX AND WORK IN CHINA

The informal mode of governance that has become so prevalent in post-Mao China suggests that discussion of risk for STIs and HIV among urban Chinese businessmen and government officials is tied as much to employment as it is to sexual practices. For many men, these behaviors are an unwelcome but unofficially required aspect of their work; through these practices, men demonstrate party loyalty and thereby gain access to the state-controlled resources that determine their success.

In Ruili, men may host and entertain guests six or seven days a week, frequently dropping everything and leaving home for the evening at their bosses' request. In this politico-economic environment, party loyalty has supplanted the familial loyalty that traditional Confucian culture prescribes. Men are forced to do things that one government worker described as "offensive to your own wife" (*duibuqi ni ziji de laopo*)—referring to the unmentionable sexual activities he engages in as part of his unofficial work-related requirements. A government worker at a gender-training workshop in the provincial capital who was asked to comment about the health risks of being a man in China raised a concern about the frequent use of sex work in his work unit's hosting and entertaining activities. He said that although he did not like participating in these activities, he felt compelled to accept the services of a sex worker when hosting and entertaining with his boss in order to strengthen and maintain relations with his superiors and limit any threat to his own career that might come from a perception of disloyalty. Another man who was HIV-positive described a scenario of hosting and entertaining people five days out of every week: "When a superior [*lingdao*] came down to visit, we would go eat with them. Then, when we finished eating and finished drinking, we would all go out to sing and dance together. And after singing, we would go do chaotic things, including all the soliciting of prostitutes that comes along with it." He stated, "Our work made us do these things." Again, all of this is done in the name of demonstrating loyalty toward the party, which transforms these activities into a crucial aspect of work for businessmen who need access to state-controlled resources and for government and party workers and officials who hope to ascend in rank.

THE FUNCTIONAL AND BEHAVIORAL ROLES OF SEX WORK

The term "sex work" (*xing gongzuo*) enters Chinese from Western discourse that has aimed to transform popular and policy-oriented perceptions of prostitutes, who were commonly associated with lust, dirt, and disease. This discussion of sex work likewise is meant to help us understand how public health prevention and intervention strategies targeted at this field can be adapted to the Chinese context. This requires a broader understanding of how the term "sex work" is used and understood in the field of public health.

In 1973, the organization Call Off Your Old Tired Ethics (COYOTE) proposed supplanting the term "prostitute" with the term "sex worker" in order to disassociate women in the sex industry from negative stereotypes and instead legitimize them as a social category engaged in an income-generating occupation.[27] "Sex work" has since become integrated into global discourse—but primarily for the role it plays in preventing HIV transmission, and less for its role in promoting sex workers' rights. The sex work movement spawned many advocacy organizations, but most had trouble finding support to transform the image of a stigmatized profession. This quickly changed when the public health field recognized sex workers as a population vulnerable to HIV infection. Funding became available for sex workers' organizations willing to take a public health approach in their advocacy.[28] Advocacy around sex work also changed, shifting toward disease prevention that strongly associated sex workers with a highly stigmatized virus, after a previous focus on reducing stigma and discrimination against women employed in a legitimate occupation. The new public health programs that appropriated the sex work agenda also took their cues from international legal discourse focused primarily on keeping people out of prostitution rather than promoting sex workers' rights. So, while many programs have been developed to prevent and treat HIV infection in women who can be identified as sex workers, little progress has been made on efforts to legitimize sex workers or protect their rights. Ultimately, this defeats the public health agenda, as a lack of advocacy leaves women vulnerable to laws that criminalize sex work and deprive them of the occupational control and legal protection they need to achieve the necessary rights that can protect them from HIV infection.[29]

Many of these dilemmas result from a pragmatic need to target a concentrated population associated with a high-risk behavior. Sex workers provide a good target population for HIV prevention programs because their occupation easily associates them with the disease. They are also typically concentrated in a location associated with sex and risk for infection. In addition, sex workers present an efficient "sentinel" population for epidemiologic surveillance of the disease, which depends on large concentrations of people potentially infected with HIV.[30] A population group associated with

     ELANAH URETSKY

risk, however, is also branded with a reputation related to danger and immoral behavior that leads to stigma and discrimination.[31] As a result, well-intentioned strategies designed to target sex workers have had an unintended consequence: reifying stigma and discrimination against women often implicated as the primary vectors of sexually transmitted HIV. Programs that focus on individual determinants of health—or, in this case, sexual behavior—decontextualize behaviors from their social, cultural, economic, and political foundations; this approach neglects important factors that shape sexual experiences and mediate risk for disease.[32] A focus on the behaviors associated with sex work and the pragmatic considerations for public health has, further, resulted in neglect of the men who are also vulnerable to sexually transmitted HIV through sex work.

Behavioral interventions identify the men who consume commercial sex as "clients of sex workers."[33] But these highly mobile men who constantly move between work, home, and occasionally the brothel are mistakenly identified with an enduring status that they can easily eschew once they leave the brothel and return to work or home. For many, sexuality is a means to build relationships with one another, and not something that can be associated with negative risk. These types of relational factors, illustrated here in an examination of men's sexual practices in China, often motivate men globally to engage in sex work; but their identity distinguishes them from the categories targeted by most public health interventions.[34]

THE SOCIAL ORGANIZATION OF SEX WORK IN CHINA

Anne Allison's pioneering work on female hostesses in Tokyo nightclubs illustrated the functional role sex work plays in the everyday lives of Japanese businessmen.[35] We have similarly seen the functional role sex work plays in political and economic relationships among men in Korea, China, and Vietnam.[36] Despite widespread popular recognition of the function that sex work plays for Chinese men, their engagement in commercial sex is still analyzed as a behavioral category. Chinese discourse on sex work, which is perhaps more developed than any other global discourse on sex work, recognizes the various social functions of the women engaged in transactional sex. Women in sex work are associated with specific functional identities that range from elite mistresses (*ernai*) who maintain an exclusive relationship with one man in exchange for luxurious provisions like houses, cars, and expensive clothes to women referred to as "tent dwellers," so called because they exchange sex for basic housekeeping services with myriad construction workers who live in makeshift tents or other temporary housing structures. The gap in between is occupied by a variety of entertainment establishment–based sex workers—for example, "three-accompaniment misses" (*sanpei xiaojie*), who accompany men in singing, dancing, and drinking in karaoke clubs, or "calling misses," who call hotel rooms to offer massage and hair-washing (as a euphemism for sexual services)—as well as brothel-based sex workers (*falangmei*, or "hair salon sisters," since many brothels are officially registered as hair salons) and streetwalkers (*jienü*).[37] Men, meanwhile, are recognized as consumers of sex—but they can veil the role that sex plays in their work behind their official capacities and social roles, unlike the women whose social roles are associated with the provision of sex.

The scant research on men who consume sex work in China takes a behavioral approach that identifies them as "clients of sex workers."[38] Examination of the composition of these clients, though, points to a different motivation for their engagement in sex work. China's commercial sex industry is fueled by men in management and entrepreneurial positions, who account for a disproportionate rate of HIV associated with clients of sex workers, and perhaps even a much greater proportion of HIV than women identified as sex workers.[39] Few, if any of these men, however, would be willing to step forward as a "client of a sex worker." Highlighting their individual connection to a disease that is associated with illegal practices is politically sensitive, in view of China's current crisis of party legitimacy. This reinforces the need to examine the social context that motivates wealthy businessmen and government officials in contemporary urban China to frequently engage the services of commercial sex workers.

The term "sex work" was developed to highlight the functional role of prostitution. It demonstrated that women who engage in prostitution do so as a way to generate income. Development of the term aimed to transform prostitutes from a population identified as immoral and diseased into a legitimate part of the workforce. Public health efforts to prevent sexual transmission of HIV have once again framed "sex worker" as an identity associated with disease. The authority that public health brings with this behavioral association has branded these women with a perceived ownership over sexually transmitted HIV that is both stigmatizing and counterproductive to HIV prevention efforts.

The example I provide in this chapter of politically and economically powerful Chinese men demonstrates the functional role sex work serves in the work of men (and women) in urban China. What many (including the international public health organizations that conduct HIV/AIDS prevention

 ELANAH URETSKY

and intervention programs in China) view as a consumerist act of pleasure does serve an occupational role for men seeking economic and political success in China. But unlike the sex workers who have become branded with this designated occupational identity, the men who visit sex workers do not acquire an enduring identity associated with sex because sex is not perceived as part of their occupational role, although for many it is a requirement for success in their work. Even in China, where engagement with commercial sex workers is integral to the functions of a man's work, they work in a capacity that is defined differently and associated with a much different identity. The men and women who have described to me the expectation to smoke and drink heavily, eat indulgently, and engage in commercial sex as a way to gain social capital in their social field and climb up the political or economic ladder recognize these activities as an occupational hazard rather than a public health hazard. Public health practitioners and researchers should consequently reframe their conception of the intersection of sex and work to recognize that these activities are structured more by social and cultural practices—in China and elsewhere—than by the individual behaviors prioritized in public health models. Acknowledging the social functions that sex work serves, for both women and men, will benefit public health programs targeting risky behaviors.

NOTES

This chapter builds on my 2015 article "'Sex'—It's Not Only Women's Work."

1   A reference to Xi Jinping's approach to stamping out official corruption in China; Xi he vowed to go after officials at both higher and lower municipal levels of government.

2   He, "Yunnan Official Tried Suicide, Report Says."

3   These identities, all constructed within the public health paradigm, are meant to describe individual behavioral categories and do not necessarily engage individual identities. In the field of public health, these categories of identities are condensed into three-letter acronyms: Commercial sex workers are CSWs, injection drug users are IDUs, and men who have sex with men are MSM. They are subsumed under a common umbrella of MARPs (most at-risk populations). For more on the challenges of applying the MSM category, please see Boellstorff, "But Do Not Identify as Gay."

4   Marx, *Capital.*

5   Furth, "Rethinking Van Gulik"; and Micollier, "Social Significance of Commercial Sex Work."

6   Henriot, *Prostitution and Sexuality in Shanghai*; Hershatter, *Dangerous Pleasures*; and Ruan, *Sex in China.*

7   Peterson, *Bitter Gourd.*

8   Bauman, "On Postmodern Uses of Sex"; and Micollier, "Social Significance of Commercial Sex Work."

9   See Zhang, "China's Sexual Revolution."

10   Bauman, "On Postmodern Uses of Sex," 122.

11   Gutmann, *The Meanings of Macho.*

12   Bourdieu and Wacquant, *An Invitation to Reflexive Anthropology.*

13   Uretsky, *Occupational Hazards.*

14   See also Yang, *Gifts, Favors, and Banquets*; Wank, *Commodifying Communism*; Osburg, *Anxious Wealth*; and Mason, *Infectious Change.*

15   *Ci hai.*

16   Smart, "Cognac, Beer, Red Wine or Soft Drinks?"

17   Bourdieu and Wacquant, *An Invitation to Reflexive Anthropology.*

18   Mars and Altman, "Alternative Mechanism of Distribution in a Soviet Economy."

19   Hershatter, *Dangerous Pleasures.*

20   Mason, *Infectious Change.*

21   Bourdieu and Wacquant, *An Invitation to Reflexive Anthropology.*

22   Ibid.; and Williams, "Theorising Class, Health and Lifestyles."

23   Entwistle and Henderson, *Re-drawing Boundaries.*

24   Walder, *Communist Neo-traditionalism*; and Meisner, *Mao's China and After.*

25   Yang, *Gifts, Favors, and Banquets*; Yan, *The Flow of Gifts*; Kipnis, *Producing Guanxi*; Gold et al., "An Introduction to the Study of Guanxi"; and Tsai, *Capitalism without Democracy.*

26   Marx, *Capital.*

27   Kempadoo, "Introduction"; Farley, "'Bad for the Body, Bad for the Heart'"; and Weitzer, "Sociology of Sex Work."

28   Doezma, "Forced to Choose."

29   Huang et al., "HIV/AIDS Risk Among Brothel-Based Female Sex Workers in China"; and Gruskin and Ferguson, "Government Regulation of Sex and Sexuality."

30   De Zalduondo, "Prostitution Viewed Cross-Culturally."

31   Douglas, "Risk as a Forensic Resource"; and Lupton, "Risk as Moral Danger."

32   De Zalduondo, "Prostitution Viewed Cross-Culturally"; Parker and Aggleton, *Culture, Society, and Sexuality*; Parker et al., *Framing the Sexual Subject*; and Hirsch et al., *The Secret.*

33   See, for example, Shannon et al., "Structural and Environmental Barriers to Condom Use Negotiation with Clients among Female Sex Workers."

34   Bernstein, "The Meaning of the Purchase"; Hirsch et al., *The Secret*; and Weitzer, "Sociology of Sex Work."

35   Allison, *Nightwork.*

36   See Allison, *Nightwork*; Cheng, "Assuming Manhood"; Uretsky, "Mobile Men with Money"; and Phinney, "'Eaten One's Fill and All Stirred Up.'"

37   Pan, *Cunzai yu huangming*; and Huang et al., "HIV/AIDS Risk Among Brothel-Based Female Sex Workers in China."

38   See, for example, Yang et al., "HIV, Syphilis, Hepatitis C and Risk Behaviours among Commercial Sex Male Clients in Sichuan Province, China."

39   Pan, "AIDS in China"; Wang et al., "The 2007 Estimates for People at Risk for and Living with HIV in China"; and Pan et al., "Clients of Female Sex Workers in China."

GLOSSARY OF CHINESE CHARACTERS

For orthographic consistency, all characters here appear in the traditional/
complex (*fanti*) style.

ban canfei 半殘廢
ban gulao 伴孤老
bankai men 半開門
banti 半體
Bao Jingyan 鮑敬言
Bao Tianxiao 包天笑
Bao'er 寶兒
bianxingren 變性人
biji 筆記
bimao 鼻毛
Bu 卜
bu zhongyong 不中用
buchong cailiao 補充材料

caizhan 採戰
Caizhen jiyao 採真機要
caizi jiaren 才子佳人
Cao Qujing 曹去晶
Cao Xueqin 曹雪芹
Chan zhen houshi 禪真後史
Chan zhen yishi 禪真逸史
Changsha 長沙
Chen Bainian 陳百年
Chen Jianshan 陳建山
Chenghua 成化
Chongzhen 崇禎
chuanqi 傳奇

Chuanyinglou huiyilü 釧影樓回憶錄
chumu 出母
*Chunyang yanzheng Fuyou Dijun jiji
    zhenjing* 純陽演正孚祐帝君既濟
    真經
Chunyu Zhang 淳于長
ci 雌
cifuxiong 雌孵雄
cimu 慈母

da Qing bing 大清兵
da Qing tianbing 大清天兵
Daliyuan 大理院
daqi 大妻
Daimu 代目
dakuaier 大塊兒
danwei 單位
Daode jing 道德經
Daxue 大學
dazi bao 大字報
Deng Xiaonan 鄧小南
Dengcao heshang 燈草和尚
di 娣
dimu 嫡母
Ding Yaokang 丁耀亢
diqi 嫡妻
dizi 嫡子

dianqie 典妾
dongbei zei 東北賊
Dongxuanzi 洞玄子
doufen 豆粉
Du Xiaoying 杜小英
duibuqi ni ziji de laopo 對不起你自己
　的老婆
duoqi zhidu 多妻制度
Duoyin 多銀

ernai 二奶

falangmei 髮廊妹
Fanghong buyi 房中補益
fanti 繁體
fanzui shishi 犯罪事實
fayu weiquan zhi nanzi 發育未全之
　男子
Feng Menglong 馮夢龍
Fengyue meng 風月夢
Fu Junlian 伏俊璉
Funü zazhi 婦女雜誌
fuqi tongti 夫妻同體
fuqi yiti 夫妻一體

ganhuo 肝火
Gao Rimei 高日枚
Ge Hong 葛洪
gongzuo 工作
"Guanju" 關雎
guanggun 光棍
guanxi 關係
Gujin xiaoshuo 古今小説
Guo, Empress of Wei 文德郭皇后
guoli Shanghai yixueyuan 國立上海
　醫學院
Guwangyan 姑妄言

Haishanghua 海上花
Han Ziyun 韓子雲
Hanshang Mengren 邗上蒙人
Hao 郝
haochi 皓齒

haonan'er 好男兒
He yinyang 合陰陽
heqi 合氣
heng 哼
Hong Mai 洪邁
Hong Yuan 洪淵
Hongguang 弘光
Honglou meng 紅樓夢
houmu 後母
Huan E 宦萼
Huang Xun 黃訓
Huangting jing 黃庭經
Huangting neijing yujing 黃庭内景
　玉經
Huangting waijing yujing 黃庭外景
　玉經
huangzhong ren 黃種人
"Huanwen ge yi" 歡聞歌一
Hu 惠
*Huitu Haishang mingji si da jingang
　qishu* 繪圖海上名妓四大金剛
　奇書

Ishimpō 醫心方

Jia Nanfen 賈南風
Jia Wenwu 賈文物
jiamu 嫁母
Jiang of Yi 夷姜
jianquan 健全
jiantiao 兼祧
Jiaojiao 皎皎
jiaojiao huangniao 交交黃鳥
jiaopi nenrou 嬌皮嫩肉
jiaren 佳人
jie yin shuo fa 借淫說法
jienü 街女
jiji 雞雞
jijian 雞姦
jijian zui 雞姦罪
jimu 繼母
Jin 晉
Jin ping mei 金瓶梅

Jindan jieyao 金丹節要
Jindan jiuzheng pian 金丹就正篇
Jindan zhenchuan 金丹真傳
Jingbao 晶報
jingshen shuairuobing 精神衰弱病
Jingshi tongyan 警世通言
Jinpingmei cihua 金瓶梅詞話
Jinshi 進士
jiqie 妓妾
Juyan 居延

Ke 客

Lanling Xiaoxiao Sheng 蘭陵笑笑生
laobaixing 老百姓
laodong 勞動
Laozi zhongjing 老子中經
Li Du 李杜
Li Yu 李漁
Li Zicheng 李自成
liangtou da 兩頭大
Lianhebao 聯合報
liefu 烈婦
Lienü zhuan 烈女傳
lingdao 領導
lingsui jia 零碎嫁
Liu Bannong 劉半農
Liu Jin 劉瑾
Liu Mengying 劉夢瑩
Liu Qingxing 劉慶荇
Liu Rushi 柳如是
Liu Wenru 劉文如
liumang zui 流氓罪
luanjiao 亂交
"Lun fangzhong jingdian *Sunüjing* yu
    Xuannüjing" 論房中經典《素女
    經》與《玄女經》
Lüye xianzong 綠野仙踪

Mao 毛
Mao Qiling 毛奇齡
Mao Wenjie 毛文杰
Mao Xiang 冒襄

Mawangdui yishu 馬王堆醫書
Mawangdui 馬王堆
meimu 美目
miaojian 廟見
Minduo zazhi 民鐸雜誌
Mudan ting 牡丹亭
muzhi 墓誌

nacai 納采
naji 納吉
nanke 男科
nannü zhibie 男女之別
nanxing meiyao 男性媚藥
naqie 納妾
nazheng 納徵
ni huibuhui liujing 你會不會流精
*Niwan Li zushi nüzong shuangxiu
    baofa* 泥丸李祖師女宗雙修
    寶筏
Nügong zhengfa 女功正法
nühuanan 女化男
Nüjindan yaofang 女金丹要方

Pan Guangdan 潘光旦
Pei 裴
pianqi 偏妻
pidou 批鬥
piping yu ziwo pipan 批評與自我批評
Pu Songling 蒲松齡

qi 妻
Qian Gui 錢貴
Qian Qianyi 錢謙益
qianmu 前母
Qiaoqiao hua 悄悄話
qie 妾
Qijie 奇姐
Qing 清
Qinglou meng 青樓夢
Qinglou wenxue 青樓文學
Qinglou yunyu 青樓韻語
qingqi 請期
qinying 親迎

qiti 齊體
quanren 全人

renyao 人妖
Rong 容
Rouputuan 肉蒲團
Ruan Dacheng 阮大成
rujia 儒家
Ruyijun zhuan 如意君傳

Sai Jinhua gushi 賽金花故事
Saijinhua benshi 賽金花本事
sanjiao gui yi 三教歸一
sanpei xiaojie 三陪小姐
sao 騷
Se Lu 瑟盧
Shanghai baobei 上海寶貝
shanghuo 上火
Shangqing huangshu guodu yi 上清
　　黃書過度儀
Shangqing jiudan shanghua taijing zhongji jing 上清九丹上化胎精
　　中精記
Shen Defu 沈德符
Shenbao 申報
shenghuo zai shuishen huore zhi zhong 生活在水深火熱之中
shengmu 生母
shenjing shuairuobing 神經衰弱病
Shi Kefa 史可法
Shijing 詩經
shinü 石女
shiqie 侍妾
shiqin 侍寢
Shiwen 十問
shouxin 獸心
shu yu tian 叔于田
shumu 庶母
shushi 術師
shuzi 庶子
Shun 舜
Sunü miaolun 素女妙論
Sunüfang 素女方

Sunüjing 素女經
suoyangzheng 縮陽症

tanbai jiaodai 坦白交代
Tang Song nüxing yu shehui 唐宋女性
　　與社會
Tang Xianzu 湯顯祖
Tao Sijin 陶思瑾
Tao Yuanqing 陶元慶
Taohua shan 桃花扇
Taohua ying 桃花影
Tiandi yinyang jiaohuan dale fu
　　天地陰陽交歡大樂賦
"*Tiandi yinyang jiaohuan dale fu chutan*" 天地陰陽交歡大樂賦
　　初探
Tianqi 天啟
Tianxia zhidao tan 天下至道談
tian'yan 天閹
Tianyu hua 天雨花
tizhi 體質
Tong Zida 童自大
tongxing'ai 同性愛
tongxing lian'ai 同性戀愛
tongxun 通訊
tongzhi 同志

Wan Guifei 萬貴妃
Wang Duanshu 王端淑
Wang Xiuchu 王秀楚
Wang Yihui 王逸慧
Wang Ziyao 王自瑤
Wei 魏
Wei Zhongxian 魏忠賢
Weiyang Sheng 未央生
Wendi Laoba 文第老八
wenming 問名
wo bing 我兵
wo chao 我朝
Wu 吳
Wu Gang 吳綱
Wu He 鄔合
Wu Jianren 吳趼人

Wu Juenong 吳覺農
Wu Weiye 吳偉業
Wu Zetian 武則天
Wugenshu 無根樹

Xi Han shiqi de xing guannian 西漢
　　時期的性觀念
xia 俠
xianyao 纖腰
Xianzong 憲宗
xiao 孝
Xiao Jianyi 蕭健一
Xiao Yan 蕭衍
xiaoqi 小妻
xiaqi 下妻
Xie An 謝安
Xie Jianshun 謝尖順
xing 幸
Xing 刑
xing gongzuo 性工作
xingbu 性部
Xinghua tian 杏花天
xingnengli 性能力
xingqiguan 性器官
Xingshi hengyan 醒世恆言
Xingshi yinyuan 醒世姻缘
Xingshi yinyuan zhuan 醒世姻緣傳
xingzhuang 行狀
Xinqingnian 新青年
xinshen haoruo 心神耗弱
xinshu 心術
Xinwenbao 新聞報
xinxing daode 新性道德
xiong 雄
xiucai 秀才
Xiuta yeshi 繡榻野史
xiuxi 休息
Xiwangmu nüxiu zhengtu shize 西王母
　　女修正途十則
Xu Guangqi 徐光啟
Xu Jin Ping Mei 續金瓶梅
Xu Naili 徐乃禮
Xu Qinwen 許欽文

Xuan, Lord of Wei 衛宣公
Xuanying 玄英
xunyi 薰衣
xunzang 殉葬

Yan Fuqing 顏福慶
Yan Tingzhi 嚴挺之
Yan Wu 嚴武
Yang 陽
yangbu 陽部
yangguizi 洋鬼子
yangju 陽具
yangmu 養母
yangren 洋人
yangwu 陽物
Yangzhou shiri ji 揚州十日記
Yao 堯
Yao Jinping 姚錦屏
Yao Yotang 姚有堂
Yao Zhen 姚震
Ye Dehui 葉德輝
Yesou puyan 野叟曝言
Yi jian zhi 夷堅志
Yi Yuren 易于仁
Yin 陰
ying 媵
yingchou 應酬
yingqie 媵妾
yinyao 淫妖
yishi gonghui jianwei 醫師公會監委
you fantian 游梵天
You Xialiu 游夏流
"You xianku" 游仙窟
youshengxue 優生學
Yu Da 俞達
Yu Huai 余懷
Yuan Dianzhang 元典章
yubi 御婢
Yuchi lian 玉池蓮
yudiao 御屌
Yufang mijue 玉房秘訣
Yufang zhiyao 玉房指要
yujingxiao 玉莖小

yunu 鬱怒
Yunü sunyyi 禦女損益
Yushi mingyan 喻世明言
Yutai xin yong 玉臺新詠
yuzhi 玉指

zai shui yi fang 在水一方
zei 賊
Zhang Jingsheng 張競生
Zhang Mengwei 張夢微
Zhang Xichen 章錫琛
zhenfu 貞婦
zheng 烝
Zhengde you Jiangnan 正德游江南
Zhengfeng 鄭風
zhi 姪

Zhong Qing 鍾情
"Zhong si" 螽斯
Zhongguo Kelisiding 中國克麗斯汀
Zhonghua Ribao 中華日報
Zhongyang ribao 中央日報
Zhou Jianren 周建人
Zhou Yimou 周貽謀
zhuanglian 妝奩
zhuchun 朱脣
*Zijin Guangyaodaxian xiuzhen
　　yanyi* 紫金光燿大仙修真
　　演義
ziyou lianai 自由戀愛
ziyou lihun 自由離婚
zuo shengyi 做生意
Zuozhuan 左傳

BIBLIOGRAPHY

ABBREVIATIONS

DFZZ *Dongfang zazhi* 東方雜誌 (Eastern miscellany)
DMM *Damimi* 大秘密 (Big secret)
DWB *Dawanbao* 大晚報 (China evening news)
FNZZ *Funü zazhi* 婦女雜志 (Ladies' journal)
JB *Jingbao* 晶報 (Crystal)
LHB *Lianhebao* 聯合報 (United daily news)
LL *Linglong* 玲瓏 (Lin-loon ladies magazine)
SB *Shenbao* 申報 (Shanghai news)
SB2 *Shibao* 時報 (Eastern times)
XWB *Xinwenbao* 新聞報 (The news)

SOURCES CONSULTED

Ahmed, Sara. "Affective Economies." *Social Texts* 22, no. 2 (2004): 117–39.

"'Ai' de ziwei" '愛'的次味 (The taste of love). *SB2*, May 1932.

Aldrich, Robert. *Colonialism and Homosexuality*. New York: Routledge, 2004.

———, ed. *Gay Life and Culture: A World History*. London: Thames and Hudson, 2006.

Alexander, Jeffrey C. *Trauma: A Social Theory*. Cambridge, UK: Polity, 2012.

Allison, Anne. *Nightwork: Sexuality, Pleasure, and Corporate Masculinity in a Tokyo Hostess Club*. Chicago: University of Chicago Press, 1994.

Anonymous. *Sunü miaolun* 素女妙論 (The wondrous commentary of the plain girl). Beijing: Zhongguo Xiju Chubanshe, 2007.

Arondeka, Anjali. "In the Absence of Reliable Ghosts: Sexuality, Historiography, South Asia." *differences* 25, no. 3 (2014): 98–122.

Baecque, Antoine de. *The Body Politic: Corporeal Metaphor in Revolutionary France, 1770–1800*. Translated by Charlotte Mandell. Stanford, CA: Stanford University Press, 1997.

Bai Bi 白比. "Nühua nanshen" 女化男身 (Woman to man). *Xinsheng zhoukan* 新生週刊 (New life weekly) 2, no. 9 (1935): 182–3.

Balazs, Etienne. *Chinese Civilization and Bureaucracy: Variations on a Theme*. Translated by H. M. Wright. Edited by Arthur F. Wright. New Haven: Yale University Press, 1964.

Barbieri-Low, Anthony J., and Robin D. S. Yates. *Law, State, and Society in Early Imperial China: A Study with Critical Edition and Translation of the Legal Texts from Zhangjiashan Tomb No. 247*. Leiden: Brill, 2015.

Barlow, Tani. *The Question of Women in Chinese Feminism*. Durham: Duke University Press, 2004.

Barlow, Tani, and Gary J. Bjorge, eds. *I Myself Am a Woman: Selected Writings of Ding Ling*. Boston: Beacon Press, 1989.

Barnhart, Richard M., Yang Xin, Nie Chongzheng, James Cahill, Lang Shoujun, and Wu Hung. *Three Thousand Years of Chinese Painting*. New Haven: Yale University Press, 1997.

Bauer, Heike, ed. *Sexology and Translation: Cultural and Scientific Encounters across the Modern World, 1880–1930*. Philadelphia: Temple University Press, 2015.

Bauman, Zygmunt. "On Postmodern Uses of Sex." *Theory, Culture, and Society* 15, nos. 3–4 (1998): 215–42.

Benjamin, Harry. *The Transsexual Phenomenon*. New York: The Julian Press, 1966.

Bernhardt, Kathryn. *Women and Property in China, 960–1949*. Stanford: Stanford University Press, 1999.

Bernstein, Elizabeth. "The Meaning of the Purchase: Desire, Demand and the Commerce of Sex." *Ethnography* 2, no. 3 (2001): 389–420.

Beurdeley, Michel, ed. *Jeux des nuages et de la pluie* (The clouds and the rain: The art of love in China). Frieburg: Office du Livre, 1969.

Bhabha, Homi K. *The Location of Culture*. New York: Routledge, 1994.

Bi Huankui 畢煥奎. "Sheping: Shenjingshuairuo yu qingnian: Zhuangcheng gongxiangei qin'aide qingnian xueyoumen" 社評：神經衰弱與青年：專誠貢獻給親愛的青年學友們 (Social commentary: Neurasthenia and youth; Sincerely for dear youthful friends). *Yiyao pinglun* 醫藥評論 (Medical review), no. 32 (1930): 12–16.

Birge, Bettine. "Levirate Marriage and the Revival of Widow Chastity in Yuan China." *Asia Major* 8, no. 2 (1995): 107–46.

——. *Women, Property, and Confucian Reaction in Sung and Yüan China (960–1368)*. Cambridge, UK: Cambridge University Press, 2002.

——. "Sexual Misconduct in Mongol-Yuan Law, with Some Observations on Chinggis Khan's Jasagh." *Mongolica: An International Annual of Mongol Studies* 22 (2009): 287–97.

Birrell, Anne. *New Songs from a Jade Terrace: An Anthology of Early Chinese Love Poetry.* Boston: Allen & Unwin, 1982.

———. *Chinese Mythology: An Introduction.* Baltimore: Johns Hopkins University Press, 1993.

Black, Dora. "Young China: Hints on Building the New Civilization." Lecture held in China, 90000, 2–3, Bertrand Russell Archive, McMaster University, Hamilton.

———. "Zhongguo de nüquanzhuyi yu nüxing gaizao" 中國的女權主義與女性改革 (Chinese feminism and the female reform movement). Translated by Yun He. *FNZZ* 9, no. 1 (1923): 51.

Bleys, Rudi. *The Geography of Perversion: Male-to-Male Sexual Behavior Outside the West and the Ethnographic Imagination, 1750–1918.* New York: New York University Press, 1995.

Boellstorff, Tom. "But Do Not Identify as Gay: A Proleptic Genealogy of the MSM Category." *Cultural Anthropology* 26, no. 2 (2011): 287–312.

Bossler, Beverly. *Courtesans, Concubines, and the Cult of Female Fidelity: Gender and Social Change in China, 1000–1400.* Cambridge, MA: Harvard University East Asia Center, 2013.

———. "Faith Wives and Heroic Maidens: Politics, Virtue, and Gender in Song China." In *Tang Song nüxing yu shehui* 唐宋女性與社會 (Women and society in Tang–Song China), edited by Deng Xiaonan, 751–84. Shanghai: Shanghai Cishu Chubanshe, 2003.

———. *Faithful Wives and Heroic Martyrs: State, Society, and Discourse in the Song and Yuan.* Tokyo: Tokyo Metropolitan University Press, 2002.

———. *Powerful Relations: Kinship, Status, and the State in Sung China (960–1279).* Cambridge, MA: Harvard University East Asia Center, 1998.

———. "Shifting Identities: Courtesans and Concubines in Song China." *Harvard Journal of Asiatic Studies* 62, no 1 (2002): 5–37.

Bourdieu, Pierre, and Loic Wacquant. *An Invitation to Reflexive Anthropology.* Chicago: University of Chicago Press, 1992.

Boyd, Nan A., and Horacio N. Roque Ramirez. *Bodies of Evidence: The Practice of Queer Oral History.* Oxford: Oxford University Press, 2012.

Bray, Francesca. *Technology and Gender: Fabrics of Power in Late Imperial China.* Berkeley: University of California Press, 1997.

Brennan, Samantha J. *"Pornography, the Theory: What Utilitarianism Did to Action* (review)." *Victorian Studies* 49, no. 1 (2006): 155–56.

Brockey, Liam Matthew. *Journey to the East: The Jesuit Mission to China, 1579–1724.* Cambridge, MA: Harvard University Press, 2007.

Brownell, Susan. *Training the Body for China: Sports in the Moral Order of the People's Republic.* Chicago: University of Chicago Press, 1995.

Buffington, Robert M., Eithne Luibhéid, and Donna J. Guy, eds. *A Global History of Sexuality: The Modern Era.* Malden: Wiley Blackwell, 2014.

"Burang Kelisiding zhuanmei yuqian dabing jiang bianchen xiaojie" 不讓克麗絲汀專美於前 大兵將變成小姐 (Christine will not be America's exclusive: Soldier destined to become a lady). *LHB*, August 21, 1953.

Canaday, Margot. "Thinking Sex in the Transnational Turn: An Introduction." *American Historical Review* 114, no. 5 (2009): 1250–57.

Canguilhem, Georges. *The Normal and the Pathological*. New York: Zone Books, 1991.

Cao Qujing 曹去晶. *Guwangyan* 姑妄言 (Preposterous words). Taipei: Taiwan Daying Baike Gufen Youxian Gongsi, 1997.

Cao Xuesong 曹雪松. "Sanjiaolian'ai jiejuefa" 三角戀愛解決法 (Resolving romantic triangles). *FNZZ* 11, no. 3 (1925): 394–99.

Cao Yaxia 曹亞俠. "Taolun: Wode sanjiaolian'ai jiejuefa (weiwan)" 討論: 我底三角戀愛解決法 (未完) (Discussion: My method for resolving romantic triangles [not concluded]). *Funü pinglun* 婦女評論 (Women's review), no. 96 (1923): 1–2.

———. "Taolun: Wode sanjiaolian'ai jiejuefa (xu)" 討論: 我底三角戀愛解決法 (續) (Discussion: My method for resolving romantic triangles [continued]). *Funü pinglun*, no. 95 (1923): 2–3.

———. "Taolun: Wode sanjiaolian'i jiejuefa (xu)" 討論: 我底三角里奈解決法 (續) (Discussion: My method for resolving romantic triangles [continued]). *Funü pinglun*, no. 98 (1923): 3–4.

Carlitz, Katherine. "Shrines, Governing-Class Identity, and the Cult of Widow Fidelity in Mid-Ming Jianan." *Journal of Asian Studies* 56, no. 3 (1997): 612–40.

Castiglia, Christopher, and Christopher Reed. *If Memory Serves: Gay Men, AIDS, and the Promise of the Queer Past.* Minneapolis: University of Minnesota Press, 2012.

Cauldwell, David. "Psychopathia Transexualis." *Sexology* 16 (1949): 274–80.

Chai Fuyuan 柴福沅. *Xingxue ABC* 性學 ABC (ABC of sexology). Shanghai: Shijie Shuju, 1932 [1928].

Chao, Buwei Yang, and Yuen Ren Chao. *Autobiography of a Chinese Woman*. New York: John Day, 1947.

Chauncey, George. *Gay New York: Gender, Urban Culture, and the Making of the Gay Male World, 1890–1940*. New York: Basic Books, 1994.

Chen, Jianshan 陳建山. "Youshengxue he ji ge xing de wenti" 優生學和幾個性的問題 (Eugenics and some problems related to sex). *Minduo zazhi* 民鐸雜誌 (People's tocsin) 5, no. 4 (1925): 52–61.

Chen Biyun 陳碧云. "Nüxing jidude jiepou" 女性忌妒的解剖 (Dissecting female jealousy). *Nüsheng* 女聲 (Women's voice) 2, no. 11 (1934): 6–7.

Chen Guyuan 陳顧遠. *Zhongguo hunyin shi* 中國婚姻史 (History of Chinese marriage). Changsha: Yuelu, 1998.

Chen Qiyou 陳奇猷. *Han Feizi xin jiaozhu* 韓非子新校注 (A new annotation of Han Feizi). Shanghai: Guji, 2000.

Chen Ruoshui 陳弱水. *Tangdai de funü wenhua yu jiating shenghuo* 唐代的婦女文化與家庭生活 (Women's culture and family life in Tang China). Taipei: Yunchen wenhua, 2007.

Chen Shou 陳壽 (233–97). *Sanguo zhi* 三國志 (Three kingdoms). Beijing: Zhonghua, 1959.

Chen Yiyuan 陳益源. *Cong "Jiaohong ji" dao "Honglou meng,"* 從嬌紅記到紅樓夢 (From *Jiaohong ji* to *Honglou meng*). Shenyang: Liaoning Guji Chubanshe, 1996.

———. *"Guwangyan* sucai laiyuan chukao" 姑妄言素材來源初考 (A study of sources in *Guwangyan*, part one). In *"Cong 'Jiaohong ji' dao 'Honglou meng,'"* 從嬌紅記到紅樓夢 (From *Jiaohongji* to *Honglou meng*), by Chen Yiyuan, 304–19. Shenyang: Liaoning Guji Chubanshe, 1996.

———. *"Guwangyan* sucai laiyuan erkao" 姑妄言素材來源二考 (A study of sources in *Guwangyan*, part two). *Ming Qing xiaoshuo yanjiu* 明清小說研究 (Research on Ming–Qing novels) 46, no. 4 (1997): 127–36.

Chen Zhaorong 陳昭容. "Liang-Zhou hunyin guanxi zhong de 'ying' yu 'yingqi'—Qingtongqi mingwen zhong de xingbie, shenfen yu jiaose yanjiu zhi er" 兩周婚姻關係中的「媵」與「媵器」—青銅器銘文中的性別、身分與角色研究之二 (Marriage practices and dowry objects in Zhou dynasty marriage relations—Gender, status, and role in bronze inscriptions, part two). *Zhongyang Yanjiuyuan Lishi Yuyan Yanjiusuo jikan* 中央研究院歷史語言研究所集刊 (Bulletin of the Institute of History and Philology, Academia Sinica) 77, no. 2 (2006): 193–278.

Cheng, Sea-ling. "Assuming Manhood: Prostitution and Patriotic Passions in Korea." *East Asia: An International Quarterly* 18, no. 4 (2000): 40–78.

Chiang, Howard. *After Eunuchs: Science, Medicine, and the Transformations of Sex in Modern China*. New York: Columbia University Press, 2018.

———. "Archiving Peripheral Taiwan: The Prodigy of the Human and Historical Narration." *Radical History Review*, no. 120 (2014): 204–25.

———. "The Conceptual Contours of Sex in the Chinese Life Sciences: Zhu Xi (1899–1962), Hermaphroditism, and the Biological Discourse of *Ci* and *Xiong*, 1920–1950." *East Asian Science, Technology, and Society* 2, no. 3 (2008): 401–30.

———. "Epistemic Modernity and the Emergence of Homosexuality in China." *Gender and History* 22, no. 3 (2010): 629–57.

———. "Gender Transformations in Sinophone Taiwan." *positions: asia critique* 25, no. 3 (2017): 527–63.

———. "Revisiting Foucault: Thinking with *The History of Sexuality* at Forty." *Cultural History* 5, no. 2 (2016): 115–21.

Chien, Ying-Ying. "Feminism and China's New 'Nora': Ibsen, Hu Shi, and Lu Xun." *Comparatist* 19 (May 1995): 97–113.

Chin, Tamara T. *Savage Exchange: Han Imperialism, Chinese Literary Style, and the Economic Imagination*. Cambridge, MA: Harvard University East Asia Center, 2014.

Chou, Wah-shan. *Tongzhi: Politics of Same-Sex Eroticism in Chinese Societies*. New York: Haworth Press, 2000.

Chu, Pao-liang. *Twentieth-Century Chinese Writers and Their Pen Names*. Boston: G. K. Hall, 1977.

Ch'ü, T'ung-Tsu. *Law and Society in Traditional China.* Paris: Mouton, 1961.

Chung, Juliette Yuehtsen. *Struggle for National Survival: Eugenics in Sino-Japanese Contexts, 1896–1945.* New York: Routledge, 2002.

Ci hai 辭海 (Sea of words). Shanghai: Shanghai Cishu Chubanshe, 1979.

"Ciduo huixiede riji" 詞多穢褻之日記 (Diary with many dirty words). *SB2,* May 29, 1932.

The Criminal Code of the Republic of China. Translated by S. L. Burdett and Lone Liang. Shanghai: Shanghai Provisional Court, 1928.

Crompton, Louis. *Homosexuality and Civilization.* Cambridge, MA: Belknap Press, 2003.

Cvetkovich, Ann. *An Archive of Feelings: Trauma, Sexuality, and Lesbian Public Cultures.* Durham: Duke University Press, 2003.

"Dai Tao nüshi dugengzheng" 代陶女士讀更正 (Correction on behalf of Miss Tao). *Hangzhou minguo ribao* 杭州民國日報 (Hangzhou Republican daily), July 1932.

Damimi 大秘密 (The big secret). Shanghai, 1920s–1930s.

Dan Weng 丹翁. "Nühuanan" 女化男 (Woman-to-man). *JB,* March 20, 1935.

Dardess, John. *Blood and History: The Dongling Faction and Its Repression, 1620–1627.* Honolulu: University of Hawai'i Press, 2002.

Darnton, Robert. *The Forbidden Bestsellers of Pre-Revolutionary France.* New York: Norton, 1995.

Davidson, Arnold I. *The Emergence of Sexuality: Historical Epistemology and the Formation of Concepts.* Cambridge, MA: Harvard University Press, 2001.

Dawanbao 大晚報 (China evening news). Shanghai, 1932–1949.

De Villiers, Nicholas. *Opacity and the Closet: Queer Tactics in Foucault, Barthes, and Warhol.* Minneapolis: University of Minnesota Press, 2012.

De Weerdt, Hilde. *Competition over Content: Negotiating Standards for the Civil Service Examinations in Imperial China (1127–1279).* Cambridge, MA: Harvard University East Asia Center, 2007.

De Zalduondo, Barbara. "Prostitution Viewed Cross-Culturally: Toward Recontextualizing Sex Work in AIDS Intervention Research." *Journal of Sex Research* 28, no. 2 (1991): 223–48.

DeJean, Joan. "The Politics of Pornography: *L'École des Filles.* In *The Invention of Pornography,* edited by Lynn Hunt, 109–23. New York: Zone Books, 1993.

D'Emilio, John. *The World Turned: Essays on Gay History, Politics, and Culture.* Durham: Duke University Press.

Deng Xiaonan 邓小南, ed. *Tang Song nüxing yu shehui* 唐宋女性與社會 (Women and society in Tang–Song China). Shanghai: Shanghai Cishu Chubanshe, 2003.

Despeux, Catherine. *Immortelles de la Chine ancienne: Taoïsme et alchimie féminine.* Puiseaux: Pardès, 1990.

Despeux, Catherine, and Livia Kohn. *Women in Daoism.* Honolulu: University of Hawai'i Press, 2003.

Diamant, Neil J. *Revolutionizing the Family: Politics, Love, and Desire in Urban and Rural China, 1949–1968.* Berkeley: University of California Press, 2000.

Dikötter, Frank. *Imperfect Concepts: Medical Knowledge, Birth Defects, and Eugenics in China*. New York: Columbia University Press, 1998.

———. *Sex, Culture and Modernity in China: Medical Science and the Construction of Sexual Identities in the Early Republican Period*. Honolulu: University of Hawai'i Press, 1995.

Dittmer, Lowell. "The Structural Evolution of 'Criticism and Self-Criticism.'" *China Quarterly* 56 (1973): 708–29.

Doan, Laura. *Disturbing Practices: History, Sexuality, and Women's Experience of Modern War*. Chicago: University of Chicago Press, 2013.

Doezma, Jo. "Forced to Choose: Beyond the Voluntary v. Forced Prostitution Dichotomy." In *Global Sex Workers: Rights, Resistance, and Redefinition*, edited by Kamala Kempadoo and Jo Doezma. New York: Routledge, 1998.

Dong Jiazun 董家遵. *Zhongguo gudai hunyin shi yanjiu* 中國古代婚姻史研究 (Research on marriage in classical China). Edited by Bian Encai 卞恩才. Guangzhou: Guangdong renmin, 1995.

Douglas, Mary. "Risk as a Forensic Resource." *Daedalus* 119, no. 4 (1990): 1–16.

Du, Lanlan. "From Taboo to Open Discussion: Discourses of Sexuality in *Azalea Mountain* and *Red Azalea*." *Comparative Literature Studies* 52, no. 1 (2015): 130–44.

"Du. Dangrande jieguo" 妒。當然的結果 (The preordained outcome of jealousy). *SB2*, October 10, 1932.

Du He. "Nühua nanshen" 女化男身 (Woman-to-man bodily transformation). *XWB*, March 18, 1935.

Du You 杜佑. *Tongdian* 通典 (Comprehensive institutions). Edited by Wang Wenjin 王文錦. Beijing: Zhonghua, 1988.

Du Zhengsheng 杜正勝. *Gudai shehui yu guojia* 古代社會與國家 (Ancient state and society). Taipei: Yunchen Wenhua, 1992.

Duberman, Martin, Martha Vicinus, and George Chauncey, eds. *Hidden from History: Reclaiming the Gay and Lesbian Past*. New York: Meridian, 1990.

Duggan, Lisa. *Sapphic Slashers: Sex, Violence, and American Modernity*. Durham: Duke University Press, 2000.

———. "The Trials of Alice Mitchell: Sensationlism, Sexology, and the Lesbian Subject in Turn-of-the-Century America." *Signs* 18, no. 4 (1993): 791–814.

Dull, Jack L. "Marriage and Divorce in Han China: A Glimpse at 'Pre-Confucian' Society." In *Chinese Family Law and Social Change in Historical and Comparative Perspective*, edited by David C. Buxbaum, 23–74. Seattle: University of Washington Press, 1978.

Ebner von Eschenbach, Silvia Freiin. "In den Tod mitgehen: Die Totenfolge in der Geschichte Chinas." In *Auf den Spuren des Jenseits: Chinesische Grabkultur in den Facetten von Wirklichkeit, Geschichte und Totenkult*, edited by Angela Schottenhammer, 167–91. Frankfurt: Peter Lang, 2003.

Ebrey, Patricia Buckley. *The Inner Quarters: Marriage and the Lives of Chinese Women in the Sung Period*. Berkeley: University of California Press, 1993.

———. *Women and the Family in Chinese History*. London: Routledge, 2003.

Ebron, Paulla, and Anna Lowenhaupt Tsing. "From Allegories of Identity to Sites of Dialogue." *Diaspora: A Journal of Transnational Study* 4, no. 2 (1995): 125–51.

Ellis, Havelock. *Psychology of Sex: A Manual for Students*. New York: R. Long & R. R. Smith, 1933.

———. *Studies in the Psychology of Sex*. Vol. 2, *Sexual Inversion*. 3rd ed. Philadelphia: F. A. Davis, 1921.

———. *The Problem of Race-Regeneration*. New York: Moffat, Yard & Co, 1911.

Elman, Benjamin. *On Their Own Terms: Science in China, 1550–1900*. Cambridge, MA: Harvard University Press, 2005.

Eng, David. "The Queer Space of China: Expressive Desire in Stanley Kwan's *Lan Yu*." *positions: east asia cultures critique* 18, no. 2 (2010): 459–88.

Entwistle, Barbara, and Gayle Henderson. *Re-drawing Boundaries: Work, Households, and Gender in China*. Berkeley: University of California Press, 2000.

Epstein, Maram. *Competing Discourses: Orthodoxy, Authenticity, and Engendered Meanings in Late Imperial Chinese Fiction*. Cambridge, MA: Harvard University Press, 2001.

Evans, Harriet. *Women and Sexuality in China: Dominant Discourses of Female Sexuality and Gender Since 1949*. Cambridge, UK: Polity, 1997.

"Fabiao Xie Jianshun mimi weifan yishifa buwu shidangchu" 發表謝尖順祕密 違反醫師法 不無失當處 (Publicizing Xie Jianshun's secret goes against the legal regulation of medicine). *LHB*, October 29, 1955.

Faderman, Lillian. "The Morbidification of Love between Women by Nineteenth-Century Sexologists." *Journal of Homosexuality* 4, no. 1 (1978): 73–90.

Fang, Gang 方剛. *Tongxinglian zai Zhongguo* 同性戀在中國 (Homosexuality in China). Changchun: Jilin People's Press, 1995.

Fang Fei 芳菲. "Nüzhuan nanshen de yanjiu" 女轉男身的研究 (Research on female-to-male transformation). *JB*, March 21, 1935.

Fang Ruhao方汝浩. *Chanzhen houshi* 禪真後史 (Later tales of the true way). Hangzhou: Zhejiang Guji Chubanshe, 1987.

Fang Xuanling 房玄齡. *Jinshu* 晉書 (The history of the Jin). Beijing: Zhonghua Shuju, 1974.

Fanon, Frantz. *The Wretched of the Earth*. New York: Grove Press, 1963.

Farley, Melissa. "'Bad for the Body, Bad for the Heart': Prostitution Harms Women Even if Legalized or Decriminalized." *Violence Against Women* 10 (2004): 1087–125.

Feng Menglong 馮夢龍. *Xingshi hengyan* 醒世恆言 (Constant words to awaken the world). Taipei: Shijie Shuju, 1973.

Feng Yuming 馮玉明and Zhu Yongfeng 朱勇鋒. "300 li songchi ji boqi yinjing celiang baogao" 300 例鬆弛及勃起陰莖測量報告 (A report on the flaccid and erect penis sizes of three hundred men). *Nanxingxue zazhi* 男性學雜誌 (Chinese journal of andrology) 8, no. 4 (1994): 236–37.

Feng Zi 鳳子. "Lianai ziyou jieda kewen di yi" 戀愛自由解答客問第一 (An explanation on the freedom of love—1). *FNZZ* 8, no. 8, coll. vol. 33 (1922): 15,151–53.

———. "Lianai ziyou jieda kewen di si" 戀愛自由解答客問第四 (An explanation on the freedom of love—4). *FNZZ* 9, no. 2, coll. vol. 35 (1923): 16,286–87.

———. "Lianai ziyou jie ji pian" 戀愛自由解續篇 (A piece interpreting freedom of love). *FNZZ* 9, no. 2, coll. vol. 35 (1923): 16,289–90.

Ferguson, Frances. *Pornography, the Theory: What Utilitarianism Did to Action.* Chicago: University of Chicago Press, 2004.

Fong, Grace. "Signifying Bodies: The Cultural Significance of Suicide Writings in Ming-Qing China." *Nannü: Men, Women, and Gender in China* 3, no. 1 (2001): 105–42.

Foucault, Michel. *The History of Sexuality, Vol. 1: An Introduction.* Translated by Robert Hurley. New York: Random House, 1978.

Freeman, Elizabeth. *Time Binds: Queer Temporalities, Queer Histories.* Durham: Duke University Press, 2010.

Frühstück, Sabine. *Colonizing Sex: Sexology and Social Control in Modern Japan.* Berkeley: University of California Press, 2003.

Fu Junlian 伏俊璉. "*Tiandi yinyang jiaohuan dale fu* chutan" 天地陰陽交歡大樂賦初探 (A preliminary study of love, happiness, and joy between heaven and earth). *Guizhou daxue xuebao* 貴州大學學報 (Journal of Guizhou University) 21, no. 4 (2003).

Fuechtner, Veronika, Douglas E. Haynes, and Ryan Jones, eds. *A Global History of Sexual Science, 1880–1960.* Berkeley: University of California Press, 2017.

Funü pinglun 婦女評論 (Women's review). Supplement to *Minguo ribao* 民國日報 (Republican daily). Shanghai, 1921–47.

Funü zazhi 婦女雜志 (Ladies' journal). Shanghai, 1915–31.

Furth, Charlotte. "Androgynous Males and Deficient Females: Biology and Gender Boundaries in Sixteenth- and Seventeenth-Century China." *Late Imperial China* 9, no. 2 (1988): 1–31.

———. *A Flourishing Yin: Gender in China's Medical History, 960–1665.* Berkeley: University of California Press, 1999.

———. "The Patriarch's Legacy: Household Instructions and the Transmission of Orthodox Values." In *Orthodoxy in Late Imperial China,* edited by Kwang-Ching Liu, 187–211. Berkeley: University of California Press, 1990.

———. "Rethinking Van Gulik: Sexuality and Reproduction in Traditional Chinese Medicine." In *Engendering China: Women, Culture, and the State,* edited by Christina K. Gilmartin, Gail Hershatter, Lisa Rofel, and Tyrene White, 125–46. Cambridge, MA: Harvard University Press, 1994.

———. "Rethinking van Gulik Again." *Nan Nü: Men, Women and Gender in China* 7, no. 1 (2005): 71–78.

Furuya Toyoko 古屋登代子. "Tongxing'ai zai nüzi jiaoyushangde xinyiyi" 同性愛在女子教育上的新意義 (The new significance of same-sex love in female education). Translated by Weisheng 薇生. *FNZZ* 11, no. 6 (1925): 1064–69.

"Gaofayuan jinchen kaishen" 高法院今晨開審 (Supreme Court begins deliberations this morning). *DWB*, July 26, 1932.

Ge Longpu to Zhang Xichen 章錫琛. "Xuhun fachu de biyao" 許婚廢除的必要 (The necessity of abolishing arranged marriages). *FNZZ* 8, no. 9, coll. vol. 33 (1922): 15, 111–12.

Glosser, Susan L. *Chinese Visions of Family and State, 1915–1953*. Berkeley: University of California Press, 2003.

Gold, Thomas, Doug Guthrie, and David Wank. "An Introduction to the Study of Guanxi." In *Social Connections in China*, edited by Thomas Gold, Doug Guthrie, and David Wank, 3–20. New York: Cambridge University Press, 2002.

Goldin, Paul R. "Copulating with One's Stepmother—Or Birth Mother?" In *Behaving Badly in Early and Medieval China*, edited by Harry N. Rothschild and Leslie V. Wallace, 56–69. Honolulu: University of Hawai'i Press, 2017.

———. "The Cultural and Religious Background of Sexual Vampirism in Ancient China." *Theology & Sexuality* 12, no. 3 (2006): 285–307.

———. *The Culture of Sex in Ancient China*. Honolulu: University of Hawai'i Press, 2002.

———. "Gender and Sexuality in Pre-Modern China: Bibliography of Materials in Western Languages." www.sas.upenn.edu/ealc/paul-r-goldin#tabset-tab-4.

Gruskin, Sofia, and Laura Ferguson. "Government Regulation of Sex and Sexuality: In their Own Words." *Reproductive Health Matters* 17, no. 34 (2009): 108–18.

Gu Yin 顧寅. "Cong TaoLiu dusha shuodao nüzi tongxing'ai he nüxing fanzui yu xingjineng (zhong)" 從陶劉妒殺說到女子同性愛和女性犯罪與性機能 (中) (Speaking of women's criminality and sexual function from the perspective of the Tao Liu jealousy murder [middle]). *Doubao* 斗報 (Struggle) 2, no. 10 (1932): 5–7.

———. "Cong TaoLiu dusha shuodao nüzi tongxing'ai he nüxing fanzui yu xingjineng (xia) "從陶劉妒殺說到女子同性愛和女性犯罪與性機能 (下) (Speaking of women's criminality and sexual function from the perspective of the Tao Liu jealousy murder [final]). *Doubao* 2, no. 11 (1932): 3–5.

———. "Nüzide shouyuin" 女子的手淫 (Women's masturbation). *Shengming yu jiankang* 生命歟健康 (Life and health), no. 42 (1926): 3–5.

Guai 怪. "Sanjiao tongxinglian'aizhi zha" 三角同性戀愛之戰 (The battle of triangular homosexuality). *Beiyang huabao* 北洋畫報 (Beiyang pictorial), September 26, 1928.

Guo, Xiaofei 郭曉飛. *Zhongguo fashiyexiade tongxinglian* 中國法視野下的同性戀 (Homosexuality under the horizon of Chinese law). Beijing: Zhishi Chanquan Publishing House, 2007.

Gutmann, Matthew. *The Meanings of Macho: Being a Man in Mexico City*. Berkeley: University of California Press, 1996.

Halberstam, Jack [Judith]. *In a Queer Time and Place: Transgender Bodies, Subcultural Lives*. New York: New York University Press, 2005.

Hall, Stuart, and Paul du Gay. *Questions of Cultural Identity.* Sage Publications, 1996.

Halperin, David. *One Hundred Years of Homosexuality: And Other Essays on Greek Love.* New York: Routledge, 1990.

Halperin, David, John Winkler, and Froma Zeitlin, eds. *Before Sexuality: The Construction of Erotic Experience in the Ancient Greek World.* Princeton: Princeton University Press, 1990.

Hanan, Patrick. *The Invention of Li Yu.* Cambridge, MA: Harvard University Press, 1988.

Harper, Donald. *Early Chinese Medical Literature: The Mawangdui Medical Manuscripts.* London: Kegan Paul International, 1998.

———. "The Sexual Arts of Ancient China as Described in a Manuscript of the Second Century BC." *Harvard Journal of Asiatic Studies* 47, no. 2 (1987): 539–93.

Harrison, Henrietta. *The Making of the Republican Citizen: Political Ceremonies and Symbols in China, 1911–1929.* Oxford: Oxford University Press, 2000.

Hausman, Bernice L. *Changing Sex: Transsexualism, Technology, and the Idea of Gender.* Durham: Duke University Press, 1995.

He, Huifeng. "Yunnan Official Tried Suicide, Report Says." *South China Morning Post,* May 11, 2014. www.scmp.com/news/china/article/1509337/yunnan-official-allegedly-being-probed-graft-attempts-suicide-report-says.

Heathorn, Stephen. "Explaining Russell's Eugenic Discourse in the 1920s." *Russell Journal* 25, no. 2 (2005): 107–39.

Heinrich, Ari Larissa. *The Afterlife of Images: Translating the Pathological Body between China and the West.* Durham: Duke University Press, 2008.

Henriot, Christian. *Prostitution and Sexuality in Shanghai: A Social History, 1849–1949.* Translated by Noël Castelino. Cambridge, UK: Cambridge University Press, 2001.

Hershatter, Gail. *Dangerous Pleasures: Prostitution and Modernity in Twentieth-Century Shanghai.* Berkeley: University of California Press, 1997.

———. *The Gender of Memory: Rural Women and China's Collective Past.* Berkeley: University of California Press, 2011.

"Heyiwei Xie Jianshun" 何以慰謝尖順 (How to console Xie Jianshun). *LHB,* October 29, 1955.

Hinsch, Bret. *Passions of the Cut Sleeve: The Male Homosexual Tradition in China.* Berkeley: University of California Press, 1992.

———. *Women in Early Imperial China.* 2nd ed. Lanham, MD: Rowman & Littlefield, 2011.

Hirsch, Jennifer, Holly Wardlow, Daniel Jordan Smith, Harriet Phinney, Shanti Parikh, and Constance Nathanson. *The Secret: Love, Marriage, and HIV.* Nashville: Vanderbilt University Press, 2009.

Ho, Clara Wing-chung. *Overt and Covert Treasures: Essays on the Sources for Chinese Women's History.* Hong Kong: Chinese University Press, 2012.

Holmgren, Jennifer. "The Economic Foundations of Virtue: Widow Remarriage in Early and Modern China." *Australian Journal of Chinese Affairs* 13 (1985): 1–27.

"Hongchuan Hui'an quanxian Luo Rongzong nanhua weinü: Keyu Yao Jinping xiangying chengqu" 轟傳惠安全縣駱榮宗男化為女: 可與姚錦屏相映成趣 (The male-to-female transformation of Luo Rongzong shocked Hui'an county: An interesting parallel to Yao Jinping). *Nanyang Shangbao* 南洋商报 (South sea business), April 29, 1935.

Honig, Emily. "Socialist Sex: The Cultural Revolution Revisited." *Modern China* 29, no. 2 (2003): 143–75.

Honig, Emily, and Gail Hershatter. *Personal Voices: Chinese Women in the 1980s.* Stanford: Stanford University Press, 1988.

Honig, Emily, and Xiaojian Zhao. "Sent-Down Youth and Rural Economic Development in Maoist China." *China Quarterly* 222 (2015): 499–521.

Hoshina Sueko 保科季子. "Kandai no josei chitsujo—Myōbu seido engen kō" 漢代の女性秩序—命婦制度淵源考 (The social order of women during the Han: The origins of the system of *ming-fu*). *Tōhō gaku* 東方學 (Eastern culture) 108 (2004): 22–34.

Hsieh, Daniel. *Love and Women in Early Chinese Fiction.* Hong Kong: Chinese University of Hong Kong Press, 2008.

Hsieh Bao Hua. *Concubinage and Servitude in Late Imperial China.* Lanham, MD: Lexington, 2014.

Hsu, Rachel Hui-Chi. "The 'Ellis Effect': Translating Sexual Science in Republican China (1911–1949)." In *Towards a Global History of Sexual Science, 1870–1950*, edited by Douglas E. Haynes, Veronika Feuchtner and Ryan Jones, 186–210. Berkeley: University of California Press, 2017.

Hu Yunwei 胡雲薇. "Qianli huanyou cheng dishi, meinian fengjing shi taxiang—Shilun Tangdai de huanyou yu jiating" 千里宦遊成底事, 每年風景是他鄉—試論唐代的宦遊與家庭 (Thousands of miles of official travel to the end, the scenery is a hometown each year—On official travel and the family in the Tang dynasty). *Taida lishi xuebao* 臺大歷史學報 (Bulletin of the Department of History of National Taiwan University) 41 (2008): 65–107.

Huang, Hans Tao-Ming. *Queer Politics and Sexual Modernity in Taiwan.* Hong Kong: Hong Kong University Press, 2011.

Huang, Martin W. *Desire and Fictional Narrative in Late Imperial China.* Cambridge, MA: Harvard University Press, 2001.

———, ed. "Male Friendship in Ming China." Special issue, *Nan Nü: Men, Women and Gender in China* 9 (2007).

———. "Male-Male Sexual Bonding and Male Friendship in Late Imperial China." *Journal of the History of Sexuality* 23, no. 1 (2014): 312–31.

———. *Negotiating Masculinities in Late Imperial China.* Honolulu: University of Hawai'i Press, 2006.

Huang, Philip C. C. "Divorce Law Practices and the Origins, Myths, and Realities of Judicial 'Mediation' in China." *Modern China* 31, no. 2 (2005): 151–203.

Huang, Yingying, Gail Henderson, Suiming Pan, and Myron Cohen. "HIV/AIDS Risk Among Brothel-Based Female Sex Workers in China: Assessing the Terms, Content, and Knowledge of Sex Work." *Sexually Transmitted Diseases* 31, no. 11 (2004): 695–700.

Huang Yufeng 黃宇烽and Xu Ruiji 許瑞吉. *Nanke zhenduanxue* 男科診斷學 (Diagnostics of men's medicine). Shanghai: Dier Junyi Daxue Chubanshe, 1999.

Hunt, Lynn. "Introduction: Obscenity and the Origins of Modernity, 1500–1800." In *The Invention of Pornography*, edited by Lynn Hunt, 9–45. New York: Zone Books, 1993.

———, ed. *The Invention of Pornography: Obscenity and the Origins of Modernity.* New York: Zone Books, 1993.

———. "Pornography and the French Revolution." In *The Invention of Pornography*, edited by Lynn Hunt, 301–39. New York: Zone Books, 1993.

Jeffreys, Elaine, and Haiqing Yu. *Sex in China.* Cambridge, UK: Polity, 2015.

Jia, Ben-ray 翟本瑞. "Zongguoren 'xing' guan chutan" 中國人「性」觀初談 (A preliminary investigation of the Chinese view on sex). *Si yu yan* 思與言 (Thought and language) 33 (1995): 27–75.

Jia, Jinhua, Xiaofei Kang, and Ping Yao, eds. *Gendering Chinese Religion: Subject, Identity, and Body.* Albany: State University of New York Press, 2014.

Jiang, Quanbao, and Jesús J. Sánchez-Barricarte. "Bare Branches and Social Stability: A Historical Perspective from China." *Frontiers of History in China* 6, no. 4 (2011): 538–61.

Jiang Yu 江漁, Wang Yixin 王益鑫, Ji Ming 季明, Han Yinfa 韓銀發, Chen Zhenxing 陳振興, and Qian Xianmin 錢憲民. "470 li nanxing qingshaonian xingfayu qingkuang diaocha" 470 例男性青少年性發育情況調查 (An investigation of sexual development of 470 young and adolescent males). *Zhonghua miniao waike zazhi* 中華泌尿外科雜誌 (Chinese journal of urology) 6, no. 4 (1985): 230–32.

Jin Changtao 金昌燾, Min Yongxie 閔永燮, Jin Fenshan 金粉善, and Li Bingqiu 李炳求. "Chaoxianzu yu hanzu qingzhuangnian yinjing daxiao de bijiao" 朝鮮族與漢族青壯年陰莖大小的比較 (A comparison in penis size between ethnic Han and Korean young and middle-aged males). *Nanxingxue zazhi* 男性學雜誌 (Chinese journal of andrology) 3, no. 2 (1988): 113.

Jin Zhonghua 金仲華and Huang Huajie 黃華節. "Funü yu jiatinglan: renleixuejia suojian tongxing'aide yuanyin" 婦女與家庭欄： 人類學家所見同性愛的原因 (Women and family column: Causes of same-sex love observed by anthropologists). *DFZZ* 30, no. 21 (1933): 13–17.

Jiying 繼影. "Tongxinglian'aide mimi" 同性戀愛的秘密 (The secrets of same-sex love). *DMM*, February 3, 1929.

Jiyun 紀雲. "Tao'an taolunhui: Tao'an gai shei fuze?" 陶案討論會： 陶案該誰負 責? (Tao case symposium: Who should bear responsibility?). *DWB*, August 6, 1932.

Kang, Wenqing. "The Decriminalization and Depathologization of Homosexuality in China." In *China in and beyond the Headlines*, edited by Timothy Weston and Lionel Jensen, 231–48. Lanham: Rowman & Littlefield, 2012.

———. *Obsession: Male Same-Sex Relations in China, 1900–1950*. Hong Kong: Hong Kong University Press, 2009.

Katz, Jonathan Ned. *The Invention of Heterosexuality*. Chicago: University of Chicago Press, 2007.

Kelsky, Karen. *Women on the Verge: Japanese Woman, Western Dreams*. Durham: Duke University Press, 2001.

Kempadoo, Kamala. "Introduction: Globalizing Sex Workers' Rights." In *Global Sex Workers: Rights, Resistance, and Redefinition*, edited by Kamala Kampadoo and Jo Doezma, 1–28. New York: Routledge, 1998.

Key, Ellen. *The Century of the Child*. New York: G. P. Putnam's Sons, 1912.

———. *Love and Marriage*. New York: Source Book Press, 1970.

Kipnis, Andrew B. *Producing Guanxi: Sentiment, Self, and Subculture in a North China Village*. Durham: Duke University Press, 1997.

Kipnis, Laura. *Bound and Gagged: Pornography and the Politics of Fantasy in America*. New York: Grove Press, 1996.

Kleinman, Arthur, Yunxiang Yan, Jing Jun, Sing Lee, Everett Zhang, Pan Tianshu, Wu Fei, and Guo Jinhua. *Deep China: The Moral Life of the Person*. Berkeley: University of California Press, 2011.

Ko, Dorothy. *Cinderella's Sisters: A Revisionist History of Footbinding*. Berkeley: University of California Press, 2005.

Ko, Dorothy, and Wang Zheng, eds. *Translating Feminisms in China*. London: Wiley-Blackwell, 2007.

Kuriyama, Shigehisa. "Angry Women and the Evolution of Chinese Medicine." In *National Healths: Gender, Sexuality and Health in a Cross-Cultural Context*, edited by Michael Worton and Nana Wilson-Tagoe, 179–90. London: UCL Press, 2004.

Lagerwey, John. *Taoist Ritual in Chinese Society and History*. New York: MacMillan, 1987.

Lanser, Susan S. *The Sexuality of History: Modernity and the Sapphic, 1565–1830*. Chicago: University of Chicago Press, 2014.

Laqueur, Thomas. *Making Sex: Body and Gender from the Greeks to Freud*. Cambridge, MA: Harvard University Press, 1990.

Larson, Wendy. "Never This Wild: Sexing the Cultural Revolution." *Modern China* 25, no. 4 (1999): 423–50.

Laurence, Patricia Ondek. *Lily Briscoe's Chinese Eyes: Bloomsbury, Modernism, and China*. Columbia: University of South Carolina Press, 2003.

Lean, Eugenia. *Public Passions: The Trial of Shi Jianqiao and the Rise of Popular Sympathy in Republican China*. Berkeley: University of California Press, 2007.

Leary, Charles. "Intellectual Orthodoxy, the Economy of Knowledge, and the Debate over Zhang Jingsheng's Sex Histories." *Republican China* 18 (1994): 99–137.

Lee, Haiyan. *Revolution of the Heart: A Genealogy of Love in China, 1900–1950*. Stanford: Stanford University Press, 2007.

Lee, Jen-der [Li Zhende]. "Querelle des femmes? Les femmes jalouses et leur contrôle au début de la Chine médiévale." Translated by Gilles Despeux and Pénélope Ribaud Duran. In *Education et instruction en Chine*, edited by Christine Nguyen Tri and Catherine Despeux, 67–97. Paris: Peeters, 2004.

Lee, Peter A., and Edward O. Reiter. "Genital Size: A Common Adolescent Male Concern." *Adolescent Medicine Clinics* 13, no. 1 (2002): 171–80.

Leo, Jessieca. *Sex in the Yellow Emperor's Basic Questions: Sex, Longevity, and Medicine in Early China*. Dunedin: Three Pines, 2011.

Levenson, Joseph R. *Revolution and Cosmopolitanism*. Berkeley: University of California Press, 1971.

Lewis, Mark Edward. *The Construction of Space in Early China*. Albany: State University of New York Press, 2006.

Li, Yinhe 李銀河, and Xiaobo Wang 王小波. *Tamende shijie: Zhongguo nantongxinglianqunluo toushi* 他們的世界：中國男同性戀群落透視 (Their world: Male homosexual subculture in China). Taiyuan: Shanxi Renmin Chubaoshe, 1992.

Li Jishuo 李繼碩. "Zhongguo ren chengnian nanzi shenzang de yanjiu" 中國人成年男子腎臟的研究 (A study of the kidneys of adult Chinese men). *Zhonghua xinyixuebao* 中華新醫學報 (Journal of Chinese new medicine) 2, no. 5 (1951): 327–38.

Li Jiugong 李九功. *Lixiu yijian* 勵修一鑑 (Encourage a lesson). In *Tianzhujiao dongchuan wenxian sanbian* 天主教東傳文獻三編 (Documents of Catholic missions in Asia), edited by Ai Rulüe 艾儒略 [Giulio Aleni]. Taipei: Xuesheng, 1984.

Li Ling 李零. *Zhongguo fangshu zhengkao* 中國方術正考 (A study of Chinese *fangshu*). Beijing: Zhonghua Shuju, 2006.

Li Ling 李零 and Keith McMahon, "The Contents and Terminology of the Mawangdui Texts on the Arts of the Bedchamber." *Early China* 17 (1992): 145–85.

Li Wai-yee. "The Late Ming Courtesan: Invention of a Cultural Ideal." In *Writing Women in Late Imperial China*, edited by Ellen Widmer and Kang-I Sun Chang, 46–73. Palo Alto: Stanford University Press, 1997.

———. *Women and National Trauma in Late Imperial Chinese Literature*. Cambridge, MA: Harvard University Press, 2014.

Li Yu 李漁. *Rouputuan* 肉浦團 (The carnal prayer mat). Hong Kong: Lianhe Chubanshe, 1976.

Li Zhende 李貞德 [Jen-der Lee]. "Han Tang zhi jian nüxing caichanquan shitan" 漢唐之間女性財產權試探 (Women's property rights between Han and Tang dynasties). In *Zhongguoshi xinlun: Xingbieshi fence* 中國史新論：性別史分冊 (New Chinese historiography: Gender volume), edited by Li Zhende, 191–238. Taipei: Lianjing, 2009.

"Lian'ai fasheng yu tongxing wei jingshenshuairuo zhi mingzheng?" 戀愛發生於同性為精神衰弱之明證? (Is the development of love between people of the same sex evidence of neurasthenia?), *SB2*, May 8, 1932.

"Liang nüsheng zhi yimu canju" 兩女生0之一幕慘劇 (The tragedy of female students). *DWB*, February 24, 1932.

Liao Yifang 廖宜方. *Tangdai de muzi guanxi* 唐代的母子關係 (Mother-son relationship in the Tang dynasty). Taipei: Daoxiang, 2009.

Lindquist, Lisa J. "Images of Alice: Gender, Deviancy, and a Love Murder in Memphis." *Journal of the History of Sexuality* 6, no. 1 (1995): 30–61.

Ling Xiaoqiao 凌筱嶠. "Yilu yindu zhi can: Jie *Xixiang ji* yuedu *Hailing yishi*" 夷虜淫毒之慘: 借《西廂記》閱讀《海陵佚史》 (A reading of *Hailing yishi* through *The Western Chamber*). *Qinghua zhongwen xuebao* 清華中文學報 (Tsinghua journal of Chinese literature)12 (2014): 153–200.

Linglong 玲瓏 (Lin-loon ladies magazine). Shanghai, 1931–1937.

Lionnet, Françoise. *Autobiographical Voices: Race, Gender, Self-Portraiture.* Ithaca: Cornell University Press, 1989.

Liu, Kwang-Ching, ed. *Orthodoxy in Late Imperial China.* Berkeley: University of California Press, 1990.

Liu, Lydia H. "Life as Form: How Biomimesis Encountered Buddhism in Lu Xun." *Journal of Asian Studies* 68 (2009): 21–54.

———. *Translingual Practice: Literature, National Culture, and Translated Modernity—China, 1900–1937.* Stanford: Stanford University Press, 1995.

Liu, Petrus. *Queer Marxism in Two Chinas.* Durham: Duke University Press, 2015.

Liu Dalin 劉達臨. *Zhongguo gudai xing wenhua* 中國古代性文化 (Sex in ancient Chinese culture). Rev. ed. Yinchuan: Ningxia Renmin, 2003.

Liu Guozhen 劉國振 and Cao Jian 曹堅. "Zhongguo chengren nanzi wai shengzhiqi zhengchang biaozhun" 中國成人男子外生殖器正常標準 (The criteria for normal external reproductive organ size of Chinese adult males). *Jiepouxue tongbao* 解剖學通報 (A bulletin of anatomy) 4, no. 2–3 (1981): 178–83.

Liu I-ch'ing 劉義慶. *Shih-shuo hsin-yü* 世說新語. Translated by Richard B. Mather as *A New Account of Tales of the World*. 2nd ed. Ann Arbor: Center for Chinese Studies, University of Michigan, 2002.

Liu Jingzhen 劉靜貞. "Zheng wei yu nei? Songdai nüxing de shenghuo kongjian" 正位於內? —宋代女性的生活空間 (Located inside? Female living space in Song dynasty). *Qian Mu Xiansheng Jinianguan guankan* 錢穆先生紀念館館刊 (Bulletin of Qian Mu Memorial Museum) 6 (1997): 57–71.

Liu Piji 劉丕基. *Renjian wujie de shengwu* 人間誤解的生物 (Common misinterpretations of biology). Shanghai: Commercial Press, 1935.

Liu Ruilin 劉瑞麟. "Qingnian yu shenjing shuairuo" 青年與神經衰弱 (Youth and neurasthenia). *Xiandai qingnian* 現代青年 (Modern youth) 1, no. 4 (1935): 20–22.

Liu Xinning 劉欣寧. *You Zhangjiashan Hanjian Ernian lüling lun Hanchu de jicheng zhidu* 由張家山漢簡《二年律令》論漢初的繼承制度 (On the succession system of Han dynasty as written by Zhangjiashan's *Han Dynasty Bamboo Slips of the Second Year*). Taipei: Guoli Taiwan Daxue, 2007.

Liu Yibin 劉宜賓. "Zhengchang ertong 464 li gaowan he yinjing de celiang fenxi" 正常兒童464 例睪丸和陰莖測量分析 (An analysis of the result of measuring

464 normal children's scrotums and penises). *Hunan yixueyuan xuebao* 湖南醫學院學報 (Journal of Hunan Medical College) 11, no. 3 (1986): 280–85.

Liu Zenggui 劉增貴. "Wei Jin Nanbeichao shidai de qie" 魏晉南北朝時代的妾 (Concubines in Wei Jin Northern and Southern dynasties). *Xin shixue* 新史學 (New history) 2 (1991): 1–36.

Liu Zongyuan 柳宗元. "Hejian zhuan" 何鍵傳 (A biography of Hejian). In *Liu Hedong ji* 柳河東集 (A collection of Liu Hedong's works), 794–95. Based on the 1960 Zhonghuashuju Shanghai Bianjisuo edition. Shanghai: Shanghai Renmin Chubanshe, 1974.

Louie, Kam. *Theorizing Chinese Masculinity: Society and Gender in China*. New York: Cambridge University Press, 2002.

Love, Heather. *Feeling Backward: Loss and the Politics of Queer History*. Cambridge, MA: Harvard University Press, 2007.

Lu, Weijing. "Abstaining from Sex: Mourning Ritual and the Confucian Elite." In "Sexuality in Chinese History," edited by Weijing Lu. Special Issue, *Journal of the History of Sexuality* 22, no. 2 (2013): 230–52.

———. "The Chaste and the Licentious: Female Sexuality and Moral Discourse in Ming and Early Qing China." *Early Modern Women: An Interdisciplinary Journal* 5 (2010): 183–87.

———. "Introduction." In "Sexuality in Chinese History," edited by Weijing Lu. Special Issue, *Journal of the History of Sexuality* 22, no. 2 (2013): 201–6.

———, ed. "Sexuality in Chinese History." Special Issue, *Journal of the History of Sexuality* 22, no. 2 (2013).

———. *True to Her Word: The Faithful Maiden Cult in Late Imperial China*. Stanford: Stanford University Press, 2008.

Lu Jingyi 盧靜儀. *Qingmo Minchu jiachan zhidu de yanbian: Cong fenjia xichan dao yichan jicheng* 清末民初家產制度的演變: 從分家析產到遺產繼承 (The evolution of the property system in late Qing and early Republican China: From separation to inheritance analysis). Taipei: Yuanzhao, 2012.

Lu Xun. "My Views on Chastity." In *Women in Republican China: A Sourcebook*, edited by Hua R. Fong and Vanessa L. Fong, 10–16. Armonk, New York: M. E. Sharpe, 1999.

"Lujun diyi zongyiyuan xuanbu Xie Jianshun shoushu chenggong" 陸軍第一總醫院宣佈 謝尖順變性手術成功 (No. 1 Hospital announces the completion and success of Xie Jianshun's sex change operation). *LHB*, October 28, 1955.

Luo Mingjian 羅明堅 [Michele Ruggieri]. *Tianzhu shengjiao shilu* 天主聖教實錄 (The Holy Bible). In *Tianzhujiao dongchuan wenxian xubian* 天主教東傳文獻續編 (Documents of the diffusion of Catholicism into the East: Continuation), edited by Xu Guangqi 徐光啟. Taipei: Xuesheng, 1966.

Lupton, Deborah. "Risk as Moral Danger: The Social and Political Functions of Risk Discourse in Public Health." *International Journal of Health Services* 23, 3 (1993): 425–35.

"Lüshi dabianlun jingshenbing nanduanding" 律師大辯論精神病難斷定 (Lawyers debate the difficulty of determining mental illness). *DWB*, April 12, 1932.

Ma, Yuxin, "Male Feminism and Women's Subjectivities: Zhang Xichen, Chenxuezhao and the New Woman." *Twentieth Century China* 29, no. 1 (2003): 1–37.

MacCormack, Geoffrey. "A Reassessment of the 'Confucianization of the Law' from the Han to the Tang." In *Zhongguoshi xinlun: Falüshi fence* 中國史新論:法律史分冊 (New Chinese historiography: Legal history volume), edited by Liu Liyan 柳立言, 397–442. Taipei: Lianjing, 2008.

Man, Eva Kit Wah. "Discourses on Female Bodily Aesthetics and Its Early Revelations in *The Book of Songs*." In *Overt and Covert Treasures: Essays on the Sources for Chinese Women's History*, edited by Clara Wing-chung Ho, 113–30. Hong Kong: Chinese University Press, 2012.

Mann, Susan. *Gender and Sexuality in Modern Chinese History*. Cambridge, UK: Cambridge University Press, 2011.

———. *Precious Records: Women in China's Long Eighteenth Century*. Stanford: Stanford University Press, 1997.

Mao Qiling 毛奇齡. *Xihe ji* 西河集 (Collection of Xihe). *Wenyuange Siku quanshu* 文淵閣四庫全書.

Mars, Gerald, and Yochanan Altman. "Alternative Mechanism of Distribution in a Soviet Economy." In *Constructive Drinking: Perspectives on Drink from Anthropology*, edited by Mary Douglas, 270–79. New York: Cambridge University Press, 1987.

Marshall, Daniel, Kevin Murphy, and Zeb Tortorici. "Queering Archives: Historical Unravelings." *Radical History Review*, no. 120 (2014): 1–11.

———. "Queering Archives: Intimate Tracings." *Radical History Review*, no. 122 (2015): 1–10.

Marx, Karl. *Capital: A Critique of Political Economy, Volume 1*. Translated by B. Fowkes. Harmondsworth: Penguin, 1976 [1867].

Mason, Katherine. *Infectious Change: Reinventing Chinese Public Health after an Epidemic*. Stanford: Stanford University Press, 2016.

McClintock, Anne. *Imperial Leather: Race, Gender, and Sexuality in the Colonial Contest*. New York: Routledge, 1995.

McMahon, Keith. "Eroticism in Late Ming, Early Qing Fiction: The Beauteous Realm and the Sexual Battlefield." *Toung Pao*, Second Series, 73. livr. 4/5 (1987): 217–64.

———. *Misers, Shrews, and Polygamists: Sexuality and Male-Female Relations in Eighteenth-Century Chinese Fiction*. Durham: Duke University Press, 1995.

———. *Polygamy and Sublime Passion: Sexuality in China on the Verge of Modernity*. Honolulu: University of Hawai'i Press, 2009.

———. "The Polyandrous Empress: Imperial Women and Their Male Favorites." In *Wanton Women in Late-Imperial Chinese Literature: Models, Genres,*

Subversions, and Traditions, edited by Mark Stevenson and Wu Cuncun, 29–53. Leiden: Brill, 2017.

———. "The Potent Eunuch: The Story of Wei Zhongxian." *Journal of Chinese Literature and Culture* 1, nos. 1–2 (2014): 1–28.

Meisner, Maurice. *Mao's China and After: A History of the People's Republic of China*. 3rd ed. New York: Free Press, 1999.

Meng, Yue. "Female Images and National Myth." In *Gender Politics in Modern China: Writing and Feminism*, edited by Tani E. Barlow, 118–36. Durham: Duke University Press, 1993.

Meyerowitz, Joanne. *How Sex Changed: A History of Transsexuality in the United States*. Cambridge, MA: Harvard University Press, 2002.

Micollier, Evelyne. "Social Significance of Commercial Sex Work: Implicitly Shaping a Sexual Culture?" In *Sexual Cultures in East Asia: The Social Construction of Sexuality and Sexual Risk in a Time of AIDS*, edited by Evelyne Micollier, 3–22. New York: Routledge, 2004.

Min, Anchee. *Red Azalea*. London: Bloomsbury, 2009.

Ming. "Luosuo he nannü guanxi" 羅素和男女關系 (Russell and the relationship between men and women). *Juewu* 覺悟 (Awakening), supplement to *Minguo ribao* 民國日報副刊 (Republican daily), 10, no. 17 (1920).

"Mingriqi benbao zhuri pilou Tao Sijin yuzhong riji" 明日起本報逐日批露陶思瑾獄中日記 (Tomorrow this newspaper begins an exposé of Tao Sijin's prison diary). *DWB*, July 26, 1932.

Minguo ribao 民國日報 (Republican daily). Shanghai, 1921–1947.

Minton, Henry L. *Departing from Deviance: A History of Homosexual Rights and Emancipatory Science in America*. Chicago: University of Chicago Press, 2001.

Mitter, Rana. *A Bitter Revolution: China's Struggle with the Modern World*. Oxford: Oxford University Press, 2004.

Murphy, Kevin P., and Jennifer M. Spear, eds. *Historicising Gender and Sexuality*. London: Wiley-Blackwell, 2011.

Murray, Stephen. *Homosexualities*. Chicago: University of Chicago Press, 2000.

Najmabadi, Afsaneh. "Beyond the Americas: Are Gender and Sexuality Useful Categories of Analysis?" *Journal of Women's History* 18, no. 1 (2006): 11–21.

———. *Professing Selves: Transsexuality and Same-Sex Desire in Contemporary Iran*. Durham: Duke University Press, 2013.

"Nannüxuesheng lian'aide mimi" 男女學生戀愛的秘密 (The secrets of romance between male and female students). *DMM*, June 10, 1929.

"Nanshi faxian yinyangren jiangdong shoushu bian nannü" 南市發現陰陽人 將動手術辨男女 (A hermaphrodite discovered in Tainan: Sex to be determined after surgery). *LHB*, August 14, 1953.

Nivard, Jacqueline. "L'évolution de la presse féminine chinoise de 1898 à 1949." *Études chinoises* 5, nos. 1–2 (1986), 157–84.

Norberg, Kathryn. "The Libertine Whore: Prostitution in French Pornography from Margot to Juliette." In *The Invention of Pornography*, edited by Lynn Hunt, 225–52. New York: Zone Books, 1993.

"Nübian nanshen" 女變男身 (Woman to man). *Juxing* 聚星 (Stars) 2, no. 3 (1934): 10.

"Nübiannan" 女變男 (Female to male). *Xinzhonghua zazhi* 新中華雜誌 (New China magazine) 2, no. 6 (1934): 52.

"Nühua nanshen zhi Yao Jinping yeyi di Hu" 女化男身之姚錦屏業已抵滬 (The woman-to-man Yao Jinping has arrived in Shanghai). *SB*, March 17, 1935.

"Nüxuesheng jisude damimi" 女學生寄宿的大秘密 (The big secrets of female students' lodging). *DMM*, April 16, 1929.

"Nüxuesheng tongxinglian'aizhi eguo" 女學生同性戀愛之惡果 (The untoward result of girl students' same-sex love). *SB2*, March 24, 1932.

"Nüxueshengde damimi" 女學生的大秘密 上 (The big secrets of female students, part 1). *DMM*, April 12, 1929.

Nyström, Louise Sofia Hamilton, and Anna E. B. Fries. *Ellen Key: Her Life and Her Work*. New York: G. P. Putnam's Sons, 1913.

Oosterhuis, Harry. *Stepchildren of Nature: Krafft-Ebing, Psychiatry, and the Making of Sexual Identity*. Chicago: University of Chicago Press, 2000.

Osburg, John. *Anxious Wealth: Money and Morality among China's New Rich*. Stanford: Stanford University Press, 2013.

Ouyang Xiu 歐陽修. *Xin Tangshu* 新唐書 (The new book of Tang). Beijing: Zhong-hua, 1975.

Pan, Lynn. *When True Love Came to China*. Hong Kong: Hong Kong University Press, 2015.

Pan Guangdan 潘光旦. "TaoLiu dusha'ande shehui zeren" 陶劉妬殺案的社會責任 (Social responsibility for the Tao-Liu jealousy murder case). *Huanian* 華年 (Huanian weekly) 1, no. 2 (1932): 25–26.

——. "Wudu yououde tongxing jiansha'an" 無獨有偶的同性姦殺案 (Same-sex murder cases are rare but not unique). *Huanian* 華年 1, no. 11 (1932): 205.

——. "Zaiti TaoLiu dusha'an" 再提陶劉妒殺案 (On the Tao-Liu jealousy murder case again). *Huanian* 華年 1, no. 5 (1932): 82–83.

Pan Suiming 潘绥铭. "AIDS in China: How Much Possibility Is There in Sexual Transmitting?" Paper presented at the First China Conference on AIDS/STDs, Beijing, November, 2001.

——. *Cunzai yu huangming: Zhongguo dixia xing chanye kaocha* 存在與荒謬：中國地下 "性產業" 考察 (Existence and ridicule: A survey of the underground sex industry in China). Beijing: Qun Yan Chubanshe, 1997.

——. "Transformations in the Primary Life Cycle: The Origins and Nature of China's Sexual Revolution." In *Sex and Sexuality in China*, edited by Elaine Jeffreys, 21–42. Abingdon, UK: Routledge, 2006.

——. *Zhongguo Xinggeming Zonglun* 中國性革命總論 (Discussing China's sex revolution). Xiaoxiong: Wanyou Press, 2006.

Pan Suiming, William Parrish, and Yingying Huang. "Clients of Female Sex Workers in China: Prevalence and Risk Factors." Sex Work in Asia symposium, Harvard University, October 1–2, 2010.

Parker, Richard G., and Peter Aggleton, eds. *Culture, Society, and Sexuality: A Reader*. London: UCL Press, 1997.

Parker, Richard G., Maria Barbosa, and Peter Aggleton, eds. *Framing the Sexual Subject: The Politics of Gender, Sexuality, and Power*. Berkeley: University of California Press, 2000.

Peterson, Willard. *Bitter Gourd: Fang I-chih and the Impetus for Intellectual Change*. New Haven: Yale University Press, 1979.

Pfister, Rudolf. "The Production of Special Mental States within the Framework of Sexual Body Techniques—As Seen in the Mawangdui Medical Corpus." In *Love, Hatred, and Other Passions: Questions and Themes on Emotions in Chinese Civilization*, edited by Paolo Santangelo and Donatella Guida, 180–94. Leiden: Brill, 2006.

Pflugfelder, Gregory M. *Cartographies of Desire: Male-Male Sexuality in Japanese Discourse, 1600–1950*. Berkeley: University of California Press, 1999.

———. "'S' Is for Sister: Schoolgirl Intimacy and 'Same-Sex Love' in Early Twentieth-Century Japan." In *Gendering Modern Japanese History*, edited by Barbara Molony and Kathleen Uno, 133–90. Cambridge, MA: Harvard University Asia Center, 2005.

Phinney, Harriet. "'Eaten One's Fill and All Stirred Up': Doi Moi and the Reconfiguration of Masculine Sexual Risk and Men's Extramarital Sex in Vietnam." In *The Secret: Love, Marriage, and HIV*, edited by Jennifer Hirsch, Holly Wardlow, Daniel Jordan Smith, Harriet M. Phinney, Shanti Parikh, and Constance A. Nathanson, 108–35. Nashville: Vanderbilt University Press, 2009.

Plaenkers, Tomas. *Landscapes of the Chinese Soul: The Enduring Presense of the Cultural Revolution*. London: Karnac, 2010.

Puar, Jasbir. *Terrorist Assemblages: Homonationalism in Queer Times*. Durham: Duke University Press, 2007.

Qian Mali 錢瑪利. "'Du' shi nanzimen de zhuanlipinma?" '妒'是男子們的專利品嗎? (Is "jealousy" patented by men?). *LL* 1, no. 21 (1931): 745–46.

Qin Zhengxing 覃正興, Zhou Shuwen 周樹紋, and Zhang Zhijian 張志堅. "500 ming nanxing yinjing celiang jieguo fenxi" 500 名男性陰莖測量結果分析 (An analysis of the result of measuring five hundred men's penis size). *Guangxi yixue* 廣西醫學 (Guangxi medical journal) 21, no. 4 (1999): 638–39.

Qing Ye. "The Private, Metaphor, and Masculinity: Reading the Mid-Qing Novel *Guwangyan* (Preposterous Words)." Paper delivered at the annual AAS conference, Chicago, Illinois, April, 2015.

Raz, Gil. "The Way of the Yellow and the Red: Sexual Practice in Early Daoism." *Nan Nü: Men, Women and Gender in China* 10 (2008): 86–120.

Ren, Wei. "The Writer's Art: Tao Yuanqing and the Formation of Modern Chinese Deisgn (1900–1930)." PhD diss., Harvard University, 2015.

Ren Peichu 任培初. "Tongxing'aizhi buliang jieguo" 同性愛之不良結果 (The untoward result of same-sex love). *LL* 2, no. 56 (1932): 247.

"Renwu: Tao Sijin nüshi" 人物: 陶思瑾女士 (People: Miss Tao Sijin). *Pingmin yuekan* 平民月刊 (Common people monthly) 12, no. 4 (1936): 15.

Roberts, Rosemary. *Maoist Model Theatre: The Semiotics of Gender and Sexuality in the Chinese Cultural Revolution (1966–1976)*. Leiden: Brill, 2009.

Robertson, Jennifer. "Dying to Tell: Sexuality and Suicide in Imperial Japan." *Signs: Journal of Women in Culture and Society* 25, no. 11 (1999): 1–35.

Robinet, Isabelle. *La révélation du Shangqing dans l'histoire du taoïsme*. Paris: Ecole Française d'Extrême-Orient, 1984.

Rocha, Leon Antonio. "*Xing*: The Discourse of Sex and Human Nature in Modern China." *Gender and History* 22, no. 3 (2010): 603–28.

Rofel, Lisa. *Desiring China: Experiments in Neoliberalism, Sexuality, and Public Culture*. Durham: Duke University Press, 2007.

Ruan, Fang Fu. *Sex in China: Studies in Sexology in Chinese Culture*. New York: Plenum Press, 1991.

Rogaski, Ruth. *Hygienic Modernity: Meanings of Health and Disease in Treaty-Port China*. Berkeley: University of California Press, 2004.

Rupp, Leila J. *Sapphistries: A Global History of Love between Women*. New York: New York University Press, 2011.

Russell, Bertrand. Personal correspondence, 1920. Bertrand Russell Archive, McMaster University, Hamilton, ON.

———. *The Problem of China*. London: George Allen & Unwin, 1922.

Russell, Dora. *The Tamarisk Tree: My Quest for Liberty and Love*. New York: Putnam, 1975.

Sakamoto, Hiroko. "The Cult of Love and Eugenics in May Fourth Movement Discourse." *positions: east asia cultures critique* 12, no. 2 (2004): 329–76.

Sang, Tze-lan. *The Emerging Lesbian: Female Same-Sex Desire in Modern China*. Chicago: University of Chicago Press, 2003.

Sanger, Margaret. *World Trip Journal 1922*. Margaret Sanger Papers Project, New York University, New York.

Santangelo, Paolo, and Donatella Guida, eds. *Love, Hatred, and Other Passions: Questions and Themes on Emotions in Chinese Civilization*. Leiden: Brill, 2006.

Santos, Gonçalo, and Steven Harrell, eds. *Transforming Patriarchy: Chinese Families in the Twentieth Century*. Seattle: University of Washington Press, 2017.

Sasaki Mami 佐佐木滿實. "Handai hunyin xingtai xiaokao—Guanyu *Ernian lüling* suojian 'xiaqi,' 'pianqi'" 漢代婚姻形態小考—關於《二年律令》所見"下妻"、"偏妻" (An investigation into the varieties of marriage during the Han dynasty—"Lower wives" and "side-wives" appeared in the *Statutes and Ordinances of the Second Year*). In *Jianbo wenxian yu gudaishi: Di erjie chutu wenxian qingnian xuezhe guoji luntan lunwenji* 簡帛文獻與古代史: 第二屆出土文獻青年學者國際論壇論文集 (Bamboo and silk documents and ancient history: Collected papers from the Second International Young Scholars' Symposium on Excavated Documents), edited by the Department of History of Fudan University, 157–64. Shanghai: Zhongxi, 2015.

Schipper, Kristofer. "Science, magie et mystique du corps: Notes sur le taoïsme et la sexualité." In *Jeux des nuages et de la pluie*, edited by Michel Beurdeley, 11–42. Frieburg: Office du Livre, 1969.

———. *The Taoist Body*. Berkeley: University of California Press, 1994.

Schwarcz, Vera. *The Chinese Enlightenment: Intellectuals and the Legacy of the May Fourth Movement of 1919*. Berkeley: University of California Press, 1986.

Se Lu 瑟盧. "Luosuo yu funü wenti" 羅素與婦女問題 (Bertrand Russell and the woman problem). *FNZZ* 6, no. 1. Reprinted in *Juewu* 覺悟 (Awakening), supplement to *Minguo ribao* 民國日報副刊 (Republican daily), 8, no. 20 (1920): 2–3.

———. "Wenming yu dushen" 文明與獨身 (Civilization and spinsterhood), *FNZZ* 8, no. 10 (1922): 2–7.

Sedgwick, Eve Kosofsky. *Epistemology of the Closet*. Berkeley: University of California Press, 1990.

———. *Touching Feeling: Affect, Pedagogy, Performativity*. Durham: Duke University Press, 2003.

Sensheng 森聲. "Qingnian nannü yu xingde shenjingshuairuo" 青年男女與性的神經衰弱 (Male and female youth and sexual neurasthenia). *Jiankang shenghuo* 健康生活 (Health and life) 9, no. 4 (1937): 12–13.

Shahani, Nishant. *Queer Retrosexualities: The Politics of Reparative Return*. Bethlehem: Lehigh University Press, 2012.

Shannon, Kate, Steffanie Strathdee, Jean Shoveller, Melanie Rusch, and Mark Tyndall. "Structural and Environmental Barriers to Condom Use Negotiation with Clients among Female Sex Workers: Implications for HIV-Prevention Strategies and Policy." *American Journal of Public Health* 99, no. 4 (2009): 659–65.

Shanzai 善哉. "Funü tongxinzhi aiqing" 婦女同性之愛情 (Women's same-sex love). *Funüshibao* 婦女時報 (Women's times) 1, no. 7 (1911): 36–38.

Shapiro, Hugh. "The Puzzle of Spermatorrhea in Republican China." *positions: east asia cultures critique* 6, no. 3 (1998): 551–96.

"Sharende xiaojie" 殺人的小姐 (The murdering miss). *SB2*, May 9, 1932.

"Sharenzhe zisha" 殺人者自殺 (Murderer commits suicide). *SB*, June 19, 1932.

Shen Defu 沈德符. *Wanli yehuo bian buyi* 萬曆野獲編補遺 (Supplement to Wanli gleanings). Beijing: Zhonghua Shuju, 1980.

Shen Zemin 沈澤民. "Tongxing'ai yu jiaoyu" 同性愛與教育 (Same-sex love and education). *Jiaoyu zazhi* 教育雜誌 (Chinese educational review) 8, no. 15 (1923): 1–10.

Shenbao 申報 (Shanghai news). Shanghai, 1872–1949.

Shi Chengli 史成禮, Liu Guodong 劉國棟, and Zhang Hualin 張華麟. "Yinjing tiji celiang baogao: Bing lung ji guochan yinjingtao guige" 陰莖體積測量報告並論及國產陰莖套規格 (A report measuring penis size and the size of condoms

made in China). *Lanzhou yixueyuan xuebao* 蘭州醫學院學報 (Journal of Lanzhou Medical College), no. 1 (1963): 121–26.

Shibao 時報 (Eastern times). Shanghai, 1904–1939.

Shih, Shu-mei. *The Lure of the Modern: Writing Modernism in Semicolonial China, 1917–1937.* Berkeley: University of California Press, 2001.

"Shisheng lian'aizhi mimi" 師生戀愛之秘密 (The secrets of teacher-student romance). *DMM*, March 31, 1929.

Shuiguo 水國. "Tao Sijin chaodu qingchou" 陶思瑾超度情仇 (Tao Sijin's excessive romantic revenge). *Xinghua*星華 (Star of China) 1, no. 1 (1936): 6.

"Sici shoushu yibianerchai Xie Jianshun bianxing jingguo" 四次手術易弁而釵 謝尖順變性經過 (Male to female transformation after four surgeries: The sex change experience of Xie Jianshun). *LHB*, October 28, 1955.

Smart, Josephine. "Cognac, Beer, Red Wine or Soft Drinks? Hong Kong Identity and Wedding Banquets." In *Drinking Cultures: Alcohol and Identity*, edited by Thomas Wilson, 107–28. New York: Berg, 2005.

Snitow, Ann, Christine Stansell, and Sharon Thompson, eds. *Powers of Desire: The Politics of Sexuality.* New York: Monthly Review Press, 1983.

Somerson, Wendy. "Under the Mosquito Net: Space and Sexuality in *Red Azalea.*" *College Literature* 24, no. 1 (1997): 98–115.

Sommer, Matthew H. "The Gendered Body in the Qing Courtroom." *Journal of the History of Sexuality* 22, no. 2 (2013): 281–311.

———. *Polyandry and Wife-Selling in Qing Dynasty China: Survival Strategies and Judicial Interventions.* Oakland: University of California Press, 2015.

———. *Sex, Law, and Society in Late Imperial China.* Stanford: Stanford University Press, 2000.

Song Qiang 宋強, Zhang Zangzang 張藏藏, and Qiao Bian 喬邊. *Zhongguo keyi shuo bu* 中國可以說不 (China can say no). Beijing: Zhonghua Gongshang Lianhe Chubanshe, 1996.

Stein, Edward, ed. *Forms of Desire: Sexual Orientation and the Social Construction Controversy.* New York: Garland Publishing, 1990.

Stevenson, Mark. "Sound, Space and Moral Soundscapes in *Ruyijun zhuan* and *Chipozi zhuan.*" *Nan Nü* 12, no. 2 (2010): 255–310.

Stevenson, Mark, and Cuncun Wu, eds. *Homoeroticism in Imperial China: A Sourcebook.* London: Routledge, 2013.

Stoler, Ann Laura. *Carnal Knowledge and Imperial Power: Race and the Intimate in Colonial Rule.* Berkeley: University of California Press, 2002.

Stone, Charles R. *The Fountainhead of Chinese Erotica: The Lord of Perfect Satisfaction (Ruyijun zhuan).* Honolulu: University of Hawai'i Press, 2003.

Tai Yen-hui. "Divorce in Traditional Chinese Law." In *Chinese Family Law and Social Change in Historical and Comparative Perspective*, edited by David C. Buxbaum, 75–106. Seattle: University of Washington Press, 1978.

Tamba Yasuyori 丹波康賴, ed. *Yixinfang [Ishinpo]* 醫心方 (Medical knowledge). Annotated by Gao Wenzhu. Beijing: Huaxia Chubanshe, 2011.

Taniguchi Yasuyo 谷口やすよ. "Kandai no kōgō ken" 漢代の皇后權 (Queenship in the Han dynasty). *Shigaku zasshi* 史學雜誌 (Historial magazine) 87, no. 11 (1978): 1578–96.

"Tao Liu an panjue quanwen" 陶劉案判決全文 (Complete judgment of the Tao-Liu case). *SB2*, May 18, 1932.

"Tao Sijin jinmian yisi" 陶思瑾僅免一死 (Tao Sijin narrowly avoids death). *SB2*, May 21, 1932.

"Tao Sijin yuzhong songjing" 陶思瑾獄中誦經 (Tao Sijin chants sutras in prison). *Sheying huabao* 攝影畫報 (Photography illustrated) 10, no. 2 (1934): 3.

Taylor, John. "The Long, Hard Days of Dr. Dick." *Esquire*, September 1995: 120–30.

Terry, Jennifer. *An American Obsession: Science, Medicine, and Homosexuality in Modern Society.* Chicago: University of Chicago Press, 1999.

Thatcher, Melvin P. "Marriages of the Ruling Elite in the Spring and Autumn Period." In *Marriage and Inequality in Chinese Society*, edited by Rubie S. Watson and Patricia Buckley Ebrey, 25–57. Berkeley: University of California Press, 1991.

Theiss, Janet M. *Disgraceful Matters: The Politics of Chastity in Eighteenth-Century China.* Berkeley: University of California Press, 2004.

———. "Managing Martyrdom: Female Suicide and Statecraft in Mid-Qing China." *Nan Nü* 3, no. 1 (2001): 47–76.

T'ien Ju-K'ang. *Male Anxiety and Female Chastity.* Leiden: Brill, 1988.

Tran, Lisa. *Concubines in Court: Marriage and Monogamy in Twentieth-Century China.* Lanham, MD: Rowman & Littlefield, 2015.

Traub, Valerie. *Thinking Sex with the Early Moderns.* Philadelphia: University of Pennsylvania Press, 2015.

Tsai, Kellee. *Capitalism without Democracy: The Private Sector in Contemporary China.* Ithaca: Cornell University Press, 2007.

Tsai, Shunchang Kevin. "Ritual and Gender in the 'Tale of Li Wa.'" *Chinese Literature: Essays, Articles, Reviews* 26 (2004): 99–127.

Tsu, Jing. *Failure, Nationalism, and Literature: The Making of Modern Chinese Identity, 1895–1937.* Stanford: Stanford University Press, 2005.

"Two Young Americans in Murder and Suicide Tragedy." *China Weekly Review*, June 25, 1932: 141.

Ullén, Magnus. "Pornography and Its Critical Reception: Toward a Theory of Masturbation." *Jump Cut* 51 (2009). www.ejumpcut.org/archive/jc51.2009 /UllenPorn/index.html.

Uretsky, Elanah. "Mobile Men with Money: The Socio-cultural and Politico-economic Context of 'High-Risk' Behavior among Wealthy Businessmen and Government Officials in Urban China." *Culture, Health, and Sexuality* 10, no. 8 (2008): 1–14.

———. *Occupational Hazards: Sex, Business, and HIV in Post-Mao China.* Stanford: Stanford University Press, 2016.

———. "'Sex'—It's Not Only Women's Work: A Case for Refocusing on the Functional Role That Sex Plays in Work for Both Women and Men." *Critical Public Health* 25, no. 1 (2015): 78–88.

van Gulik, Robert Hans. *Sexual Life in Ancient China: A Preliminary Survey of Chinese Sex and Society from ca. 1500 B.C. till 1644 A.D.* Leiden: Brill, 2003.

Vance, Carol S., ed. *Pleasure and Danger: Exploring Female Sexuality.* Boston: Routledge & Kegan Paul, 1984.

Vankeerberghen, Griet. "A Sexual Order in the Making: Wives and Slaves in Early Imperial China." In *Sex, Power, and Slavery*, edited by Gwyn Campbell and Elizabeth Elbourne, 121–39. Athens: Ohio University Press, 2014.

Vitiello, Giovanni. "Family Affairs: *A Crazed Woman* and Late Ming Pornography." In *A Life Journey to the East: Sinological Studies in Memory of Giuliano Bertuccioli (1923–2001)*, edited by Antonio Forte, 245–62. Kyoto: Italian School of East Asian Studies, 2002.

———. *The Libertine's Friend: Homosexuality and Masculinity in Late Imperial China.* Chicago: University of Chicago Press, 2011.

Volpp, Sophie. "Classifying Lust: The Seventeenth-Century Vogue for Male Love." *Harvard Journal of Asiatic Studies* 61, no. 1 (2001): 77–117.

Vukovich, Daniel. *China and Orientalism: Western Knowledge Production and the PRC.* New York: Routledge, 2012.

Walder, Andrew George. *Communist Neo-traditionalism: Work and Authority in Chinese Society.* Berkeley: University of California Press, 1986.

Waltner, Ann. "Infanticide and Dowry in Ming and Early Qing China." In *Chinese Views of Childhood*, edited by Anne Behnke Kinney, 193–217. Honolulu: University of Hawai'i Press, 1995.

Wang, Hui. *China's New Order: Society, Politics, and Economy in Transition.* Cambridge, MA: Harvard University Press, 2003.

Wang, Jessica Ching-Sze. *John Dewey in China: To Teach and to Learn.* Albany: State University of New York Press, 2007.

Wang, Lu, Ning Wang, Liyan Wang, Dongmin Li, Manhong Jia, Xing Gao, Shuquan Qu, Qianqian Qin, Yanhe Wang, and Kumi Smith. "The 2007 Estimates for People at Risk for and Living with HIV in China: Progress and Challenges." *Journal of Acquired Immune Deficiency Syndromes* 50, no. 4 (2009): 414–18.

Wang, Y. Yvon. "Shame, Survival, Satisfaction: Legal Representations of Sex between Men in Early Twentieth-Century Beijing." *Journal of Asian Studies* 75, no. 3 (2016): 703–24.

Wang, Yuejin. "*Red Sorghum*: Mixing Memory and Desire." In *Perspectives on Chinese Cinema*, edited by Chris Berry, 80–103. London: BFI Publishing, 1991.

Wang Cunzhang 王存章, Gu Wanzhao 谷萬昭, and Zhou Changyou 周長友. "Ziboshi chengren yinjing zhengchang biaozhun" 淄博市成人陰莖正常標準 (The normal size of the penises of adult males in Zibo city). *Nanxingxue zazhi* 男性學雜誌 (Chinese journal of andrology) 1, no. 2 (1987): 119.

Wang Dang 王讜. *Tang yulin jiaozheng* 唐語林校證. Edited by Zhou Xunchu 周勛初. Beijing: Zhonghua, 1987.

Wang Huiming 王褘茗. "Lishishang de 'pingqi' xianxiang jiqi falü wenti chutan" 歷史上的"平妻"現象及其法律問題初探 (A historical investigation into "equal-status wives" and relevant legal issues). *Jinan xuebao (Zhexue shehui kexue ban)* 暨南學報(哲學社會科學版) (Jinan academic journal) 38, no. 3 (2016): 43–50.

Wang Jing. *High Culture Fever: Politics, Aesthetics and Ideology in Deng's China.* Berkeley: University of California Press, 1996.

Wang Xin 王鑫. "*Funü zazhi* yanjiu: Guanyu Zhongguo xiandai nüxing huayu de ge an fenxi" 《婦女雜誌》研究——關於中國現代女性話語的個案分析 ("Research on the *Ladies' Journal*: A Case Study and Analysis of the Language on the Chinese Modern Woman"). PhD diss., Beijing Normal University, 2009.

Wang Zheng. *Finding Women in the State: A Socialist Feminist Revolution in the People's Republic of China, 1949–1964.* Oakland: University of California Press, 2016.

———. *Women in the Chinese Enlightenment.* Berkeley: University of California Press, 1999.

Wang Zijin 王子今. *Gushi xingbie yanjiu conggao* 古史性別研究叢稿 (Gender studies in ancient history). Beijing: Shehui Kexue Wenxian, 2004.

Wank, David. *Commodifying Communism: Business, Trust, and Politics in a Chinese City.* New York: Cambridge University Press, 1999.

Weil, Rachel. "Sometimes a Scepter Is Only a Scepter: Pornography and Politics in Restoration England." In *The Invention of Pornography*, edited by Lynn Hunt, 125–53. New York: Zone Books, 1993.

Weitzer, Ronald. "Sociology of Sex Work." *Annual Review of Sociology* 35 (2009): 213–34.

Wells, Scott, and Ping Yao. "Discourses on Gender and Sexuality." In *The Cambridge World History*, edited by Craig Benjamin, 154–78. Cambridge, UK: Cambridge University Press, 2015.

Wengshan Zhudi 翁山柱砥 and He Mengmei 何夢梅. *Baimudan* 白牡丹 (White peony). Changsha: Yuelu Shushe, 2004.

White, Melissa Autumn. "Archives of Intimacy and Trauma: Queer Migration Documents as Technologies of Affect." *Radical History Review*, no. 120 (2014): 75–93.

Wile, Douglas. *Art of the Bedchamber: The Chinese Sexual Yoga Classics including Women's Solo Meditation Texts.* Albany: State University of New York Press, 1992.

Williams, Linda. *Hardcore: Power, Pleasure and the Frenzy of the Visible.* Berkeley: University of California Press, 1989.

———, ed. *Porn Studies.* Durham: Duke University Press, 2004.

———. "Porn Studies: Proliferating Pornographies On/Scene: An Introduction." In *Porn Studies*, edited by Linda Williams, 1–23. Durham: Duke University Press, 2004.

Williams, Simon. "Theorising Class, Health and Lifestyles: Can Bourdieu Help Us?" *Sociology of Health and Illness* 17, no. 5 (1995): 577–604.

Windscript, Shan. "Hopes and Collisions: How to Write a Diary in Mao's New China." Paper delivered at the Association for Asian Studies conference, Kyoto, Japan, 2016.

Woju 蝸居 (Dwelling narrowness). Shanghai Television, July 2009.

Wong, Alvin K. H. "Transgenderism as a Heuristic Device: On the Cross-Historical and Transnational Adaptations of the *Legend of the White Snake*." In *Transgender China*, edited by Howard Chiang, 127–58. New York: Palgrave Macmillan, 2012.

Wong, Jan. "'I Lived in Darkness. There Was Nowhere to Look for Help.'" *Globe and Mail*, November 14, 1993.

Wong, Ka F. "The Anatomy of Eroticism: Reimagining Sex and Sexuality in the Late Ming Novel *Xiuta Yeshi*." *Nan Nü* 9, no. 2 (2007): 284–329.

Wu, Cuncun. *Homoerotic Sensibilities in Late Imperial China.* Oxford: Routledge, 2004.

Wu, Cuncun, and Mark Stevenson. "Karmic Retribution and Moral Didacticism in Erotic Fiction from the Late Ming and Early Qing." *Ming Qing Studies* (2011): 467–86.

———. "Speaking of Flowers: Theatre, Public Culture, and Homoerotic Writing in Nineteenth-Century Beijing." *Asian Theatre Journal* 27, no. 1 (2010): 100–29.

Wu, Juenong 吳覺農. "Ai Lunkai de ziyou lihun lun" 愛倫凱的自由離婚論 (Ellen Key's free divorce theory). *FNZZ* 8, no. 4, coll. vol. 32 (1922): 14,481–87.

Wu, Yu-Chuan. "A Disorder of Qi: Breathing Exercise as a Cure for Neurasthenia in Japan, 1900–1945." *Journal of the History of Medicine and Allied Sciences* 71, no. 3 (2016): 322–44.

Wu Weicheng 吳偉成, Yang Wenzhi 楊文質, Zhao Yong 趙永, Peng Xuanfu 彭宣芙, Luo Kangping 羅康平, Lu Pei 魯培, and Zhang Min 張敏. "Yinjing celiang fangfa de tantao ji zhengchang biaozhun" 陰莖測量方法的探討及正常標準 (An exploration of the method of measuring the penis and its normality). *Zhonghua miniao waike zazhi* 中華泌尿外科雜誌 (Chinese journal of urology) 13, no. 6 (1992): 449–52.

Wuchen 無塵. "Guanyu tongxinglian'ai" 關於同性戀愛 (On same-sex love). *Shehui ribao* 社會日報 (Social daily news), June 25, 1932.

Xiao Jianyi 肖健一. "Xi Han shiqi de xing guannian" 西漢時期的性觀念 (Views of sex in the Western Han dynasty). *Wenbo* 文博 (Fair) 4 (2003):19–29.

Xiao Ying 小英. "Yin Yao Jinping huixiang A'nidu" 因姚錦屏迴想阿尼度 (Reminded of A'nidu because of Yao Jinping). *JB*, March 20, 1935.

———. "Yin Yao Jinping nüshen xiangqi taijian" 因姚錦屏女身想起太監 (Reminded of eunuchs because of Yao Jinping's female body). *JB*, March 24, 1935.

"Xiaoyangnü Fu Xiuxia zhu Tatong Jiaoyangyuan" 小養女傅秀霞 住大同教養院 (Little girl Fu Xiuxia boarding at Ta Tong Relief Institute). *LHB*, June 7, 1959.

Xie Dexian 謝德銑. *Zhou Jianren pingzhuan* 周建人評傳 (Zhou Jianren's critical biography). Chongqing: Chongqing Chubanshe, 1991.

     BIBLIOGRAPHY

"Xie Jianshun gaizao shoushu huo jianglai Taibei kaidao" 謝尖順改造手術 或將來台北開刀 (Xie Jianshun's alteration surgery might take place in Taipei). *LHB*, September 24, 1953.

"Xie Jianshun guanxiongfu" 謝尖順慣雄伏 (Xie Jianshun adjusting to feminine psyche). *LHB*, November 11, 1959.

"Xie Jianshun xiaojie de yintong" 謝尖順小姐的隱痛 (The pain of Miss Xie Jianshun). *LHB*, October 17, 1953.

Xie Yuhua 謝育華, Huang Xianhua 黃顯華, and Lin Lin 林冧. "2,906 li chengnian nanxing gaowan yinjing celiang jieguo fenxi" 2,906 例成年男性睪丸陰莖測量結果分析 (An analysis of the results of measuring 2,906 adult males' scrotums and penises). *Nanxingxue zazhi* 男性學雜誌 (Chinese journal of andrology) 6, no. 3 (1992): 49–50.

Xing Guowu 邢國武 and Tian Shifeng 田世峰. "1,149 yihunnanxing shengzhi qiguan celiang baogao" 1,149 已婚男性生殖器官測量報告 (A report on the results of measuring the penises of 1,149 married men). *Nankexue zazhi* 男性學雜誌 (Chinese journal of andrology) 3 (1990): 173.

"Xiri dabing tongzhi jianglai fulian huiyuan" 昔日大兵同志 將來婦聯會員 (Former soldier comrade a future member of women's association). *LHB*, October 10, 1956.

"Xiri shachang zhanshi jinze jingru chuzi" 昔日沙場戰士 今則靜如處子 (Former battle warrior a present quiet virgin). *LHB*, September 17, 1958.

"Xiuzhen xinwen: Tao Sijinjiehun" 袖珍新聞: 陶思瑾結婚 (News briefs: Tao Sijin marries). *Xianshi* 現實 (Reality), no. 1 (1939): 38.

Xu, Gary. "Ethics of Form: Qing and Narrative Excess in *Guwangyan*." In *Dynastic Decline and Cultural Innovation: From the Late Ming to the Late Qing and Beyond*, edited by David Wang and Shang Wei, 235–63. Cambridge, MA: Harvard University Asia Center, 2005.

Xu, Wenying. "Agency via Guilt in Anchee Min's *Red Azalea*." *MELUS* 25, nos. 3–4 (2000): 203–19.

Xu Changling 徐昌齡. "Ruyijun zhuan" 如意君傳 (Lord of perfect satisfaction). In *Ruyijun zhuan/Chipozi zhuan/Sengni niehai/Chunmen suoyuan* 如意君傳/癡婆子傳/僧尼孽海/春夢瑣言, vol. 24 of *Si wu xie hui bao* 思無邪滙寶, edited by Chen Qinghao and Wang Qiugui. Taipai: Taiwan Daying Baike Gufen Youxian Gongsi, 1994.

Xu Meiyu Nüshi 徐美玉女士. "Tongxinglian 'ai yu sanjiaolian'ai" 同性戀愛歟 三角戀愛歟 (Same-sex love and romance triangles). *LL* 1, no. 49 (1932): 2003.

"Xu Qinwen fangwenji" 許欽文訪問記 (Interview with Xu Qinwen). *DWB*, May 15, 1932.

Xu Youwen 徐友文. "Nübiannan qiwen" 女變男奇聞 (News of female to male). *Libailiu* 禮拜六 (Saturday) 605 (1935): 97.

Yan, Yunxiang. *The Flow of Gifts: Reciprocity and Social Networks in a Chinese Village*. Stanford: Stanford University Press, 1996.

Yan Shi 晏始. "Pingtan: Nannüde geli yu tongxing'ai" 評壇：男女的隔離與同性愛 (Comment: the social separation of men and women and same-sex love). *FNZZ* 9, no. 5 (1923): 14–15.

Yang, C., C. Latkin, R. Luan, C. Wang, and K. Nelson. "HIV, Syphilis, Hepatitis C and Risk Behaviours among Commercial Sex Male Clients in Sichuan Province, China." *Sexually Transmitted Infections* 86, no. 7 (2010): 559–64.

Yang, Mayfair Mei-hui. "From Gender Erasure to Gender Difference: State Feminism, Consumer Sexuality, and Women's Public Sphere in China." In *Spaces of Their Own: Women's Public Sphere in Transnational China*, edited by Mayfair Yang, 35–67. Minneapolis: University of Minnesota Press, 1999.

———. *Gifts, Favors, and Banquets: The Art of Social Relationships in China*. Ithaca: Cornell University Press, 1994.

———, ed. *Spaces of Their Own: Women's Public Sphere in Transnational China*. Minneapolis: University of Minnesota Press, 1999.

Yang Bojun 楊伯峻. *Chunqiu Zuozhuan zhu* 春秋左傳注 (Spring and autumn annals note). 2nd ed. Beijing: Zhonghua, 1990.

Yang Mingzhao 楊明照. Baopuzi *waipian jiaojian* 抱朴子外篇校箋 (The annotation of the *Baopuzi*'s unofficial chapters). Beijing: Zhonghua, 1991–97.

Yao, Ping. "Changing Views on Sexuality in Early and Medieval China." *Journal of Daoist Studies* 8 (2015): 52–68.

———. "Historicizing Great Bliss: Erotica in Tang China (618–907)." *Journal of the History of Sexuality* 22, no. 2 (2013): 207–29.

———. "The Status of Pleasure: Courtesans and Literati Connection in Tang China (618–906)." *Journal of Women's History* 14, no. 2 (2002): 26–53.

"Yao Jinping huanan fangwen ji" 姚錦屏化男訪問記 (Interview with Yao Jinping about her sex transformation). *SB*, March 18, 1935.

"Yao Jinping nühua nanshen" 姚錦屏女化男身 (Yao Jinping's body transformed into a man's). *XWB*, March 19, 1935.

"Yao Jinping wanquan nüershen" 姚錦屏完全女兒身 (Yao Jinping is a complete woman). *SB*, March 21, 1935.

"Yao Jinping xi fushen huananti" 姚錦屏係副腎化男體 (Yao Jinping's masculinization of the adrenal gland). *SB*, March 19, 1935.

"Yao Jinping yanxi wanquan nüshen" 姚錦屏驗係完全女身 (Yao Jinping has been confirmed to be a complete woman). *XWB*, March 22, 1935.

"Yao Jinping yeyi di Hu" 姚錦屏業已抵滬 (Yao Jinping has arrived in Shanghai). *XWB*, March 17, 1935.

"Yao Jinping zuoru yiyuan jianyan" 姚錦屏昨入醫院檢驗 (Yao Jinping entered the hospital yesterday for examination). *SB*, March 20, 1935.

"Yaoshi Zhang Mojun lai shenli LiuTao'an Tao Sijin jue wushengwang" 要是張默君來審理劉陶案陶思瑾決無生望 (If Zhang Mojun judges the Liu-Tao case, Tao Sijin has no hope). *SB2*, June 16, 1932.

Yasuyori Tamba, Emil C. H. Hsia, Ilza Veith, and Robert Geertsma. *The Essentials of Medicine in Ancient China and Japan: Yasuyori Tamba's* Ishimpō. Leiden: Brill, 1986.

YD [Wu Juenong] 高山. "Luosuo furen de zhongguo nuquan yundong guan" 羅素夫人的中國女權運動觀 (Mrs. Russell's view on the Chinese women's rights movement). *Xiandai funü* 現代婦女 (Modern woman) 16 (1923): 2.

———. "Ziyou lianai yu lianai ziyou" 自由戀愛與戀愛自由 (Free love and freedom of love). *FNZZ* 9, no. 2, coll. vol. 35 (1923): 16,287–94.

Ye, Sang. "Keeping a Diary in China: Memories for the Future." *China Story*, June 4, 2015. www.thechinastory.org/2015/06/keeping-a-diary-in-china-memories-for -the-future/.

Yin Muqiang 殷木强. *Xing de shengli he bingtai* 性的生理和病態 (Physiology and abnormality of sex). Beijing: Zhonghua Shuju, 1950.

"Yinyangren jingshenti" 陰陽人淨身體 (Hermaphrodite cleans body). *Taiwan xinshengbao* 台灣新生報 (Taiwan new life daily news), August 19, 1953.

"Yinyangren shinan shinü jintian fenxiao" 陰陽人是男是女今天分曉 (Heramphrodite's sex determined today). *Zhonghua ribao* 中華日報 (China daily news), August 20, 1953.

"Yinyangren Xie Jianshun jinkaidao biancixiong" 陰陽人謝尖順 今開刀辨雌雄 (Hermaphrodite Xie Jianshun: Sex determined today through surgery). *LHB*, August 20, 1953.

"Yishi chuangzao nüren wunian duding qiankun" 醫師創造女人 五年篤定乾坤 (Doctors building a woman: sex determined in five years). *LHB*, September 4, 1958.

You Xuezhou 尤學周. "Xingyu yu duji" 性慾與妒忌 (Sexual desire and jealousy). *Changshou* 長壽 (Longevity), no. 61 (1933): 81.

"Young American Ex-Banker Sought in Fatal Shooting of Fellow Countryman Here." *China Press*, June 18, 1932.

Yu Dong, Chelsea Morgan, Yurii Chenenov, Ligang Zhou, Wenquan Fan, Xiaolin Ma, and Kate Pechenkina. "Shifting Diets and the Rise of Male-Biased Inequality on the Central Plains of China during Eastern Zhou." *Proceedings of the National Academy of Sciences* 114, no. 5 (2017): 932–37.

"Yuejing yu chunü mo" 月經與處女膜: 陶思瑾生理上研究 (Menstruation and the hymen: On Tao Sijin's physiology). *SB2*, June 9, 1932.

Yuen, Sun-pong, Pui-lam Law, and Yuk-ying Ho. *Marriage, Gender, and Sex in a Contemporary Chinese Village*. Translated by Fong-ying Yu. Armonk, NY: M. E. Sharpe, 2004.

Yuen Yeuk-laam. "China Census Shows Continuing Gender Imbalance, Aging Population." *Global Times*, January 21, 2015.

Zamperini, Paola. *Lost Bodies: Prostitution and Masculinity in Chinese Fiction*. Leiden: Brill, 2010.

Zeitlin, Judith T. *Historian of the Strange: Pu Songlin and the Chinese Classical Tale*. Stanford: Stanford University Press, 1993.

Zhang, Ellen Cong. "Anecdotal Writing on Illicit Sex in Song China (960–1279)." *Journal of the History of Sexuality* 22, no. 2 (2013): 253–80.

Zhang, Everett Yuehong. "The Birth of *Nanke* (Men's Medicine) in China: The Making of the Subject of Desire." *American Enthnologist* 34, no. 3 (2007): 491–508.

———. "China's Sexual Revolution." In *Deep China: The Moral Life of the Person*, edited by Arthur Kleinman, Yunxiang Yan, Jing Jun, Sing Lee, Everett Zhang, Pan Tianshu, and Guo Jinhua, 106–51. Berkeley: University of California Press, 2011.

———. "Flows between the Media and the Clinic: Desiring Production and Social Production in Urban Beijing." In *Media, Erotics, and Transnational Asia*, edited by Purnima Mankaker and Louisa Schein, 139–71. Durham: Duke University Press, 2013.

———. *The Impotence Epidemic: Men's Medicine and Sexual Desire in Contemporary China*. Durham: Duke University Press, 2015.

Zhang Beichuan 張貝川. *Tongxinglian* 同性戀 (Homosexuality). Jinan: Shandong Kexue Jishu Press, 1994.

Zhang Jingsheng 張競生. *Zhang Jingsheng wenji* 張競生文集 (A collection of articles by Zhang Jingsheng). Guangzhou: Guangzhou Chubanshe, 1998.

Zhang Jun 張均. "Tao nüshi chanhuiji" 陶女士懺悔記 (Tao Sijin's regrets). *Foxue banyuekan* 佛學半月刊 (Buddhism bimonthly) 5, no. 24 (1935): 14–15.

Zhang Kecheng 張克成. *Nannü shengzhiqi xing shenjingshuairuozhi yufang ji zhiliao* 男女生殖器性神經衰弱之預防及治療 (The prevention and cure of male and female sexual neurasthenia). Shanghai: Shenghuo Yiyuan, 1934.

Zhang Kuo 張廓. *Duoqi zhidu—Zhongguo gudai shehui he jiating jiegou* 多妻制度—中國古代社會和家庭結構 (Polygamy: Ancient Chinese society and family structure). Tianjin: Guji, 1999.

Zhang Puzhong 張普忠, Song Xiang 宋祥, Liu Xiangming 劉向明, Wu Yinzhong 吳印忠, Zou Xiaofei 邹小飛, and Zhou Jianfeng 周健峰. "220 li zhengchang nanxing yinjing boqi changdu de celiang baogao" 220 例正常男性陰莖勃起長度的測量報告 (A report of 220 normal males' penis lengths in erection). *Zhongguo nankexue zazhi* 中國男科學雜誌 (Chinese journal of andrology) 13, no. 3 (1999): 161.

Zhang Qingyue 張清樾. "Tao'an taolunhui: yuyi sharen" 陶案討論會：偶意殺人 (Symposium on the Tao case: Killing by chance). *DWB*, August 2, 1932.

Zhang Sixiao 張思孝, Tang Xiaoda 唐孝達, and Yang Yuru 楊宇如. "2,029 li chengnian nanxing shengzhiqiguan diaocha baogao" 2,029 例成年男性生殖器官調查報告 (An investigation of 2,029 adult males' reproductive organs). *Zhonghua miniaowaike zazhi* 中華泌尿外科雜誌 (Chinese journal of urology) 9, no. 6 (1988): 328–31.

Zhang Xiaofeng 張小鋒. "Shi Zhangjiashan Hanjian zhong de 'yubi'" 釋張家山漢簡中的"御婢" (Interpretation of Zhang Jiashan Han Jian in the "Royal bi"). *Chutu wenxian yanjiu* 出土文獻研究 (Research on Chinese excavated classics) 6 (2004): 125–29.

Zhang Xichen 章錫琛. "Du Chen Jianshan Xiansheng 'Youshengxue he ji ge xing de wenti'" 讀陳建山先生 "優生學和幾個性的问题" (Reading Mr. Chen Jianshan's "Eugenics and some problems related to sex"). *Minduo zazhi* 民鐸雜誌 6, no. 2 (1925): 1–11.

———. "Du Feng Zi Nüshi he YD Xiansheng de taolun" 讀鳳子女士與Y.D.先生的討論 (Reading the debate between Miss Feng Zi and Mr. YD). *FNZZ* 9, no. 2, coll. vol. 35 (1923): 16,294–95.

———. "Tongxun" 通訊 (Letter). *FNZZ* 8, no. 9, coll. vol. 33 (1922): 15,403.

———, ed. *Xin xing daode taolunji* 新性道德討論集 (The collected debates on the new sexual morality). Shanghai: Kaiming Shudian, 1925.

"Zhao Mengnan cansi Xihu" 趙夢南慘死西湖 (Zhao Mengnan's tragic death at West Lake). *SB*, May 3, 1929.

"Zhao Mengnan wei tongxinglian'ai ersi" 趙夢南為同性戀愛而死 (Zhao Mengnan died for same-sex love). *Zhongguo sheyingxuehui huabao* 中國攝影學會畫報 (Chinese photography association bulletin) 4, no. 188 (1929): 298.

"Zhao Mengnande sishi" 趙夢南的死事 (Zhao Mengnan's death). *Zhongguo sheyingxuehui huabao* 中國攝影學會畫報 4, no. 188 (1929): 297.

Zheng Yaru 鄭雅如. *Qinggan yu zhidu: Wei Jin shidai de muzi guanxi* 情感與制度：魏晉時代的母子關係 (Emotion and system: Mother-child relationship in Wei and Jin dynasties). Taipei: Guoli Taiwan Daxue, 2001.

Zhenlan Nüshi 珍蘭女士. "Tongxing'ai shi shenshengdema?" 同性愛是神聖的嗎? (Is same-sex love sacred?). *LL* 2, no. 62 (1932): 533–34.

Zhentan 偵探. "Nan maiyinde mimi" 男賣淫的秘密 (The secrets of men selling sex). *DMM*, September 10, 1929.

Zhong, Xueping. *Masculinity Besieged? Issues of Modernity and Male Subjectivity in Chinese Literature of the Late Twentieth Century*. Durham: Duke University Press, 1999.

Zhou, Dan 周丹. *Aiyue yu guixun: Zhongguoxiandaixingzhong tongxingyuwangde falixianxiang* 愛悅與規訓：中國現代性中同性慾望的法理想像 (Desires and discipline: Legal interpretations of same-sex desires in Chinese modernity). Guilin: Guangxi Normal University Press, 2009.

Zhou, Jianren 周建人. "Du 'Zhongguo zhi yousheng wenti'" 讀中國之優生問題 (Reading "China's eugenic problems"). *DFZZ* 22, no. 8 (1925).

———. *Zhou Jianren Wenxuan* 周建人文選 (Selected writings of Zhou Jianren). Beijing: Zhongguo Wenhua Chubanshe, 1988.

Zhou, Xiaoyi. "*Salomé* in China: The Aesthetic Art of Dying." In *Wilde Writings: Contextual Conditions*, edited by Joseph Bristow, 295–316. Toronto: University of Toronto Press, 2003.

Zhou Yimou 周貽謀. "Lun fangzhong jingdian *Sunüjing* yu *Xuannüjing*" 論房中經典《素女經》與《玄女經》(Discuss bedchamber classics: *The Classic of the Plain Girl* and The *Classic of the Mysterious Girl*). *Zhongguo xingkexue* 中國性科學 (Chinese sexology) 14, no. 1 (2005).

Zhu Huibin 朱惠斌 and Chen Kai 陳凱. "Gaowan yinjing daxiao yu shengyu guanxi de tantao" 睪丸陰莖大小與生育關係的探討 (A discussion of the relationship between scrotum and penis size and marital or reproductive life). *Nanxingxue zazhi* 男性學雜誌 (Chinese journal of andrology) 7, no. 2 (1993): 88–91.

Zhu Huibin 朱惠斌, Zhang Jun 張軍, Yu Rongqing 于榮慶, Fu Jiangnan 傅江南, and Chen Kai 陳凱. "Shanghaishi 990 li hunling nanzi yinjing he gaowan celiang fenxi Jieguo" 上海990 例婚齡男子陰莖和睪丸測量分析結果 (An analysis of the measurement of the penises and scrotums of 990 men in Shanghai as premarital checkup). *Nanxingxue zazhi* 男性學雜誌 (Chinese journal of andrology) 4, no. 1 (1990): 25–28.

Zilbergeld, Bernie. *The New Male Sexuality*. New York: Bantam, 1992.

"Ziyoulianai'de mimi" 自由戀愛的秘密 (The secrets of free love). *DMM*, April 9, 1929.

Žižek, Slavoj. *The Metastases of Enjoyment: On Women and Causality*. London: Verso, 2005.

"Zuo song Shanghai yiyuan jianyan" 昨送上海醫學院檢驗 (Entered the Shanghai hospital for examination). *XWB*, March 20, 1935.

CONTRIBUTORS

PETER J. CARROLL is an associate professor of history at Northwestern University. His research interests include urban history, Chinese modernism, popular and material culture, gender/sexuality, and nationalism. He is the author of *Between Heaven and Modernity: Reconstructing Suzhou, 1895–1937* (2006), which was awarded the Best Book (Non–North American) prize by the Urban History Association in 2007, and which was published in a Chinese-language edition in 2014.

HOWARD CHIANG is an assistant professor in the department of history at the University of California, Davis. He is the author of *After Eunuchs: Science, Medicine, and the Transformations of Sex in Modern China* (2018). His edited volumes include *Transgender China* (2012), *Queer Sinophone Cultures* (2013, with Ari Larissa Heinrich), *Psychiatry and Chinese History* (2014), *Historical Epistemology and the Making of Modern Chinese Medicine* (2015), and *Perverse Taiwan* (2016, with Yin Wang).

MIRELA DAVID is an assistant professor of history and women's and gender studies at the University of Saskatchewan. Her research is situated at the intersection of modern Chinese history, gender history, intellectual and cultural history, and medical history. She is interested in different forms of eugenics in praxis, in particular birth control praxis and venereal disease policies in 1930s China, and in how ideas pertaining to eugenics insert themselves into other debates.

PAUL R. GOLDIN is a professor of East Asian languages and civilizations at the University of Pennsylvania. His research focuses on classical Chinese cultural and intellectual history, as well as the history of gender and sexuality in China. He is the author of numerous books and articles, including *The Culture of Sex in Ancient China* (2002), and has edited the new edition of Robert H. van Gulik's classic, *Sexual Life in Ancient China* (2003).

DEBBY CHIH-YEN HUANG is a PhD candidate in the department of East Asian languages and civilizations at the University of Pennsylvania. Her fields of interest include Chinese gender and cultural history from the Han to the Tang dynasties. She is the author of *The Politics of Princesses' Social Network* (in Chinese, 2013). Her current research explores how elite men differentiated degrees of interpersonal relations via the arrangement of space and objects at a home banquet during the Tang dynasty.

KEITH MCMAHON is a professor of East Asian languages and cultures at the University of Kansas. In the past decade, he has written on nineteenth-century fiction and sexuality in China; opium smoking in nineteenth- and twentieth-century China and Euro-America; the history of emperors and their wives and concubines; the institution of imperial polygamy; and the subject of queenship. He has published six books: *Causality and Containment in Seventeenth-Century Chinese Fiction* (1988); *Misers, Shrews, and Polygamists: Sexuality and Male/Female Relations in Eighteenth-Century Chinese Fiction* (1995); *The Fall of the God of Money: Opium Smoking in Nineteenth-Century China* (2002); *Polygamy and Sublime Passion: Sexuality in China on the Verge of Modernity* (2010); *Women Shall Not Rule: Imperial Wives and Concubines in China from Han to Liao* (2013); and *Celestial Women: Imperial Wives and Concubines in China from Song to Qing* (2016).

ELANAH URETSKY is a visiting assistant professor in the department of anthropology at Brandeis University. She is the author of *Occupational Hazards: Sex, Business, and HIV in Post-Mao China* (2016). An expert on masculinity, male sexuality, and HIV/AIDS in China, she has conducted extensive research on the Chinese/Burmese border. She has used her expertise to advise international public health organizations working to respond to the HIV epidemic in Yunnan; she also partnered with a local performing artist in western Yunnan to create an HIV prevention program targeted at local ethnic minority communities. She is interested in expanding her work to examine how male networking practices in urban China expose men to chronic disease.

PING YAO is a professor of history at California State University, Los Angeles. Her research interests include medieval Chinese women's experiences in everyday life and religious practice. Her English publications include *Sharing the World Stage: Biography and Gender in World History* (coauthor, 2007); *Gendering Chinese Religion: Subject, Identity, and Body* (coeditor, 2014); and more than a dozen articles. Her Chinese publications include *Women's Lives in Tang China* (2004); *Discovering History in America* (2010); *Pioneers* (2014); and *Western Scholarship on Chinese History* (coeditor, five volumes, 2016).

SHANA YE is an assistant professor of women's and gender studies at the University of Toronto Scarborough. Her research focuses on transnational feminism, queer studies, and affect studies.

EVERETT YUEHONG ZHANG is a visiting scholar in the school of social science at the Institute for Advanced Study. His research focuses on post-Mao transformations of Chinese society over the past several decades, seen through changes in the body, sexuality, and medicine. He is the author of *The Impotence Epidemic: Men's Medicine and Sexual Desire in Contemporary China* (2015), which received an honorable mention for the Diana Forsythe Prize from the General Anthropology Division of the American Anthropological Association.

INDEX

filial piety (*xiao*), 17, 39
First Opium War, 146
floating population, 173
Forel, Auguste-Henri, 92
Foucault, Michel, 4, 10, 13, 54, 125, 145,
    150, 154
free love, 76–95
Furth, Charlotte, 3, 38
fuqi tongti (husband and wife are one
    body), 19
fuqi yiti (husband and wife are one
    body), 19

Gansu, 164, 169, 170
Gao Rimei, 129
gazettes, 38
Ge Hong, 26
global health, 11
Great Leap Forward, 147, 185
Gu Yin, 116, 121
Guangdong, 115
guanggun (rootless rascals), 18
Guangxi, 169
guanxi (dyadic personalistic relation-
    ship), 196
gynecology, 81, 128–29

Halberstam, Jack (Judith), 145
Hangzhou, 9, 77, 99, 101–4, 109, 120
harmony, 8, 17, 26, 36, 38, 51–52
Harper, Donald, 35
Hebei, 165
hermaphroditism, 126, 128, 131, 133–35,
    138
Hershatter, Gail, 3
heterosexuality, 8–9, 12, 68, 102–4, 109,
    113–16, 155, 189
HIV/AIDS, 11–13, 188–201
homonationalism, 145, 159
homosexuality, 8–11, 13, 40, 45, 68, 108,
    116, 120, 142–48, 154–55
Hong Mai, 41
Honig, Emily, 4, 11, 144

hooliganism (*liumang zui*), 148
hormones, 117, 119, 126
hospital, 81, 100, 129, 135, 137–38, 179
houmu (foster mother), 25
Hu Shi, 78–79, 85
Huan E, 61, 68, 69
Humble Words of an Old Rustic (Yesou
    puyan), 53
Hunt, Lynn, 53–54

Ibsen, Henrik, 85
identity, 8, 19, 23, 27, 43, 45, 77, 133,
    135, 167–68, 173, 176, 180, 183, 189,
    191, 195, 200–201; queer, 142, 145,
    153–56
immortality, 36, 107
impotence, 7, 61–63, 69, 113, 163, 166,
    168, 175–76, 183
individualism, 8–9, 76–95, 134
infanticide, 18
infidelity, 102
inversion, 106–7, 115, 121
intersexuality, 13, 126, 133–35

January 28 Incident, 102
Jia Nanfeng, 62
Jia Wenwu, 68–69
jiamu (remarried mother), 25
Jiang of Yi, 28
Jiang Zemin, 177
jiantiao (combined succession), 24
jiaren (fine lady), 42, 58
jienü (streetwalker), 200
jiji (peepee), 61
Jilin, 169
jimu (stepmother)25, 57–58
joint burial, 19
Jorgensen, Christine, 134, 139

Key, Ellen, 8–9, 76–95
Kong Chuizhu, 188–89
Krafft-Ebing, Richard von, 115, 117,
    121

CPSIA information can be obtained
at www.ICGtesting.com
Printed in the USA
BVHW09*0900280718
522782BV00002B/4/P